IDOLS OF THE TRIBE

Also by Harold R. Isaacs

The Tragedy of the Chinese Revolution

No Peace for Asia

Two Thirds of the World

Scratches on Our Minds: American Images of China and India
(paperback edition title: Images of Asia)

Emergent Americans: A Report on Crossroads Africa

The New World of Negro Americans

India's Ex-Untouchables

American Jews in Israel

Idols of the Tribe: Group Identity and Political Change

As Editor:

New Cycle in Asia

Straw Sandals: Chinese Stories 1918–1933

IDOLS OF
THE TRIBE

GROUP IDENTITY AND POLITICAL CHANGE

HAROLD R. ISAACS

HARPER & ROW, PUBLISHERS
NEW YORK, EVANSTON
SAN FRANCISCO
LONDON

1817

FIRST EDITION

Designed by Sidney Feinberg

Library of Congress Cataloging in Publication Data

Isaacs, Harold Robert, date
  Idols of the tribe.
  Includes index.
  1. Ethnic attitudes. 2. Minorities. 3. Pluralism
(Social sciences) I. Title.
GN320.I77 1975   301.45′1042   74-1820
ISBN 0-06-012153-X

75 76 77 78 79 10 9 8 7 6 5 4 3 2 1

269055

"But I don't want to go among mad people," Alice remarked.

"Oh, you can't help that," said the Cat, "we are all mad here."

—*Lewis Carroll*

The world is always new, if your nerves are strong enough.

—*Victor Serge*

I have to forge every sentence in the teeth of irreducible and stubborn facts.

—*William James*

CONTENTS

PREFACE

Early in the work of inquiry that went into the writing of this book, I spent some time in Little Rock at the time when Federal troops were standing guard there, nine young black people were running a gauntlet of angrily jeering whites to go to school every day, and a new era was opening in the history of the American society. That was in October 1957. In this week of October 1974 as I complete this study of the nature of basic group identity, there is violence in the streets of Boston between small mobs and police and between blacks and whites over an attempt to carry out a busing program to desegregate the city's schools. On a day in this same week, October 8, the following appeared on the television page of *The New York Times:*

The Department of Health, Education and Welfare has financed a campaign of public service television spots that abandon the "melting pot" and "brotherhood" themes of previous race relations campaigns and instead concentrate on . . . recognizing that there are distinct ethnic and racial differences among people, that the minorities have not "melted" into a homogeneous society, and that the differences can have positive value although they present problems.

This book is about these differences. It is about the problems they present. These are the problems of the hostility that is built into the differences. The old TV spots about brotherhood having failed to lick these hostility-producing differences, the new TV spots are apparently joining them. This is probably as accurate a reflection as any of where we stand now in our effort to solve the riddles of our diversity in the American society.

The same reflection appeared in an account I heard at a small meeting one night about three years ago from a leading Italian-American politician from Newark, where the city's black majority had recently elected a black mayor and where the Italian-Americans were now finding themselves an embattled minority, the new "niggers" of Newark. This young ward politician had come to see that brandishing arms and threatening violence—as some of his political elders were doing—would not work in streets the whites no longer ruled. He was casting about instead for ways of negotiating a modus vivendi with the new kings of the jungle. He told about an encounter he'd had on a television panel show with a prominent black militant leader. Without other preamble, the black stabbed a finger at the Italian-American and said: "You're a racist son of a bitch." Without blinking, the Italian-American replied: "You're damned right, and so are you, you racist son of a bitch." They stared at each other for a second and then the Italian-American went on: "Well, now that we're agreed on that, can we see what else we might agree on?" And out there in front of their two watching, listening little armies of racist sons of bitches, the two spokesmen went on to talk about the issues between them. It was a remarkable vignette of the new ethnic urban politics making its way toward new combinations in the running of city affairs.

This book is about such group identities bending and shaping themselves under the pressure of political change. Only not just in Newark, not just in America, but everywhere now, everywhere in in the world. My study of the nature of group identity comes out of a long series of inquiries into encounters between different kinds of people under changing political circumstances. It began with reporting how American soldiers were perceiving and reacting to the people they encountered during the Second World War in India and China. That experience led me some years later to examine in considerable detail how Americans had acquired and over time changed their images of Chinese and Indians. I went on from there to study the impact of world affairs, especially the African emergence in the 1950s, on race relations in the American society and especially on American blacks. This is what I was doing in Little Rock in 1957.

It was from what I learned in the next five years from an extended series of intensive interviews with Negro Americans going through this wrenching experience of change that I came to see more of the depth and shape of the same experience affecting all kinds of people in all parts of the world. I went out to have a look, and explored the matter with American Jews in Israel, Untouchables in India, English-educated Chinese in Malaya, Filipinos emerging from American colonial rule, Japanese emerging from a crushing national defeat.

Having spent my entire working life trying to understand something about the nature of politics and especially political change, I found now that I had to learn more than I knew about the nature of basic group identity, and that I could best do so by starting all over from the elementary—and elemental—beginnings from which it all comes. Only then could I begin to see how this factor of group identity weaves in and out of the politics by which we are now engulfed on all sides. What I learned I have put into this book. For purposes of illustration, I have drawn heavily on much of my own past work, based mainly on interviews with individuals in various settings. Footnotes have been used to add to some of these examples, to identify sources of quotations from the works of others, and occasionally to suggest where interested readers might be able to find more about some of the many subjects so briefly touched on during our passage among them.

My quest has taken me by new paths across some old and much-traveled territory, to see some old sights with new eyes, hear some old sounds in a different key, to seek some clearer answers to some old questions. There is not a great deal "new" to be said about our bodies, our languages, our histories and our origins, our religions, our nationalities, until one tries, as I have tried here, to see how they all come together, clustering in different ways under different conditions to make us what we are in all our differing kinds. This has been a journey full of hazards and I have no doubt stumbled more even than I know. But it has been a journey of discovery for me and I hope it can serve the same function for others even though they may start from different places and want to arrive at different destinations. At the very least, as the words "ethnic" and "ethnic group" become more and more a part of our everyday vocabularies, the reader of this book will at least have a better idea of what they mean than he might otherwise have had. He will also perhaps understand better, as I now understand better than I did, why era after era, generation after generation, the deepest holdings of our bodies and our spirits keep getting in the way of our deepest hopes of coming to lead a more humane human existence.

For assistance, for sharing of ideas, for help of many different kinds in the course of this work of inquiry and writing, I owe great thanks to many people:

— to the late Vernon Eagle of the New World Foundation, for the marginal but critical financial support that made persistence in this work possible, and even more, perhaps, for his patience and his confidence

— to the M.I.T. Center for International Studies, its late director Max Millikan, and his successors Everett Hagen and Eugene Skolnikoff, for the chance I have had for so many years as a Center associate to follow my own bents wherever and however they took me, one of a company of scholars with very different bents indeed, each pursuing his own in the best tradition of open inquiry

— to colleagues and friends who have read various chapters at different times and have given me the opportunity to benefit if I could from their comments, a great debt indeed to Bruce Mazlish of M.I.T.; Walter Dean Burnham of M.I.T.; Ai-li Chin, a former colleague at M.I.T.; Jacob Neusner of Brown University; John Hope Franklin of the University of Chicago; Chai Hon-chan of the University of Malaysia; Hiroshi Wagatsuma of the University of California, Los Angeles; James Moss of the University of New York at Buffalo; Eric Lincoln of Fisk University; David Lowenthal of University College, London; William Peterson of Ohio State University; Margaret Hollenbach of the University of Washington; the Right Reverend Robert DeWitt of Pennsylvania; the Reverend John Crocker Jr. of M.I.T.

— to Fritz Stern of Columbia University, Charles Ferguson of

Stanford University, A. A. Lumsdaine of the University of Washington, and Lucian Pye of M.I.T., for particular acts of help, counsel, and courtesy

— to Irving Levine of the American Jewish Committee and Andrew Greeley of the Center for the Study of American Pluralism at the University of Chicago, for the chance I have had to benefit from exchanges of views and disagreements over aspects of this subject at various conference encounters during the last half dozen years

— to Jeannette Hopkins, editor at Harper & Row, for her enterprise and her interest, and for her painstaking and scrupulous efforts to improve this work

— to Cecilia Dohrmann, for bibliographic digging, for keeping often chaotic files, for typing, and for general logistical and moral support during the last three years; to Frances Von Mertens, for some of the same before that; and to Ann Craig Cornelius, for some late tracking down of a number of useful and illuminating references

— to the long succession of graduate students in political science at M.I.T. who took part in the seminar I offered there beginning in 1956 under the title "Changing Identities and Outlooks in World Affairs," for what they shared with me and what many of them contributed to the work I have done on this subject during these years.

— to the editors of various publications in which parts of this book have appeared in different forms during the last few years, including *Daedalus, Survey, Foreign Affairs, Washington Monthly, Bulletin* of the International House of Japan, *Ethnicity;* and to the editors and publishers of several volumes in which some of this material has also appeared, including *Color and Race,* John Hope Franklin, ed. (1968), *Racial Influences on American Foreign Policy,* George W. Shepherd, ed. (1970), and *Ethnicity in Our Time,* Nathan Glazer and Daniel P. Moynihan, eds. (1975).

There are other debts that lie beyond acknowledgment. My principal one in this work as in all the work of inquiry and writing

I have done is to Viola R. Isaacs, discusser, dissenter, editor, tolerator, collaborator, and sharer of it all. I have also to try to say what I owe to a small group of individuals whose group identities she and I have had some part in shaping simply by being the makers of the family into which they were born or into which they married, and to the five younger young people who now form the families they are making for themselves. It is to my grandchildren, Jenny, Katy, Bobby, Laura, and Jonathan, and any others who might yet enter this small circle of felicity that I dedicate this work. I hope it may have something to do one day with how they will select from their wide array of antecedents and usable pasts what they put together out of what they are to make them what they will become. I owe them thanks, meanwhile, among many other things, for what I might otherwise not have, a very personal stake in the prospects for a usable future.

—HAROLD R. ISAACS

Newton, Massachusetts
October 14, 1974

I

THE HOUSES OF MUUMBI

✦

Whirl is King, having driven out Zeus.

—ARISTOPHANES

WE ARE EXPERIENCING on a massively universal scale a convulsive ingathering of people in their numberless grouping of kinds—tribal, racial, linguistic, religious, national. It is a great clustering into separatenesses that will, it is thought, improve, assure, or extend each group's power or place, or keep it safe or safer from the power, threat, or hostility of others. This is obviously no new condition, only the latest and by far the most inclusive chapter of the old story in which after failing again to find how they can co-exist in sight of each other without tearing each other limb from limb, Isaac and Ishmael clash and part in panic and retreat once more into their caves.

In Kenya, in their oath-taking ritual—practiced in recent years in the context of tribal tensions in independent Kenya's new politics—members of the dominant Kikuyu tribe pledge: "I shall never leave the House of Muumbi." Muumbi was the progenital mother of the tribe. Her house is the womb in which all Kikuyu are born, the home in which all are nurtured. By this oath, each member of the tribe recommits himself to his tribal loyalty above all others. Not only in Kenya but everywhere in our world there are many Muumbis, mistresses of many such houses. People who live in them are huddling together more closely and more tightly packed than ever before. Those who had left to see where else one might live in the universe are streaming back. Others still out there looking for more open and spacious dwelling places are halted, not sure where they are going, or where there is to go. On all sides, Houses of Muumbi that had begun to fall apart are being shored up or rebuilt on new sites. People are swarming into them, driven by needs and fears, by new political pressures that renew, encourage, and even exploit their tribal separatenesses.

This fragmentation of human society is a pervasive fact in human affairs and always has been. It persists and increases in our own time as part of an ironic, painful, and dangerous paradox: the more global our science and technology, the more tribal our politics; the more universal our system of communications, the less we know what to communicate; the closer we get to other planets, the less able we become to lead a tolerable existence on our own; the more it becomes apparent that human beings cannot decently survive with their separatenesses, the more separate they become. In the face of an ever more urgent need to pool the world's resources and its powers, human society is splitting itself into smaller and smaller fragments.

But today's tribal caves are wired for sight and sound. Most of the television light that showed nearly a billion people the live picture of men from earth reaching the moon flickered on the walls of Houses of Muumbi. This means that the retreat is no escape, that the more groups are disconnected the more they are connected, each one trying to validate its existence by making itself and its conflicts known and, by catching the world's eye and ear, trying to win support for its survival. One result is that the current process of fragmentation and refragmentation can be examined in every day's news, indefinitely multiplied now any day, any week, anywhere in the world, be it southern Africa, southern Mindanao, or the southern Bronx, northern Luzon or northern New Jersey or northern Ireland, Alaska or Ceylon, Belgium or Biafra, Scotland or Israel, Wales or the Sudan, Uganda or Cyprus, Malaysia or Guyana, Kiev or Cleveland, Bombay or Belfast.

Most of this news is about collision and conflict. Bloody as this kind of history has always been, the present chapter has been bloodier still. The mutual massacring has taken place on a grand scale, given the unprecedented spread and scope of these collisions and the greater death-dealing capacity provided by the wonders of modern progress. It is a somber catalogue: mutual massacring of Hindus and Muslims in India; tribal civil wars in Nigeria, the Congo, Chad, Sudan; Indians killing Nagas in northeastern Assam; Malays killing Chinese in Malaysia; Indonesians killing Chinese in Indonesia; Chinese killing Tibetans in Tibet; Tutsis and Hutus killing each other in Burundi; Catholics and Protestants killing each other in Ulster; Turks and Greeks in Cyprus; Kurds and Iraqis in Iraq; Papuans fighting Indonesians in New Guinea; Israelis and Arabs; Telenganas and Andhras and other such groups in India; Filipino Christians and Filipino Muslims; and so on and on and on. One attempt to count the "ethnic/cultural fatalities" in such clashes between 1945 and 1967 listed thirty-four "major" blood-lettings and hundreds of lesser collisions and came up with an estimated total of 7,480,000 deaths.*

By 1974, this total, by conservative reckoning, had surely passed ten million. Unknown thousands of Vietnamese were killed

---

* Some of the items:

— 2,000,000 killed in the Hindu-Muslim holocaust during the partition of India and the creation of Pakistan

— 500,000 Sudanese black killed in their war against the ruling Sudanese Arabs

— 200,000 Watusi and Bahutu mutually slaughtered during the separation of Burundi and Rwanda

— 150,000 Kurds killed in their wars against the Iraqis

— 100,000 Nagas and Mizos and Ahams killed in Assam in their effort to separate from India

— 100,000 Karens, Shans, Kachins in their wars against the ruling Burmese in Burma

— 100,000 Chinese killed by Indonesians in communal attacks

— 35,000 Khambas killed by the Chinese in Tibet

— 30,000 Somalis killed by Kenyans and Ethiopians

— 10,000 Arabs eliminated by black Africans in Zanzibar

— 10,000 Berbers killed by Arabs in Morocco and Algeria

— 5,000 East Indians, Negroes, and Amerindians, mutually, in communal clashes in Guyana.

  From ROBERT D. CRANE, "Postwar Ethnic Cultural Conflicts: Some Quantitative and Other Considerations," ms., Hudson Institute, N.Y., March 1968.

by Cambodians when American and South Vietnamese armies invaded Cambodia in 1970. Close to two million died in the civil war in Biafra in 1967–70. More than half a million dark-skinned Muslim East Bengalis were killed by light-skinned Muslim Punjabis and Pathans—fellow Pakistanis all—in the war in Bangladesh in 1971. An estimated hundred thousand Hutus were massacred in Burundi in 1972–73. Figures of up to ninety thousand have been given for the numbers killed by Amin in Uganda in 1973–74 as part of the consolidation of himself and his own group in power. If we take the matter down in scale from open warfare or large-scale massacres to ethnic/cultural conflicts marked by sporadic riots, bombings, and other collisions and clashes, the list swells from scores into hundreds. If we add those situations around the world where tension and strain exist between and among groups producing acts of violence in new political settings, the number could hardly be guessed, for here we would have to include every country in which a changing political order has to try to strike new balances among contending tribal/racial/ethnic/religious/national groups. And this now means virtually every country on every continent.

This great shaking out of all power and group relations is global in extent. It has come about as a result of the collapse or weakening of power systems or larger coherences that for periods of time managed to hold their clusters of separate groups under the control of a single dominant group or coalition of groups. These systems created a certain order in which the differences and divisions were not so much submerged as held in their orbits by the gravity of the center. The force of this gravity was physical, economic, cultural and—most heavily—psychological. The rules of the game were incorporated into mystiques and mythologies of belief and behavior—e.g., all the assumptions of cultural and racial superiority/inferiority—that were internalized and accepted by all, rulers and ruled, victimizers and victims, and built into the system's institutions to keep it working. Such systems could work for given periods, producing selectively profitable economic well-being for the rulers and their chosen instruments among the lower orders, and occasionally even significant art and literature. They could keep on working only so long as both the realities and mystiques of power were maintained, both externally and internally. They could survive only so long as they could overcome or stay in balance with challenging rivals outside and only so long as each dominated group inside knew its place and accepted it.

The record shows that there could be all kinds of lags, that declines could take a long time and falls run long overdue, but that these conditions could never be indefinitely maintained. Under external or internal pressures—usually both—authority was eroded, legitimacy challenged, and in wars, collapse, and revolution, the system of power redrawn. Such, with all their differences, were the Ottoman, Hapsburg, and Romanov empires, which ruled most of eastern and central Europe, western Asia, and most of North Africa for five hundred years or more, and such too were the European empires in Asia and Africa, controlling most of the world for periods lasting from not quite one to nearly three centuries.

Ottoman rule, which lasted from 1453, when the Turks took Constantinople, to 1918, when the "sick man of Europe" finally died, extended at its peak from the Adriatic to the Persian Gulf, from the western Mediterranean to the Red Sea. Its center was in what used to be loosely called "Asia Minor" and it included all of what is now loosely called the "Middle East." It governed at one time or another all the multitudes of distinct tribes, nations, peoples, races, and kinds who lived between Algeria and the borders of Iran. It extended into southeastern Europe from the Bosphorus and the shores of the Black Sea across Greece, the Balkans, Hungary, and nearly to Vienna.

Much of the European realm of the Ottoman Empire passed in time to the Hapsburg, later known as the Austro-Hungarian, Empire, which at its peak in the half century before 1918 ruled a domain that included Germans, Hungarians, Czechs, Slovaks, Poles, Ruthenians, Ukrainians, Serbs, Croats, Slovenes, Bosnians, Macedonians, Rumanians, Italians, and scores, if not hundreds, of smaller but no less distinct groups and subgroups.

To the east of the Hapsburg and north of the Ottoman, the Russian Empire had grown over some four hundred of these years, expanding westward and southwestward into Europe and gradually eastward into Asia. It became, by that same fatal year 1918, a system that included at least twenty linguistic groups of more than a million each, and a much larger number of smaller groups. Its successor, the Soviet Union, liked to call itself a union of "a hundred nationalities," one source citing a count of 189 made in the 1920s.

Moving down other, swifter historic currents meanwhile, western Europeans were carrying trade and power into Asia and later into Africa. As Grover Clark graphically summed it up in his charts in his 1936 study, *A Place in the Sun,* Europeans, who ruled 9 percent of the earth in 1492, had come to rule a third of it by 1801, another third by 1880, nearly another fifth by 1913 on the eve of the First World War, 85 percent in all by 1935, on the eve of the Second. By that time, just under 70 percent of the world's population lived under the control of Western governments. The British alone held a quarter of the world's land and ruled a quarter of its people, more people than lived at that time in China, or in Russia, the United States, France, and Japan all put together. There had been Spain in the southern Americas until the 1820s and latecoming Germany with the pieces of Asia and Africa it had been able to seize at that century's end and hold but briefly until 1918; there was still, until World War II, in addition to the British Empire, Holland in the East Indies, the United States in the Philippines, Belgium in the Congo, France in Southeast Asia and heavily, along with Britain and Portugal, in Africa. This remarkable European takeover of the world was paralleled in extent only perhaps by the conquests of the Mongols but was infinitely greater in its effect.

Like the Hellenic and Roman and some other great power systems of the remoter past, these empires laid much more than a political imprint on the peoples they ruled. The mystiques by which they governed for so long included whole cultural systems that survived in many shapes and measures of their real or assumed superiorities, or by the sheer transforming power of what they brought with them. They left as legacies styles of life as well as of governance, often of language, art, religion, and philosophy, of the spirit and much of the practice of bureaucratic and legal systems. In many cases, a great deal of this influence primarily affected the elites of the governed peoples. Much of it survived only fleetingly; the old imperial and Graustarkian aristocracies of Europe are gone for good. But some of it, like the Spanish and Catholic mark on Latin America, survives ineradicably. English remains the lingua franca of multilingual India, as do English and French in Africa. In Israel, the political and bureaucratic style and much else was brought along intact from eastern Europe by the Zionist pioneers, while the position of the religious authorities in the country, with power over most matters of *état civil*—anomalous in a regime dominated by European socialist norms—is an explicit legacy from the Ottoman millet system, left intact by the British during their brief post-Ottoman interregnum. Many more Ottoman and Arab legacies came with the great masses of so-called Oriental Jews to confront those brought from Europe. It will take more time than has yet passed to know what the reshaping of these many Asian and African cultures will bring, but it will carry the modern European imprint heavily upon it. All the major wars and all the convulsive revolutions of this century, all the nationalist movements that have transformed the politics of the entire globe in the last century are rooted in the political, social, and philosophic evolution of western Europe during the last three hundred years. All of this history and development in all its scenes and varieties comes out of the transforming drives and ideas and technologies of industrialization, modernization, and communication that were carried from Europe more blindly and more fatefully than anything else by these moving, spreading, contending power systems across the continents. The impacts changed all the nations and societies of the world beyond any chance that they can ever return to the shapes of their past.

✦

The collapse and disappearance of these power systems, after 1918 and after 1945, threw the peoples of most of the world into the political centrifuge in which they still spin. Since the empires fell, no new larger coherences have effectively taken their place, only new nuclear-powered power blocs that have failed so far to establish and sustain a balance between themselves, much less any balancing control over all the peoples who have fallen into their orbits. None of the proffered new coherences have worked. Neither the feeble European capitalist-victor coalition represented by the Versailles settlement and the League of Nations, nor its broader-based successor, the United Nations, could create a political system in which the power struggle of the major powers—in effect reduced to two—could be contained, much less the conflicts of the greatly increased number of smaller states, with all their external and internal abrasions and collisions over national/racial/tribal/religious differences. Indeed the Soviet and American power blocs that emerged after 1945 remained fragile and uneasy combinations precisely because of the revived strength of old nationalisms and the vitality of new drives to self-assertion and self-esteem. Despite bulging nuclear muscle, neither bloc could firmly count on keeping its client states in anything resembling the older forms of proper subservience.

The superpowers have found, on the contrary, that they have been unable either at home or in the world arena to go very far in pursuit of their national/strategic interests without being pressed, decently or otherwise, to respect the opinions of this or that hitherto ignorable segment of mankind. The American system has had to give up white supremacy. The Soviet system has had to pull back from the bloodier extremes of Stalinist mass terror. In the world arena, where they had to seek some new global solution, they both found the globe disconcertingly unmanageable. They could compete in space and try to avoid mutual disaster by searching for ways to limit their escalating weaponry. They have had to play part of their twentieth-century power game by nineteenth-century rules, only they have had to do it without accomplishing nineteenth-century results. Their fleets have bumped and buzzed and nudged each other in all the oceans, enough for a hundred Agadirs, while their electronic eyes and ears have guarded nervously from afar against more fateful collisions. Their own resorts to marginal "conventional" force, whether brief and "successful" in the Russian manner (as in Hungary and Czechoslovakia) or prolonged and disastrous in the American style (as in Vietnam and Cambodia), have failed to justify their cost. Their controlling influence behind lesser conflicts (as in Vietnam, in the Arab-Israeli and India-Pakistan wars, Cyprus, etc.) has not been able to produce conclusive results.

No stable spheres take shape, no docile dependents or securely pliant tools, no permanently passive victims, not in eastern Europe, not in Cuba, not in Egypt, not in India, and not, spectacularly, in China or North Vietnam; not in western Europe, not in Japan, not even in little Santo Domingo, and not, spectacularly, in South Vietnam. And in perhaps the most spectacular of all contrasts to nineteenth-century power relations and practices, not in the Arab countries, which were able with their scimitars to hold up the nuclear-powered Western world and force it close to economic disaster by fixing cripplingly high prices for Arab oil. Clearly, the new crises in human society were churning too hard to allow anything to settle again for long, even for as long as a few decades, into the old patterns of power and conquest, submission and passivity.

It took only a few years for the bipolar power system that emerged in 1945 to be pulled into new shapes, misshapen triangles, and twisted quadrangles. Western Europe recovered from the loss of its empires, Germany and Japan rose from their ashes sooner than anyone had imagined they could, and China came to life like a long-extinct volcano, or should we say began to rumble again with the thunder so long unheard across the bay. The durability of alliances, such as it ever was in those bad old days of the last century, has gone. The process of rearrangement of power in the world is the stuff itself of the inherent instability that has already filled most of the years of this century and will surely fill all the reasonably foreseeable future. Successful re-establishment of new world power systems, even in hemispheres or semi-hemispheres, may yet be one of the ways in which new, larger coherences may be created. Given all the circumstances, however, including the proliferation of nuclear weapons, it is not the most hopeful of all visible possibilities.

If new structures based on naked force are unpromising, none of the major political or other belief systems has offered much evidence of working any better. In the so-called Middle East (i.e., western and southwestern Asia and northern Africa) over these decades, the cement of Islam proved to be much too thin to hold together any viable political structure or alliance in which the various Arab and other Muslim peoples could share any effective or durable alliance, not even in their common cause against Israel. Oil could temporarily lubricate some of their areas of friction but could not hold them together. As all Arab politics keep demonstrating and events—like West Pakistan's murderous descent upon the East Bengalis—keep confirming, Islam, like Christianity, may make men—even just Muslim men—brothers sometime somewhere else, but not now, and not on earth. In the present context of affairs, the Roman Catholic Church, the nearest thing to a universal institution the Christian religion has produced, presents one of the most striking of all current examples of a larger coherence no longer able to hold its parts together or keep its belief system intact. Neither has realization come in this half century out of the secular dream of a new socialist or proletarian internationalism as Marx had conceived it. The dream was rudely shattered by the European social democracy which broke up into its national parts in the war crisis of 1914, was dreamed again with the coming of the October Revolution in Russia, and betrayed again when the rubbing of the Bolshevik lamp produced the old-new genie of Russian national communism. Whatever was left of the socialist dream of emancipation disappeared into Stalin's concentration camps and prisons. The attempts of Hitler's Germany in Europe and of Japan in Asia to impose their own kinds of coherence on world affairs succeeded only in breaking up what was left of the power systems they challenged. Nor, finally, did the American model of a larger coherence prove in this time that it might still work. Profoundly different from all the others and still far from a failure, it was only after 1945 that it entered its most crucial testing time, still in progress.

What we are experiencing, then, is not the shaping of new coherences but the world breaking into its bits and pieces, bursting like big and little stars from exploding galaxies, each one spinning off in its own centrifugal whirl, each one straining to hold its own small separate pieces from spinning off in their turn. This is no easy scene to see clearly, even if we try, by way of summary and illustration, to do no more than distinguish some of its larger features.

POSTCOLONIAL: The ex-empires in Asia and Africa have been carved into about eighty new states since 1945, from huge India to tiny Oman to tiniest Nauru, to newest Guinea-Bissau. These new states came into being because the foreign rulers could no longer sustain their rule and because the ruled would no longer submit. In a few places, independence crowned decades of sustained nationalist struggle, as in Congress-led India or Communist-led North Vietnam. In many more places, as in most of Africa, it came as the result of the precipitous departure of the imperialists, as in the Congo, or even—as in the case of most of French Africa—the cynical recognition by the foreign ruler that the name, if not the game, had to be changed at last. In British Africa, as in Ghana, Kenya, and a few other places, there was some earlier history of nationalist disaffection; but most of the parties and institutions that figured in the politics and government of the new African states after 1957 had only been brought into being after 1948. In Portuguese Africa, independence began to come only after another decade of nationalist-guerrilla war that finally forced Portugal to withdraw—the first and the least of the empire builders, the last to go. Of Western empire in Asia, only the islands of

Hong Kong and Macao remain, and then only because once-humble China chooses to have them survive.

Whatever its course and however it came, the victory of nationalism in Asia and Africa came late. The national state had long since exhausted whatever capacity it had ever had to serve as an effective political instrument for economic development and social progress. Throwing off the foreign yoke—or having it drop away—met the powerful need of people in the colonies to regain some minimum self-respecting self-esteem. At this minimum, the new nationalists could at least replace the foreign scoundrels with local scoundrels and do away with the most egregious symbols of foreign cultural and racial superiority that had been at the core of the mystique of imperial power. In the world they had never made, creating a new state power of their own was the only way offered to accomplish this much of their purpose. But the creation of new states offered only the most limited opportunity to attack the overwhelming problems of economic development and social transformation that all these peoples faced as they came out from under foreign rule.

The governing rhetoric of Asian and African nationalism was the romantic-libertarian rhetoric of Europe's nationalisms of the previous century. But the new liberty brought very little new equality with it and, unfortunately, it brought no fraternity at all. The new day in the dawn's early light was quite bleak. Virtually none of these new states had ever existed as separate states before, certainly not in their present form. Nearly all have boundaries inherited not from their own remoter past but from the colonial era, when boundaries were usually drawn without regard for what people lived where. Most of today's African state boundaries were quite arbitrarily drawn, for example, by Europeans meeting at Berlin in 1884. Colonies were set up as political/administrative units usually inhabited by tens to scores to hundreds of distinct and mutually antagonistic peoples divided along many lines—regional, racial, religious, linguistic, tribal. With only one or two exceptions, these units were carried over intact in the transfer from colonial to sovereign status. This fact alone has dominated most of the politics and generated most of the conflict in these countries during these decades. The holy grail of self-determination in anti-colonial politics became the poison potion of group conflict, secession, rebellion, and repression in the postcolonial era.

There are few real exemptions from this condition, even among those countries that experienced the period of Western dominance in a different way. Japan, no ex-colony, is nearly homogeneous, though not without its minorities. Re-emergent China, on the other hand, has a lively "national question" of its own, with no less than half its territory—all the wide border regions along the southern mountains, through Tibet (which the Communists took and hold by armed force), Sinkiang, Mongolia—occupied by some sixty non-Chinese minorities, no less than 10 percent of China's population. For Communist China, as for Kuomintang China or imperial China before it, these minorities present important internal political problems. China's minorities continue to have the Greater Han outlook of their Chinese rulers to deal with; in the present state of China's relations with Russia, the northern and western border peoples become a particularly pressing and even critical factor in external affairs as well.

In the ex-colonial countries, however, the populations are most generally mixed in more kinds and in larger proportions, indeed in almost every possible arrangement of majorities and minorities and mutually offsetting or unevenly-grouped pluralisms, every variety producing its own kind and degree of conflict.

Thus India-Pakistan, to take a highly visible major example. It divided initially along the line of its largest division, India's Hindu majority and its Muslim minority, breaking apart amid massive slaughter and flights of populations in 1947–48, and clashing in three wars since. India was left with a Muslim minority of 45,-000,000, smaller numbers of Sikhs, Jains, and Christians, but with other even greater and deeper sources of internal tension, division, and conflict: its dozen or so strong regionalisms, its fifteen major and some fifty minor language groups, its scores of major castes and thousands of subcastes, its eighty million Untouchables outside the caste system altogether. And then, West Pakistan, itself made up of mutually tense or hostile Punjabis, Pathans, Sindis, and others, brutally imposing itself on its own Bengali East, ending in wanton massacres, rebellion, the third war with India. It had taken rivers of blood to mark new boundaries separating the Muslim brothers from the Hindus. It took new rivers of blood to separate the Muslim brothers from one another.

These conditions, varying elsewhere almost infinitely in their mixes and their kinds, have brought on most of the violence that filled the three decades following the end of World War II: the civil wars, uprisings and repressions, communal riots and massacres, language conflicts, tribally rooted coups and countercoups, irredentist struggles, etc. Most of the divisions surfacing in these conflicts survive from the precolonial past, patterns of hostility and oppression with a long history.

Certain others, however, were created in the colonial period by migrations: voluntary, induced, or forced, e.g., the massive transport of Africans into slavery; the movement of indentured or contract labor, especially from India; and the migrations, both old and new, of Chinese and Indians and Levantines to Southeast Asia, Africa, and island countries in both the Atlantic and Pacific. From these movements came a whole group of new population mixes, e.g., Sinhalese-Tamil in Ceylon; Amerindian-African-European in Latin America; Malay-Chinese-Indian in Malaysia; East Indian and sometimes Chinese combinations with Africans, as in Guyana, Trinidad, Jamaica, or with Melanesians or Polynesians, as in Fiji and elsewhere in Oceania; and the presence of Chinese minorities, large and small, in Southeast Asia and the Caribbean. Groups of still another kind, still more marginal than these, were produced by unions between colonial masters and colonial subjects, e.g., the Anglo-Indians, Anglo-Burmans, and other Eurasians; and Eurafricans, most of whom lived a pariahlike existence in their own narrow slice of the highly stratified colonial populations. These groups, as well as the communities of traders and laborers like the Chinese in Southeast Asia and the Indians in Burma and East Africa, usually became objects of hostility on their own account or the helpless scapegoat victims of other intergroup tensions in the society after independence came. In certain cases, however, by virtue of their numbers they became something more than helpless or vulnerable minorities—as in Malaysia, where Chinese make up nearly 40 percent of the population and live on in an uneasy and easily broken balance with the dominant Malays; or in Guyana, where Indians, actually a numerical majority, are in a similar position in relation to the Afro-Guyanese. In both countries this has led to recurring mob violence and bloodshed and remains the main substance of unresolved questions of power in the new postcolonial situation.

In all these fragile new states, in sum, the new men of power have to discover how to create new national identities to go with the new national sovereignties they have just acquired. They have to discover how to protect themselves from the great power rivalry that impinges on them all, how to achieve new economic development and overcome crushing poverty and backwardness. They also have to try to make coherent and viable societies out of the persistent and mutually hostile separatenesses of their conglomerations of peoples.

POSTIMPERIAL: In western Europe, which used to be the center of the world, the place from which the East was Near, Middle, and Far, and where, at Greenwich, time and longitude began, the postimperial era did not bring on the collapse and revolution the Marxists had always predicted and the imperialists had always feared. Instead the Europeans found shedding that white man's burden more a relief than a disaster. With American help in the postwar years, they found they could make do in other ways, Britain a good deal less well than France, Belgium, or Holland, and none of them as well as the new Germany that rose with such extraordinary speed from the ashes the old one had made. Trade, it turned out, could do very well without a flag to follow. There was some postimperial lag. France fought on for its grandeur—a lot harder and more doggedly than it had fought the Nazis—in Indochina and Algeria, and de Gaulle kept its appearance in view, like a wax figure at Tussaud's, for a few years more. Britain, hard-pressed to make ends meet at home, soon had to pull in the few threads of imperial mantle it had left trailing behind it east of Suez and in the Mediterranean. Displaced from the world power scene, the Europeans had to assure their own survival in the world power struggle in which they no longer had the decisive role. This meant trying again to relate to one another in new ways on their own little peninsula at Eurasia's western end. Some small moves began toward creating a "new Europe" to contain and rationalize its strongly surviving national separatenesses. These still prevailed, however, and it seemed clear that any whole they might create would continue to be weaker than its parts.

There were more "parts" to Europe, moreover, than had been noticeable for quite some time. One striking consequence of the end of empire and world power for the Europeans was the weakening of the fabric of consent, assent, or submission that had kept some subnational groups in western European societies in a condition of more or less passive subordination—or less visible discontent—for centuries. The result has been the resurfacing of hoary old separatisms; new "national" movements or drives for regaining long-lost measures of regional, linguistic, or political autonomy; or simply in militant new movements for cultural reassertion—none of these major, but none insignificant either. Thus, in varying scopes and degrees of intensity and reappearance: in Great Britain the Welsh, the Scots, even the Manx, and the reopening of Catholic-Protestant hostilities in Ulster; the Flemish-Walloon conflict in Belgium; the stirrings of the Basques in Spain, the Bretons and other regional groups in France, even the Jurassians in Switzerland; and by extension in North America, the nationalist Quebeckers in Canada.

Another fallout of the postimperial experience has been the migration to the former mother countries of sizable numbers of their ex-children: Indians, Pakistanis, Africans, and West Indians to Great Britain; Algerians to France; and Indonesian Eurasians and Amboinese to Holland. These are not, as in the past, small numbers of selected individuals come for schooling in the process of being co-opted by the colonial system, but large numbers of poor working people come to make their way down those gold-paved streets to some better condition of life. The collapse of the old authority relationship in which the lesser breeds knew their place, the class of the newcomers and their status as permanent immigrants instead of tolerated visitors, and their larger numbers have led to new internal tensions, conflicts, and riots in the streets in each of these countries. Old pretensions of relaxed attitudes about racial difference, especially in France, could not survive these new outbreaks of an old disease. This experience has created new problems for these ex-spreaders of the higher civilization and higher culture and raised new questions they have to settle about the character of their own societies and the shapes of *their* pluralisms.

✦

POSTREVOLUTIONARY: Marxist socialist doctrine promised a new international socialist world order to replace capitalist anarchy, imperialist oppression, and nationalist rivalries leading to wars. In Russia, the Bolsheviks promised a model of this kind of society, a political structure in which some of the hundred-odd nationalities in the country would enjoy territorial separateness and all would enjoy cultural and linguistic autonomy while sharing in some representative fashion in the central power. These promises were broken, precisely on the rock of the "national question," which never ceased to be a central issue in Communist theory and a very live issue in Communist politics.

Almost involuntarily from the beginning and then deliberately under Stalin, Russia became a national-Communist power. It subverted revolutionary movements elsewhere to its own national strategic goals and policies. This took place with especially crushing consequences in Germany, China, Spain, and France, aborting events that might have radically altered the course of world history in the critical decades between 1920 and 1940 had they been able to run their course independent of Russian intervention. This is a history whose threads lead directly to the subsequent cleavage between national-Communist Russia and national-Communist China, each with the device of a new socialist world order still inscribed on its banner, each readily reviving racial myths—the "yellow peril" is more vividly seen in Russia today than it ever was in America or in Hohenzollern Germany—and each making ready to annihilate the other in the name of its own national power interests.

Inside the Communist countries, the promised new order has proved equally elusive. After nearly sixty years of more or less monolithic Communist power in Russia and nearly thirty years of the same in eastern Europe, internal and intra-bloc politics still largely revolve around ancient antagonisms and unresolved issues of relations between and among the scores of "nations" or tribes that make up the populations of these countries. The structure of separate republics and other nationality-centered institutions was set up and a charade of national political/cultural autonomy continues to be played in it. But the doctrinal line of respect for national/cultural differences keeps getting tangled with the lines of authoritarian central power. Nowhere have they fallen into a design which meets the needs either of the wielders of power or of the stubborn keepers of all the many primordial bonds. The problem was not resolved in Russia, not even in the three decades of the monolithic rule of Stalin—himself a Georgian and a prime theoretician on the "national question"—when whole peoples were uprooted and deported by fiat and literally millions condemned to die at the hands of the regime. Nor, since 1945, when it gained suzerainty over eastern and southeastern Europe, has Russian power been able to keep the added nationalities of its extended empire under effective control. Neither, for that matter, have the Communist regimes inside any of these countries. The politics of Czechoslovakia still revolve around being Czech and being Slovak: Russia's armed assertion of its power in that country in 1968 made full use of this communal division. In Yugoslavia the aging Tito tried vainly in his waning years to keep that country from exploding again into its Serbian, Croatian, Montenegrin, Bosnian, and other assorted parts. Rumania and Hungary still tussle over

Transylvania, and every country uses the presence of national minorities in every other one—Albanian, Macedonian, Hungarian, or whatever—as a weapon in external pressures and counterpressures. This is the pattern not only on Russia's western frontiers but equally on the eastern, where Mongolian-Chinese antipathies are manipulated, and where, for another example, a "free Turkestan" movement has been set up to make use of the separatist restiveness of Turkic peoples under Chinese rule in Sinkiang.

Neither visionary beliefs, then, nor large-scale industrialization and urbanization, nor the passage of generations, nor concentrated centralized power, nor massive repression, nor elaborate theories, nor structural schemes have apparently been able to check the survival and the persistence of the distinctive separateness of the many nationalities or tribes of people who live under the Communist system. Socialist internationalism, like Christian brotherhood, remains an elusive myth mocked by the actualities. Resistance to Great Russian (or Great Serb or Great Czech, or Great Hungarian, or Great Rumanian, and, to be sure, Great Han, etc.) still fuels conflicts and patterns of behavior little changed from what they were in all the generations before the Communist era.

✦

POSTILLUSIONARY: In the United States, the breakdown of the worldwide white supremacy system after 1945 brought down like pricked balloons a whole cluster of illusions about the nature of the American society and raised in new ways and on a new scale the question of the character of the "American" identity. It opened up a time of wrenching change in all group relations within the society and within every group the beginning of an equally wrenching re-examination of itself.

This condition was brought on partly by the fact that the long struggle for civil rights for blacks in America finally reached the time of decision in the highest court of the land, partly by the pressure of world events. It was triggered primarily, however, by the fact that black Americans stopped accepting, stopped submitting to the old rules of the game, or the pace at which the society appeared ready to change them. The American society, which had maintained its illusions about itself by ignoring America's blacks, had to begin at last to take them into account. Black and white civil libertarians finally won the fifty-year-old battle to break down the legal barriers that had excluded blacks from the common civil rights nominally open to all. Blacks went on to challenge all the other consequences of their long subjection, to hammer at the walls of customary rejection and exclusion that still stood, and to seek to overcome all the crippling social and economic disadvantages from which they had suffered for so long. Also, perhaps most painfully and confusedly of all, they had to seek to rediscover and redefine themselves, a process that led some black Americans to go looking for their own Houses of Muumbi while waiting to discover in the new and unfamiliar circumstances just what it might still mean to be not only black but also "American" after all. They have thus raised in the sharpest possible way the issue of whether the American society, finally opening after 1945 to begin including groups long kept wholly or partially outside, would open enough to include its blacks on the same basis as it was at last coming to include everyone else—Catholics, Jews, Chinese, Japanese, etc.—in the enjoyment of rights, status, and opportunities common to all.

This crisis of "black" and "American" identity would by itself be crisis enough. But its effect in these years was to shake up all the other groups in the society located at various stations along the road from being "out" to being "in." It brought on change in the perception and self-perception of the "group" that had always been seen by all the others as "in"—the white Protestants of northern European origin who had been seen as the dominant majority "group" of the society and who now began to be so loosely and commonly lumped together under the pejorative label "Wasp." In other mostly nonwhite groups—the Mexican-Americans and other Spanish-speaking groups, the American Indians, the Chinese-Americans and Japanese-Americans—something of the black pattern began to be reproduced, with radical fringe groups appearing and reflecting—and momentarily speaking for—the much more widely felt and deeply laid feelings of whole populations that their status in the society and their image of themselves somehow had to change.

Among distinctive subgroupings in the white population, these lines were much blurrier, the responses more ambivalent and ambiguous, the effects of the turmoil much more mixed. This great turning of trend and circumstance in the American society found the Irish Catholics the farthest "in." The election of an Irish Catholic as President of the United States in 1960 marked not only a watershed in the history of the Irish in America but of anti-Catholic bigotry as well. The opening of the Catholic Church to the winds of change, the turmoil in the clergy, in Catholic education, and in the way all Catholics could hold or practice their beliefs became part of the great heaving and changing landscape for the Irish in America and for all Catholics as well.

Jews, not likely to make it to the White House any time soon, did make it through most of the barriers that still stood high against them as recently as 1945. This new experience of inclusion led some Jews to fear for the preservation of *their* House of Muumbi, and in all parts of the Jewish community there was much exhortation in this time, much effort to keep Jews inside the fold. On the other hand, there were felt limits that soon put a check on any integrationist euphoria. A division appeared between blacks and Jews, who had participated together for decades in the civil rights struggle, turning up as virulent anti-Semitism among black militant radicals and in milder form among others. It was much the same with the anti-Zionist and anti-Israel stance taken by the so-called New Left in the 1960s, a development that especially repelled those Jews who had identified themselves with the "old" Left and the much larger numbers that had always been on the side of liberal causes in American politics. There were the ambiguous attitudes that sprang up on all sides after 1967 and even more so after the October war in 1973, in attitudes about and toward Israel, both at the level of government policy and among both Protestant and Catholic religious bodies. A revived uncertainty, a sudden sense of new fragility came upon many Jews in the 1960s and 1970s, blurring again what had seemed to be coming so clear about being both "Jewish" and "American." It became more difficult to think that all the old ghosts had been laid; they were still heavily assailed by what Kurt Lewin once called "the uncertainty of belongingness." Like all other groups going through the change process in the American society, Jews were finding that the shaping of their identity was still part of the unfinished business of shaping the American identity itself.

In the other much larger sections of the white American population made up of second- and third-generation European Catholic immigrant stock, the impacts of these shock waves were still much less clearly seen. These groups, which came to be called the "white ethnics," make up a great part of the "middle" or "blue collar" classes in the population. Much began to be written about their disaffection, especially about the facts and fears of the so-called backlash that the new black aggressiveness of the 1960s ignited across occupational and neighborhood lines in the industrial centers of the northeast, and the special appeal that the candidacy of George Wallace turned out to have among these voters in the national political campaigns of 1968 and 1972. These sections of the population are still largely identified by their national origins: they are the children and grandchildren of Italians, Poles, Czechs, Slovaks, Ukrainians, Slovenes, Hungarians, Armenians, Greeks, and other immigrant groups of recent generations. Triggered by the new militancy and self-assertion among blacks, a literature and a rhetoric of ethnic reassertion began to appear in these quarters as well. This was still largely the work of either the older ethnic faithful or of new, younger ethnic enthusiasts driven by the black explosion back to their own enclaves. In the absence of adequate reporting, it remained difficult to say just how much saliency the ethnic element had in the current moods and feelings of people in these highly varied groups of the population, so painfully caught by the economic and social pressures of these years. It was clear enough, however, that, like all others, they were going through new exposures, that they were sharing in the realization that American society was not as melted as many had thought it to be, that the question of what is "American" was not as clear as they had felt it to be, that the task of redefinition that faced everyone else faced them too.

For some, this is an identity crisis, as in the case of blacks, or at least an identity problem, as among so many others. But for all, it arrives along with a whole series of other contradictions and crises in American life, all coming to some kind of head at the same time. These have had to do with persisting poverty and its consequences, rotting ghettos and beleaguered central cities, drugs, polluted environments, the great confusions of the new discovery that the industrial age has its limits, that not everything that comes out of factory smokestacks is progress. They have to do with the deeply traumatic experience of the Vietnam war, which brought into question the common belief in the essential virtue, not to say the competence, of the use of American power in the world. In the Watergate scandals that ended with the unprecedented resignation of a president under threat of impeachment, they brought into question the nature of the American political system itself. In all these major areas of national life in tumultuous events across two decades, many old illusions died or were laid very low. These were illusions about the "melting pot," about the reality of freedom and democracy in the American system, especially as it dealt with its nonwhite minorities, about the virtue of ever-advancing technological and scientific progress, about the assumed virtue of the American role in world affairs. The spasm of disaffection that appeared in its most extreme form among the most radical or disaffected youth in the late 1960s did in fact cut much more deeply and more widely among people of all ages and of every kind who thought they knew—or always unaskingly assumed that they knew—but now did not know or were much less sure what it meant to be "American."

It can be no wonder or surprise, as we stumble on our way toward new definitions and the new shapes of some new American pluralism, if many people in many groups begin to think their only real security may lie after all in the closer circle of their own tribal kin, in their own Houses of Muumbi, American style.

✦

These conditions raise new questions and new orders of questions, demand many kinds of fresh inquiry. They call us down paths either too heedlessly traveled before, or not noticed as we went down what we thought were the main roads. In all their places and their many kinds, these are massive displacements. The relative place of virtually every group of people on earth has been shifting in some way. All the lights, angles, shadows, and reflections by which people see themselves or are seen by others have moved or are moving. All postures and styles of behavior are in some way ceasing to be what they were, and more or less convulsively becoming something else. Out of the breakup of old power systems or the fragile instability of new ones comes the onset of turmoil and instability for all people in *all* their relationships. And out of this come the great new confusions that surround us. Hence the fierce holding on to vestiges of a more secure past. Hence the search for what has somewhere, somehow been lost. Hence the lunge back to the tribal caves, back to the Houses of Muumbi. It is a desperate effort to regain that condition of life in which certain needs were met, to get behind walls that enclose them once more, if only in their minds, in a place where they can feel they belong, and where, grouped with their kind, they can regain some measure of what feels like physical and emotional safety.

So we are refragmenting and retribalizing ourselves. We are doing so at a much more rapid rate, certainly, than we are moving toward any more humane kind of humanhood in the arrangement of our social and political affairs. Where this all has to go, where it can go, are still questions without answers in this time of great change. Since it is difficult to picture a superbalkanized world solving any of the most pressing of the earth's problems, one has to try to imagine what new larger coherences may come into being that might have a better chance. It could still take the form of a postnuclear quiet and thus solve everything. It can certainly, as in the past, appear as some new set of systems of concentrated power imposed and maintained by force; by all the evidence man is still more a wolf to other men than anything else. On the other hand, the belief that he might be something else dies hard. It could just be possible that the present great spasm of fragmentation could lead to the shaping of new pluralisms that will somehow better meet the old, old needs of people in the new circumstances.

If we have any chance at all to move in that direction, we have to begin, it seems to me, by asking again why the most universal needs of human beings have apparently been satisfied only in their most parochial groupings, and not satisfied well enough or at all in any broader, not to say brotherly, political systems or associations. For about two hundred years, the best and the brightest intellectuals in the Western world believed that with the advance of science, the growth of knowledge, the mastery of nature, reason would win and all earlier forms of human backwardness would just go away. This included all superstition—in which many included religion—and all the narrow tribal and other smallnesses that blocked the enlargement of the human spirit and kept human existence from being more humane. Science advanced, knowledge grew, nature was mastered, but Reason did not conquer and tribalism did not go away. It is, as Oscar Hammerstein's King of Siam said, "a puzzlement." At its worst, our current retribalization signals the end of the illusion. At its best, the present confusion of affairs arises out of a demand by all kinds of groups of people that each one should enjoy a respected and self-respecting status in society. The problem is and always has been how to make status of this kind mutually effective between groups beyond the occasional balances of terror we have been able to maintain here and there from time to time.

To try to understand our plight better than we do, we need to take a fresh look at the nature and the functioning of the basic group identities that lie at the heart of this matter. As we can so plainly see, they keep sprouting out of the ruins of empires, reappearing in the interstices of every kind of new culture and new politics, and continuing to frustrate the idealists and rationalists who stubbornly go on thinking that there has to be some better way than this to carry on the human story.

II

THE SNOWMAN

Your typical ultra-abstractionist fairly shudders at concreteness: other things equal, he positively prefers the pale and the spectral. If the two universes were offered, he would always choose the skinny outline rather than the rich thicket of reality. It is so much purer, clearer, nobler.

—WILLIAM JAMES

THE EVIDENCE of current human affairs seems to suggest that the House of Muumbi is where man really lives, that his essential tribalism is so deeply rooted in the conditions of his existence that it will keep cropping out of whatever is laid over it, like trees forcing their way through rocks on mountainsides a mile high. This may be why the various universal dreams have either remained dreams of heaven where all human beings would finally become one before God—i.e., when they are no longer human beings—or have been transmuted into power systems in which tribal differences are contained under the dominance of some particular tribe which reaches the top—i.e., when human beings are held in thrall.

Those who have aspired to some higher estate for human society have generally seen man's stubborn tribalism as a function of his backwardness. Indeed, following Paul McClean's "schizophysiology," Arthur Koestler has suggested that the gap between man's intellectual and emotional behavior, between his technological achievements and his social/human failures, is due to an evolution-

ary "mistake," i.e., the survival of the phylogenetically older reptilian or lower mammalian parts of the brain after the development
of the neocortex, the uniquely human "thinking cap" that in the
last half million years or so has brought man to where he is now.
The two have never been integrated, hence all our bewildering
contradictions. This is why man knows he must die but still rejects
the idea, peopling his universe with demons, ghosts, witches, and
other more respectable invisible presences. Coupled with the
uniquely prolonged dependence of the human on his elders and his
kin for safety in a world filled with faster and stronger enemies, this
is what has produced the quality and power of man's tribal solidarity, "his overwhelming urge to belong, to identify himself with
tribe or nation and above all with his system of beliefs."

It could not be, of course, because these matters are lodged in
the old limbic system of the brain rather than in the neocortex—
everyone knows there can be nothing reptilian or lower mammalian
about scientists and intellectuals—but it is a fact that scientists and
intellectuals who have uncovered and so precisely defined so much
else about nature have been remarkably vague and imprecise about
this aspect of human experience. Definitions, even at the simplest
level, remained elusive, loose, varied. In the dictionaries and encyclopedias, and in all the works of scholarship that touch on the
matter, words like "tribe," "clan," "nation," "nationality," "race,"
"ethnic group," and "ethnicity" continue notably blurred to this day.
Each writer has cast his definitions to suit his own particular taste,
bent, need, or discipline, or to reflect, at whatever remove, his relationship to his own House of Muumbi. This appears still to be the
case even in the considerable volume of new multidisciplinary literature about ethnicity and multiethnic societies. In recent seasons
especially, there have been dozens of academic safaris in the field,
especially American safaris, trying to track the snowman of "ethnicity," everyone sure by now that it exists and is important, more
important than most people thought, but no one sure what it looks
like, much less whether it is abominable or not.[1] This could be
because too few seekers have sought hard enough, suffering too
many blocks and meeting too many obstacles on the way. It also has

to be partly due to the fact that the reality represented by all these terms is in fact imprecise, full of contradictions and uncertainties and differing outlooks, experiences and versions. The most that can be said, perhaps, is that an effort to get sharper about matters long left vague, to seek for some new order among the old confusions, is at least under way.

Almost the first encounter on this shadowy path is with "identity," and here too the shapes are many, the meanings numerous, the usages innumerable. Among them all, moreover, the linkage between "identity" and "group identity" remains the murkiest of all, the term "group" generally serving as a blur or amalgam for all the many kinds of groups in which people appear and sort themselves. This blurring continues all the way from Charles Cooley's "primary group" to Talcott Parsons' "collectivities" or what Ali Mazrui has more recently called "total identities." In social psychology, what Gordon Allport nearly twenty years ago called "the venerable riddle of the group mind" has been getting more and more venerable despite the great increase in the volume of literature on the subject from so many different points of view.[2] As Bruce Mazlish sorrowfully remarked, the historian's thirst "for explanation in terms of group psychology and group behavior" remains unsatisfied. "The stern and demanding challenge of group psychology and its relation to history still confronts us, unsmilingly."[3]

Unsmilingly indeed. One wonders what would turn up if one went looking into the lives of scholars who have written about this matter to discover how they have related as individuals to the various Houses of Muumbi into which *they* were born. Some would never have left, and this would surely be reflected in whatever it is they wrote on the subject. On the other hand, there must be among scientists/intellectuals a fairly high ratio of individuals who became scientists/intellectuals precisely because they had pushed open the shutters of their Houses of Muumbi or had moved out looking for the wider, more open spaces in which neocortex types, unlike limbic-brain types, might find more to satisfy them. Out there they joined the large number of people who have been detribalized by all the varieties of the modernizing experience, the crossing of many lines, cultural, intellectual, national, racial, ethical, religious. Basic group identity being what it is, however—a powerful forming element in the individual psyche and individual personality—this separation too must be reflected in what they wrote or did *not* write about the subject when they dealt with it. This may have something to do with explaining why there was, for such a long time, a general tendency to blur the basic group identity, to blend or confuse it with all kinds of other less primary groupings, or to treat the basic group identity as a *given* and to look at some of its effects and not at *it*. Or, for that matter, not to look at it at all.

Perhaps, then, it is with the psychoanalysts that we should begin in this effort to begin looking *at* basic group identity, to try to see what it consists of and how it functions. This leads us to Erik Erikson, who has taken out a kind of international copyright on the very word "identity" and who went beyond his master Freud precisely in his effort to deal more specifically with the link between the individual and the group, between the child and society, between the lonely ego and the crowd.

But in Erikson too one finds the familiar blur, purposive sometimes, sophisticated sometimes, almost always literate, but still a blur. Erikson's deliberate imprecision—perhaps imprecision aforethought is the way to put it—speaks both to the high merits and the high limitations of Erikson's style. It speaks to the complexity and elusiveness of the matters he seeks to deal with—even the term "identity" itself is never pinned down in his pages but allowed, as he says, to speak for itself in its various connotations. It remains something "as unfathomable as it is all-pervasive. One can only explore it by establishing its indispensability in various contexts." But this respect for the essential disorderliness of the truth contributes more than is needful, it seems to me, to the blurry all-in or all-inclusiveness with which one is left. Something more than unavoidable vagueness is achieved by the way Erikson at different times uses "society" or "social organization" or "history" or "historical change" or just "group" as the setting in which, as he points out, the individual identity inescapably develops.

Erikson tells us that he began by "striving for greater specificity" than Freud in dealing with the social setting in which the family's influence on the child is exerted. Freud himself had paid only fleeting respects to the social sources of individual development. To be sure, he did locate them in the parents' superego, which became "the vehicle of tradition and of all the age-long values which have been handed down in this way from generation to generation . . . the past, the traditions of the race and the people." Freud also wrote that "only rarely . . . is individual psychology in a position to disregard the relations of this individual to others . . . and so from the very first individual psychology is at the same time social psychology." Group psychology, he went on, "is therefore concerned with the individual man as a member of a race, of a nation, of a caste, of a profession, of an institution, or as a component of a crowd of people who have been organized into a group at some particular time for some particular purpose."[4] When he did refer to particular kinds of groups, then, Freud took the same broadly inclusive view that we have been noting in others. His more governing view was, however, much broader and much cruder still. His word translated as "group" in *Group Psychology and the Analysis of the Ego* is actually—as the translator notes—*Masse,* German equivalent of LeBon's *foule,* i.e. "crowd" or "mob"; and indeed when Freud describes a "group" in these pages, he usually does describe a mob.[5] Freud moved quite slowly, it seems, and not very far, from this rough separation of the individual as one of a family to the individual as part of a mob. He left his school of followers with a basis for little more than an occasional ritual acknowledgment of the "social factors" in individual development. Actually Freud's central concept of "group" had to do not with the substance of various group characteristics but with the movement of individuals to identify with a leader, and thereby finding identification with each other. He "corrects" the assertion that man is a "herd animal" and suggests instead that "he is rather a horde animal, an individual in a horde led by a chief."[6]

It was in fact this thread, of *the leader,* that Erikson picked up from Freud when he set out to get more specific than Freud about the role of "society" or "history" in the development of the individual. Thus his *Luther,* thus his *Gandhi.* His psycho-biographical studies have been aimed at showing how that particular leader acquired and developed the drives that enabled him, at that right place at that right moment, to become the leader of that particular horde.

When it comes, however, to Erikson's treatment of the "society" or the "group" or the "history" which shapes individual development, we find ourselves in much vaguer territory. In an early major article on this subject—"Ego Development and Historical Change," originally written in 1946[7]—his first words are "Men who share an ethnic area, a historical era, or an economic pursuit are guided by common images of good and evil [which] assume decisive concreteness in every individual's ego development." Here we see that "group" takes in "ethnic," a shared period of time/history—e.g., all who took part, say, in a war or lived through a depression—and finally "economic pursuit," which takes us off into all possible varieties of group experience. He wants to "chart the [individual's] life cycle interwoven throughout with the history of the community," and summons social science to join psychoanalysis in this task. But the question then becomes how he sorts out the kinds/specifics of these group associations, and how or whether he differentiates among the many different kinds. The kind of interweaving resulting from, say, being black in Mississippi in 1960, or an upper-class Englishman in 1900, is going to be quite different in kind from that caused, say, by being someone who went through the Depression, the Second World War, or being a bricklayer or a lawyer.

In his core work on the life cycle, Erikson refers to the "group" or "society" usually in quite general terms. "Social life begins with each individual's beginnings." Child training is "the method by which a group's basic way of organizing experience (its group identity as we called it) is transmitted." Development through life's stages produces "a defined ego within a social reality." Or again: "The term identity . . . connotes both a persistent sameness within oneself (selfsameness) and a persistent sharing of some kind of essential character with others." In one of his more succinct statements of this relationship, he speaks of "the mutual complementation of ethos and ego, of group identity and ego identity." This goes well beyond Freud, but Erikson turns out to be as loosely inclusive as Freud about the "group" whose interaction with the individual ego identity is so decisive. In his biographical look at Shaw, he refers to Shaw's embrace of socialism as the acquisition of a group identity—i.e., a sharing in an ideology and a political movement. He speaks elsewhere of the "negative group identity formations" open to young people in "clique formations ranging all the way from neighborhood gangs and jazz mobs to dope rings, homosexual circles and criminal gangs." These highly varied associations are clearly relevant in their many different dimensions—people do belong to all kinds of groups at different times in different settings, acquiring what the sociologist Anselm Strauss has called "multiple identities." The task of achieving "greater specificity" remains, especially in distinguishing among these kinds of group identity, and most particularly, the relative meaning and place among them of the ethnic or basic group identity.

Referring to Freud's single use of the term "identity"—Freud used it in connection with his own Jewish identity—Erikson says: "Here the term identity points to an individual's link with the unique values, fostered by a unique history, of his people . . . identity of something in the individual's core with an essential aspect of the group's inner coherence . . ." Erikson stresses the extraordinary depth of the words Freud chose to describe his identity as a Jew: ". . . many obscure emotional forces which were the more powerful the less they could be expressed in words, as well as a clear consciousness of inner identity, the safe privacy of an inner mental construction . . ." The actual German words used by Freud, Erikson stresses, can hardly convey in English translation the depth of their usage. Here, he says, Freud is speaking of identity "in a most central ethnic sense," suggesting "a deep commonality known only to those who shared in it, and only expressible in words more mythical than conceptual." Identity, he says here,[8] "is a process 'located' *in the core of the individual* and yet also *in the core of his communal culture* [italics in original], a process which establishes, in fact, the identity of these two identities."

This would appear to be the starting point of a fresh examination of the nature, role, function, and impact on the individual of these powerful influences that reach him through the group into which he is born. Between them, Freud and Erikson use strong words to name these influences: "unique history" and "values," "inner coherence," "shared sameness," "obscure emotional force," "safe privacy," "inner mental construction." These are matters that bear heavily on every individual's life and have had profound positive and negative effects on the whole of human experience in all known time. Unfortunately, Erikson does not take us much further into them. In most of his later references to these basic human groupings, he shifts radically in tone, level, angle of perception. Where these references are not again general or elliptical, they have to do for the most part with broadly characterizing these groups as *pseudospecies*—as opposed to the specieshood of man—each one considering itself chosen and "considering all the others a freakish and gratuitous invention of some irrelevant deity." Each uses others as "a screen for projection of negative identities . . . a reason to slaughter each other." This system of "mortal divisions has been vastly overburdened with the function of reaffirming for each pseudospecies its superiority over all others. . . . The pseudospecies, then, is one of the more sinister aspects of all group identity." This theme is invariably coupled in these passages with urgent pleas for global-universal reform, e.g., for realizing "the fact and obligation of man's specieshood" as a condition for creating a "more universal, more inclusive human identity," which modern technology imposes and survival demands.

As any reader of Erikson can discover for himself—e.g., in his *Gandhi,* in his essays on youth and the blacks, and in his before-and-after reflections about the American identity[9]—Erikson as ideologist-prophet (religio-universalism) and student of history-politics-race is sharply distinguishable from Erikson as analyst and prober of the inwardnesses of the life cycle. The levels are quite different[10] and are worth attention, but in the context of a study of Erikson, not of group identity. Erikson tells us that "to be a special kind . . . is an important element in the human need for personal and collective identities," but he never gets much beyond telling us that this is important primarily because it represents a pseudo-solution that divides man instead of working toward his inescapable oneness. We get only this wide-cast negative or "sinister" charac-terization; here the plus-minus mix of all things fails to draw Erik-son's normally more sensitive scrutiny. Indeed, there is much evidence in his pages that he feels acute discomfort when con-fronted with the actuality of these "mortal divisions." It shows up in his writing about American blacks and is illustrated in the *Gandhi* by his intense preoccupation with the lofty heights of Hindu Oneness and his ignoring—but for an incidental mention here and there—of the lowly actualities of Hindu caste. Erikson has given us a somewhat higher threshold from which to explore the linkages between ethos and ego, but he leaves us with much "greater speci-ficity" yet to be achieved in our understanding of the basic group identities by which man has so persistently lived for so long and at such cost.

Erich Fromm, another psycho-political analyst with an ideology to grind (secular socialism), traveled a good deal further down some of these paths. He also wanted to see "individualized man" enter into "active solidarity with all men [through] spontaneous activity, love, and work, which unite him again with the world, not by pri-mary ties but as a free and independent individual."[11] He also saw the "family as the agent of society" in the shaping of the individual personality and looked upon "human nature as essentially histor-ically determined" and on man's "social character" as much more crucial in his development than Freud had indicated. He also saw "primary ties" as blocking desirable human development, standing in the way of reason and critical capacities—"they let him recog-nize himself only through the medium of his, or their, participation in a clan, a social or religious community, and not as human being."

On the other hand, Fromm acknowledged the depth and power

of the individual's need not to be isolated and alone, especially to escape what Balzac called "moral aloneness" from "lack of relatedness to values, symbols, patterns," and to *belong*. Primary ties, said Fromm, block man's development "as a free, self-determining, productive individual." But he also clearly saw that the matter also has a powerful dialectic aspect. Growing strength, integration, individuation, solidarity with other human beings also lead to "growing isolation, insecurity, and thereby growing doubt concerning one's own role in the universe, the meaning of one's life, and with all that a growing feeling of one's own powerlessness and insignificance as an individual." Over against this, the primary ties offer a positive alternative: "This identity with nature, clan, religion, gives the individual security. He belongs to, he is rooted in, a structuralized whole in which he has an unquestionable place. He may suffer from hunger or suppression, but he does not suffer from the worst of all pains—complete aloneness and doubt." The primary bonds give a person "genuine security and the knowledge of where he belongs."

This begins to touch, it seems to me, the inwardnesses of the matter: insecure men who are torn loose from all moorings cling hard to wherever they can find an "unquestionable place" where they belong, and they are finding this place more and more in this time, in what Edward Shils has called "primordial affinities" with their "ineffable significance" and their peculiarly coercive powers.

Shils offered this description in the course of a review of research and theory about groups. While he did not elaborate on it, he did stress the difference between these and other ties and suggested that his work with Talcott Parsons on primary groups and collectivities would have benefited by taking these differences into more realistic account.[12] Following Shils, the anthropologist Clifford Geertz, looking at the matter in the context of postcolonial politics, offered a more detailed description. These primordial attachments or identifications consisted, he said, of the assumed "givens" of social existence. These he identified as "immediate continuity and kin connection, mainly, but beyond them the givenness that stems from being born into a particular religious community, speaking a particular language, or even a dialect of a language, and following particular social practices," establishing a bond "of some unaccountable absolute import attributed to the very tie itself." Geertz distinguished these bonds from other kinds—class, party, business, union, profession—pointing out that the groups formed out of such bonds do not, as such, become "candidates for nationhood." He offered a brief descriptive catalogue of these identifications: *assumed blood ties, race, language, region, custom.*[13]

In a treatment of the same subject at about the same time,[14] I called these ties the "basic group identity," and offered the listing of essential characteristics which have become the subject of this book. I reported on the process by which I had come to focus not on how group identities were affecting the new politics but on how the new politics—the changing power relations—were affecting the holders of various group identities. The pursuit of this experience through a long series of concrete case studies, all of which have been reported in detail elsewhere,[15] led me directly to the need to take this much closer look at "basic group identity" itself.

In the thickets of current usage, it is usually encountered as "ethnic identity" or "ethnic group." In a vocabulary filled with imprecision the word "ethnic" is more imprecise than most. But I *am* dealing here with identity in the sense that Erikson attributed to Freud's single use of the word, i.e., in *the central ethnic sense.* It *is* the group identity formed out of what Shils and Geertz referred to as primordial affinities or attachments.

In the pages that follow, I shall be trying to sort out and describe these affinities and attachments and show how they cluster in the making of every person's basic group identity. I will try to indicate how and why these ties and connections are primordial, what functions they perform, what needs they meet, why they persist so powerfully in the human experience. I will go on then to describe by illustrative examples how these features of basic group identity appear now in the experience of many different groups as they move through the shifting patterns of power and powerlessness that fill our contemporary political affairs. I will be trying, in short, to draw a full-face picture of the snowman himself that will show him to be not mysterious at all but a creature we know well, no stranger, even in our own families. Abominable, maybe, but with a face that mothers, all our mothers, have always loved.

If the nature of group identity turns out to be, then, something we knew all the time, it could be because of the time it takes to discover how complicated simple things really are; because our past awareness of this phenomenon has clearly not prepared us for the shapes and roles it has assumed in all our lives now; and most of all, I think, because all that we were ever taught to assume as "given" about all the various groupings of human beings has now, really for the first time, been taken away. So we have to try to see it all now as if we had never actually seen it before. The only place to begin, then, is at the beginning.

III

IDOLS OF THE TRIBE

> The Idols of the Tribe have their foundation in human nature itself, and in the tribe or race of men . . . All perceptions, as well as the sense of the mind, are according to the measure of the individual and not according to the measure of the universe. And the human understanding is like a false mirror, which, receiving rays irregularly, distorts and discolors the nature of things by mingling its own nature with it.
>
> — FRANCIS BACON

To BEGIN WITH, then, basic group identity consists of the ready-made set of endowments and identifications that every individual shares with others from the moment of birth by the chance of the family into which he is born at that given time in that given place.

There is first the new baby's *body* itself, all the *shared physical characteristics* of the group acquired through the parental genes—skin color, hair texture, facial features—all that comes through the long process of selection, through what René Dubos has called the "biological remembrance of things past," plus whatever else—we still argue about *how* much else—comes through the parental membranes to give each new person the original shape of his or her unique self.*

---

* Two remarks here regarding the "his" and the "hers" of this matter:

(1) The only third person singular possessive pronoun in English besides "his" and "hers" is the neuter "its." If the use of "his" when we mean both "his" and "hers"—like the use of "men" when we mean "human beings" or

But even as it draws its first breath, hears its first sound, feels its first touch, the new infant begins to be endowed with everything else that awaits it in that family at that time in that place. These are the common holdings of the group of which the baby becomes a member, the social features, what Erikson called the "shared samenesses" that enter in all their complex ways into the making of the individual ego identity. It is quite a stock of endowments.

As an extension of its own physical characteristics, the baby is born in a place, his *birthplace,* and the kind of place it is has already had and—in most cases—will have much to do with shaping the outlook and way of life that this new baby begins to share from his first day. The baby acquires a *name,* an individual name, a family name, a group name, a first symbol for the new child in the *language* through which he will discover his world. He is already a product of the *history and origins,* of which, by being born to this family in this place at this time, he becomes heir. He automatically acquires the *religion* of his family and his group and he becomes at once an acknowledged holder of the *nationality* or other condition of national, regional, or tribal affiliation his people hold.

These legacies, with all their attached subclusters of mores, values, ethics, aesthetics, and assorted other attributes, come to the

---

"men *and* women"—does come to be seen simply as male sexist arrogance instead of acceptable surrogate usage and extension of meaning, then, as in the case of the deeply imbedded uses of the word "black," the language may need some revising. Meanwhile, as a feminist from way back who finds sexless neuterism just as offensive as sexist male *or* female chauvinism, I must keep on trying to write about these matters without mangling sensibilities or, as far as possible, the prose.

(2) Women obviously share common characteristics and some common conditions with other women across many cultures. But that does not mean that they share the same basic group identity as *women* any more than men do as *men,* not in the sense of basic group identity as I am trying to specify it here. The physical and other differences between men and women, marvelous as they are, do not make men and women candidates as such for separate nationhood. Every basic group identity is shared by the men and women in the group, with its particular terms, rules, conditions fixing the relationships between them. The struggle for equality of status for women is being fought with different degrees of success in different societies as part of the general current renovation of social and political systems. It has its problems, but as in the fight for racial justice in the American society, separation does not seem to be among the viable solutions.

child carrying the immense weight of the whole past as his family has received it. Before he has barely any consciousness at all, they shape the only reality of his existence and are made part of him. This is done formally and ritually at birth or soon thereafter, as in baptism, circumcision, and similar rites of entry into the group and again, after the conditioning of the childhood years, in the varieties of puberty rites or initiations by which young persons become fully admitted members of the group.

The new member of the group comes not only into his inheritance of the past but also into all the shaping circumstances of the present: the conditions of status that come or do not come with these legacies, his family's relative wealth or poverty, its relative position in the larger group to which it belongs, and the group's position relative to other groups in its environment—all the political-social-economic circumstances that impinge on the family and the group, with all the inward and outward effects these conditions have on the shaping of the individual's personality and the making of his life. Of these, the most decisive are the political conditions in which the group identity is held, the measure of power or powerlessness attached to it. How dominant or how dominated is the group to which this individual belongs? How static or how changing is this condition, and how, then, is he going to be able to see and bear himself in relation to others? This is the cardinal question, and it is essentially the question of the governing politics, the push and pull of power among the groups who share the scene.

Such are the holdings that make up the basic group identity. How they are seen and celebrated has provided the substance of most of what we know as history, mythology, folklore, art, literature, religious beliefs and practices. How the holdings of others are seen has provided most of the unending grimness of the we-they confrontation in human experience. Raised high or held low, these are the idols of all our tribes.

Each of these elements of the basic group identity invites fresh scrutiny. Each one exists, however, not alone but in the cluster of elements entwined and inseparable in close and intimate relation to one another. This cluster, moreover, is not a fixed, sculpted object but a live thing, changing its shape and size under varying conditions. We are now going through a time of great and heaving change in all the conditions that affect every person's life and circumstances. Changes in all power relations bring on changes in the way groups of people see themselves and relate to one another. This leads to a wrenching rearrangement of much that goes into the making of their basic group identities. I have tried to catch a closer glimpse of this process as it has been taking place in a number of different settings. This case study material, based on interviews with panels of individuals going through the experience, deals with black Americans, American Jews in Israel, Indian ex-Untouchables, English-educated Chinese Malaysians, Filipinos, and Japanese. Vignettes from these studies, most of which have been published at length elsewhere, will be turning up frequently among the examples to follow. Others will come from the public prints, filled every day with bits and pieces of this characteristic contemporary experience from just about everywhere on earth.

Each case, one finds, develops its own shapes, its own dynamics, its own peculiar intensities. There is not much about the study of the interaction of basic group identity and political change that can be reduced to single formulas or be symmetrically arranged. The various elements show up in different relationships to one another and with quite different specific gravities. Skin color and physical characteristics may be at the heart of the group identity cluster of the black American but only at the margins in the case of the blacker African, the core of whose group identity may lie in his tribal affiliation. History and origins can appear as the most powerfully positive centerpiece, say, for the Chinese with his Great Past, and as the most crushingly negative centerpiece for the ex-Untouchable in India who wants to blot his past out altogether. In Ulster it is being "Catholic" or "Protestant"—with the mix of history and religion that gives these identities their content—that governs everything about the terms on which a person in that country now is going to live or die. The common holding of Islam and fear-hate of the Hindus thrust East Bengal into a nation with the Punjabis,

Pathans, Sindis, and other Muslim peoples of India's west; geography, physical differences, language, history parted them a generation later in one of our current history's bloodier amputations.

But varied as such particulars can be, I believe it is possible to say that in all cases the *function* of basic group identity has to do most crucially with two key ingredients in every individual's personality and life experience: his sense of *belongingness* and the quality of his *self-esteem*. These come defined in many ways, and the needs they serve are met in many degrees of plus-ness and minus-ness in different cases, shaping thereby much of the behavior of the members of the group.

Obviously—and this is the point at which much blurring of "groups" takes place in the scholarly literature on the subject—these needs can be and often are satisfied at certain levels within the nuclear family itself. This can happen in some other more purely interpersonal context, or in one or more of the many other multiple and secondary group identities individuals acquire in the course of their lives in all the different collectivities to which they come to belong: class, social, educational, occupational, professional, even recreational. These are, indeed, the settings in which the literature of psychology and social psychology usually deals with the need all people have to belong and to enjoy some measure of esteem and self-esteem.[1]

But these secondary sources of belongingness and self-esteem serve only where basic group identity differences do not get in the way. This occurs within the enclosure of homogeneous groups where the basic group identity is a given, shared by all, and where differentiation takes place along other lines. It does occur also up to a point in some multigroup or heterogeneous settings—more so today in the American society than it did only yesterday, but still only up to a point. In mixed societies, however, wherever the "inside" may be, the "outside" is still quite nearby. Out there, most generally still, it becomes necessary again to face that "uncertainty of belongingness," the challenge to self-esteem, in dealings with members of other groups, be they more powerful or less. Here once more the basic group identity and the conditions of that particular pecking order determine how far these needs are met or not met.

An individual *belongs* to his basic group in the deepest and most literal sense that here he is not *alone,* which is what all but a very few human beings most fear to be. He is not only not alone, but here, as long as he chooses to remain in and of it, he cannot be denied or rejected. It is an identity he might want to conceal, abandon, or change, but it is the identity that no one can take away from him. It is *home* in the sense of Robert Frost's line, the place where, when you've got to go there, they've got to take you in—the House of Muumbi, the womb, the emotional handholds of childhood, sometimes the physical place itself.[2] Or, in this age of massive migrations, for great numbers who have been transported across great physical and cultural distances, it is the ark they carry with them, the temple of whatever rules one's forebears lived by, the "tradition" or "morality" or whatever form of creed or belief in a given set of answers to the unanswerables.

Wrapped into this affiliation is the matter of esteem and self-esteem: how individuals are seen by others, how they see themselves. Some individuals get sufficient self-esteem out of the stuff of their individual personalities alone. More people have to depend on their group associations to supply what their individualities may deny them. Most need all they can get from all sources. Again, like health or money, this matter of self-esteem derived from group identity presents no problem when the group identity and the self-acceptance it generates is an assured given, an unquestioned premise of life not in itself a source of conflict. This can be the case in a tightly homogeneous society or group, or in a stable society in which all groups from top to bottom know their place and accept it. All, including the master groups at the top and the lowest at the bottom —e.g., the Untouchables in the Hindu caste system—accept themselves as they are told they are and accept the belief system that fixes the conditions of their lives. In all its degrees, the master-subject, superior-inferior relationship has been largely based on this kind of acceptance. It has not required a higher order of status to supply the necessary measure of belongingness and self-esteem to people; a lower order can supply it just as well, provided those assigned to it believe in it and accept it without question. In the psychological sense, there have been "happy" slaves in all kinds of societies, regardless of race, creed, color, or national origin. Such frozen pecking orders have lasted for varying periods of time in different settings. In our own time and world setting, such frozen orders have been breaking up and falling apart during the last several generations. It is precisely the need for a higher, or at least an equal, order of self-esteem, the need to acquire it, feel it, assert it, that has in our own time upset all such order and become one of the major drives behind all our volcanic politics. The drive to reassert group pride fueled all the nationalist movements that broke the rule of the empires. It stoked the national/racial chauvinisms that have played decisive roles in the Russian and Chinese revolutions and their aftermaths. More than anything else, it generated the power that broke the system of white supremacy in the United States.

Identification with the aggressor, with its patterns of self-rejection and self-hate, results from negative group identities successfully imposed by stronger on weaker groups. But when members of such groups stop submitting to this condition, group identities become a problem both to victimizers and victims and sooner or later erupt into social and political conflict and crisis. This is the point at which basic group identity and politics meet. It has been the starting point of many notable lives, much notable history, hardly any more notable than the history of our own time.

It would not do, I discovered early in this inquiry,[3] simply to identify these elements and arrange them in neat boxes, giving a speciously regular appearance to what is actually a confused splatter. No mind, no personality, no individual or group identity ever looks like a set of neat boxes. In my own mind, I picture group identity as looking more like a cell of living matter with a sprawlingly irregular shape. It is part of a cluster of cells making up the ego identity, sharing elements and common membranes with that other elusive quarry, the individual personality. In it, floating or darting about, are specks and flecks, bits and pieces, big shapes and little shapes, intersecting one another or hanging loose or clinging to one another, some out at the margins, some nearer the middle, some in wide orbits around the edges, some more narrowly moving deeper inside, but each one impinging upon, drawn to, or repelled by a nuclear core that exerts its gravity upon them all and fixes the shape and content of the messages that go out along the tiny meshes of the nervous system. The arrangement and mutual relationship of these elements differ from cell to cell, and the nature of the nuclear core differs not only from cell to cell but can change within any one cell, all of these interactions having a fluid character and subject to alteration under the pressure of conditions that come in upon them from the outside.

Here, I think, in the inwardness of group identity we can learn more than we know now about the interactions of the individual, his group, and the larger politics of his time and place and more, therefore, about the nature of our common contemporary experience. There are here a thousand questions needing answers, hosts of subjects waiting their authors. In the pages that follow, I shall be touching only on a few.

IV

BODY

✦

The soul is not more than the body . . .
The body is not more than the soul.

— W A L T   W H I T M A N

THE *body* is the most palpable element of which identity—individual or group—is made. It is the only ingredient that is unarguably biological in origin, acquired in most of its essential characteristics by inheritance through the genes. Primary as they may be, all the other things that go into the making of group identity are transformable. An individual can change his name, acquire a new language, ignore or conceal his origins, disregard or rewrite his history, abandon his ancestral religion or convert to another one, adopt a different nationality, embrace new mores, ethics, philosophies, styles of life. But there is not much he can do to change his body.

Some body change can result from cultural change: e.g., Japanese are growing taller because of changes in diet. Some aspects of the body's appearance can be changed by cosmetic or other means. This has often been done in the effort to become more "beautiful" or less "ugly," usually as part of an effort to escape physical identification with one group or gain closer identification with another. Hair can be dyed, curled, straightened, weight gained or lost, muscles hardened or laxed, skin can be bleached, breasts inflated or flattened, eyelids doubled and noses or other features altered by plastic surgery. But by and large and for most people, the body remains essentially unalterable. The color and texture of its skin and hair, the shape, relative size, and mutual arrangements of its main features come to us at birth and stay with us until we die. The body is at once the most intimate and inward and most obvious and outward aspect of how we see ourselves, how we see others, and how others see us.

Much lore and sacred doctrine has held that the spirit or soul of man is some essence temporarily housed in his body, surviving —indeed, finally freed—when the body wastes away and continuing its independent existence in all the other-worlds that have been created to serve the need not to die. All the ancient religions of India saw life in the body as an interlude of suffering. The body is a stronghold made of bones, an old Buddhist sutra said, "covered with flesh and blood, and there dwell in it old age and death, pride and deceit." With that more pungent concreteness acquired during its passage through China, Zen Buddhism called the body "a stinking bag of skin." This image of the body and the idea of ascetic mortification that went with it were important in much of Indian religiosity but did not get far in China, where, as in so much else, earthier notions prevailed. Hajime Nakamura quotes an old Chinese text: "We get our body, hair, and skin from the parents. To keep it from ruin and injury is the beginning of filial piety."[1] For Plato, the body was something to be left behind when, high enough up that ladder of love, the human spirit could rise right out of its body and out of the world into the wondrous realm of pure beauty. Aristotle, in his more Chinese-like way, thought that mind and body had to live with each other in a knowable world where pure beauty—perfected man—would not readily be found. In later times, even Descartes, who continued to think he was because he thought, once acknowledged: "I do not only reside in my body [like] a pilot in his ship, but am intimately connected with it and the mixture is so blended that something like a single whole is produced."[2]

It has been more in the modern temper to think of the "single whole," of the "soul" or "spirit" or "mind" or "personality" as imbedded in a complex of which the self and the body are integral parts and joined, what is more, all but indivisibly to the society to which the individual belongs. One student of this matter suggests that the body "plays a fundamental role in our impersonal sense of social identification with 'fellow-citizens' whom we may never have met," and he provocatively calls to witness "the irrepressible metaphor for society as 'the body politic,'" used, he points out, by Plato, Aristotle, St. Thomas, Hobbes, Hegel, and Spencer, suggesting "that the features of civil society may reflect those of our individual body."[3] Coming at this along quite another disciplinary dimension, the psychoanalyst Paul Schilder joins "world, body, and personality," the problem always being to see in every individual case how each relates to the other. "The body is a social phenomenon. Our own body image is never isolated, always accompanied by the body images of others." Or, as extended by Helen Lynd: "One's body image helps to shape one's image of the world and one's image of the world affects the images one has of one's own body: both parts are essential."[4]

More than almost anything else, physical characteristics serve as a badge of identity, instantly establishing who are the "we" and who the "they" and producing solidarity or hostility as the case may be. Skin color is usually the most visible but not the only critically effective physical difference. Between the Tutsi and the Hutu, who have been slaughtering each other in Rwanda and Burundi ever since they received their independence from the Belgians in 1962, the major physical difference is between slender tallness and shorter stockiness, badges of identification that can hardly be missed when the groups of killers seek each other out.* Among the children fathered and abandoned by American soldiers in Japan, Korea, and Vietnam, the physical features that cause them to be rejected by the societies in these countries sometimes

---

* "One woman who arrived at a . . . hospital had had both her hands hacked off with a machete. This is a common reprisal, for when the short Hutu find the tall Tutsi, they often cut off their legs at the ankles." *The New York Times,* June 17, 1973.

become the only bond they have to connect them to others in an otherwise totally hostile world.*

The notion that "they"—those who are different, those who threaten the group's solidarity—are in some way *unclean* is a recurring characteristic of many cultures. The *unclean* were stoned to death outside the camp in biblical times. Elsewhere, as in Hindu India and certain other cultures, they were condemned eternally to varieties of untouchability. In somewhat milder form, this turns up as one of the most familiarly common features of prejudice patterns built up between groups in our own as well as in other cultures: *they* are "dirty"—dirty niggers, dirty Jews, dirty wops, filthy bastards—or *they* have some peculiarly offensive smell. Almost as common in the patterns of prejudice is the notion, full of fearful envy and envious fear, that *they* have sexual organs of unusual size and indefatigable sexual energy to go with them. Such ideas have turned up in Western culture about blacks and Jews, among others, and in China and Japan about Europeans as well as blacks.[5]

Indeed, distinctive physical features have been so useful for these various purposes that some groups without features to mark them apart from other groups have deliberately created them. Thus circumcision, scarifying, tattooing, filing teeth, piercing or otherwise changing the shape of nose, ears, tongue, lips, all creating signs by which to identify those who belong and those who do not, sometimes with highly complicated effect.†

Less permanent but hardly less distinctive are changes made for

---

* "At an adoption agency in Saigon, a half-black girl named Le told why Lucy was her best friend. 'Lucy looks like me. Her eyes are like me, her nose is like me, her hair is like me, she is as black as me.' . . . then she added, 'I don't like Thanh Thuy because she doesn't have curly hair.' " David K. Shipler, in *The New York Times,* August 30, 1974.

† Consider what Shakespeare has Othello the circumcised Moor say in his final speech:

> . . . In Aleppo once
> Where a malignant and turban'd Turk
> Beat a Venetian and traduced the State,
> I took by the throat the circumcised dog
> And smote him, thus (stabs himself).

the same purpose in the body's extensions, beginning with the hair: e.g., the scalplock of some North American Indians, the monk's tonsure, the sideburns of the Hasidic Jew, the uncut hair and beard of the Sikh, the recent return in America and Europe of long hair on males as a badge of the so-called youth counterculture (serving as such only until others in the culture adopted it too), the shaved head of some of London's counter-counterculturists or of some Americans seeking to look like Hindu holy men, etc. Perhaps the most dramatic recent example of hair as a symbol of changing identity patterns was the aggressive return among Negro Americans to wearing hair "natural," shedding the practices of hair-straightening or close clipping that used to conceal the tight small curls previously seen as part of their ugly nonwhiteness. The new style of hair worn in "Afros"—sometimes worn demonstratively large, and sometimes achieving its "natural" effect in the form of a wig—soon came to be recognized in Africa as distinctively "American." It was in fact, however, a powerfully liberating act of assertion of acceptance of one's own physical character and its differences from others.

Besides distinctive ways of wearing the hair, distinctive marks can be made on the body's surfaces, caste marks in India, tattoos or painted patterns on the skin as in parts of Africa and Oceania and among American Indians. Finally, clothes and styles of dress are used to distinguish between bodies that would otherwise all look more or less alike undressed. Such are all the "native costumes" that occur from nation to nation, group to group, sometimes from village to nearby village, giving to each one the identifying distinctiveness it needs to feel. Clothes, of course, also become the identifying badge for all kinds of secondary groupings in all cultures, all the special costumes or uniforms worn down through time by the holy and the unholy, priests, judges, lawyers, policemen, firemen, messengers, artisans of every description, and —perhaps most representatively of all—by the soldiers each group dresses in their identifying garb to go out to kill the soldiers of other groups dressed in *their* identifying garb.

Besides serving as the badge of identity in so many groups, the body is for all groups the main basis for its standards of beauty, the main subject by far of most art in most cultures. This begins with what is perceived in any group as sexually attractive. One can find in anthropological literature some remarkable examples of what never pales or withers in the eyes of various beholders in different places. But the portrayal of the idealized human body as an object of art also incorporates all the other complicated perceptions and values that go into the making of any culture's aesthetics. Much waits to be learned from a comparative examination of the body in the art of different cultures, with all that it can tell us about so many aspects of each one and of the points at which they meet or part. These perceptions and values appear in one form or another among all the strands of experience that go into how members of any group anywhere see what they like in the human body—ideal or real—fair or dark, blond or brunette, tall or short, classic or crude, round or lean, broad or narrow, smooth or craggy, muscular or soft, hairy or bare, large-breasted or small, round-bellied or flat, small buttocks or large. These become, then, the preferred shapes in which "we" see ourselves, and they determine how "we" deal with the negatives of all these positives that "they"—in all those other groups—hold differently in view.[6]

The physical characteristics that bear on group identity extend in critical ways to the place, the land, the soil to which the group is attached, literally, historically, mythically. We are not as far as we may think we are from the myths to which, as Mircea Eliade has shown, we keep eternally returning, and these myths have heavily to do with the places with which we identify ourselves. Much in the spirit of Eliade, Octavio Paz identifies each human being's solitude not only with the "nostalgic longing for the body from which we were cast out, but also for the place from which the body came or to which in death it will return," seen by many ancients as "the center of the world, the navel of the universe," as "paradise where the spirits of the dead dwell," and as "the group's real or mythical place of origin." He cites from Lévy-

Bruhl a primitive belief that to leave one's place is to die, illustrated by an African ritual in which movement from a place is counteracted by carrying and eating every day some of the soil of the place that was home, thus giving the social solidarity of the group "a vital organic character" and making each individual in the group literally part of a "body." Almost all the rites connected with the founding of cities or houses "allude to a search for the holy center from which we were driven out." Thus "the great sanctuaries—Rome, Jerusalem, Mecca—are at the center of the world or symbolize and prefigure it." Thus too China, whose very name means "central country," precisely in the sense suggested by Eliade, that it stood at the center of the universe, "the meeting place of the three cosmic zones: heaven, earth, and hell."[7]

Such is some of the underpinning of what appears, to begin with, as a feeling imbedded in the individual consciousness of one's birthplace: in China, people continue to identify themselves as coming from family birthplaces from which they may actually be many generations removed. The ancestral homeland, distant in time as well as in space, can become a critical ingredient in today's problems of existence; blacks in America must struggle now with the placement of Africa in their redefinition of who and what they are. Martin Buber, who was more concerned with a Jewish state of grace than with the politics of a Jewish state, saw "the physical link with the land" of Israel as crucial to the mystical and historical identity of the Jews. The mythic and the real can seem to grow very close, whether in the deserts of the Holy Land or high in mountains no less holy to the people who live among them, mountains having been seen especially from most archaic time to have been not only the gods' dwelling places, but to be the gods themselves. The notion persists, even in certain parts of godless Russia.[8]

By some readings, the attachment of a group to its "turf" is seen as something that human beings share with animals, and there can be no doubt that the defense or seizure of territory has accounted for some of the most inhuman chapters in human history. Territory has a critical role to play in maintaining group separateness; without it a "nationality" has difficulty becoming a "nation" and a "nation" cannot become a state. Loving one's "country" can involve a great deal more than the patriotic emotion—sometimes real, sometimes scoundrelly—that became part of the evolution of one's *pays* or native heath into one's *patrie* or "fatherland." It can be an extension of personal physical existence as vital as any part of the body itself. There are people like the Congo pygmies, Colin Turnbull writes, whose whole existence is centered on "their love and devotion [to] their forest world." And even the Ik, who had lost all other sense of community of every kind, "familial, economic, social, or spiritual," still clung fiercely to their identity as *kwarikik*, "mountain people." "They prefer to die of starvation and thirst rather than move out of their mountain homeland."[9]

In this most literal sense, the physical environment has to be seen as an extension of the physical being of people and a distinct factor itself in the shaping of their character, their history, mores, their patterns of life. It produces all the features attached or attributed to people because they are (or once were) mountain people or plains people or desert people, lake, river, or island people, seacoast or landlocked people, arctic, temperate, or tropical-zone people, lowland or highland, rural or urban, delta or dry-land people, etc. These differences too, in all their infinitely varied ways, are part of the stuff of which basic group identity is made.

Skin color and other physical characteristics figure critically in the shaping of every basic group identity and, with high visibility and powerful glandular effect, in relations between groups. Men have used these primary symbols of what has been called "race" as a basis for their self-esteem or their lack of it. Skin color has served as the badge of master and subject, of the enslaved and the free, the dominators and the dominated. Of all the factors involved in the great rearrangement of political and other human relationships now, none is more sensitive, more psychologically explosive, or more intimately relevant to each individual's involvement in the process of political change. Shifts in political power systems are obviously governed for the most part by considerations of numbers, geography, resources, technology, military strength, social organization. It is not necessary to argue that the element of "race"—as a physical or historical phenomenon—is co-equal with any of these in the larger determinations of our political affairs.[10] But it is present in them all in one degree or another. It may vary greatly in importance from one situation to another, but it is nowhere unimportant.

The grossest example of this in recent history has been the relation between "white" and "nonwhite" in the making and unmaking of European world empires and of the white supremacy system in the American society. The "racial" mythologies created out of differences in skin color and physical characteristics were among the prime tools of power used when white Europeans brought nonwhite Asian and African peoples under their control. The drives that brought this system to an end were fueled to no small degree by "brown" and "black" and "yellow" people intent on reasserting their own human worth. Without exception, the transfers of power in the eighty-odd new states carved out of the Western empires since 1945 have been transfers of power from whites to nonwhites. This has involved for all concerned the complicated need to overcome the long-imbedded habits and consequences of mastery and of subjection, a process that will not quickly end.

But this is hardly a matter that lies only between "whiteness" and "nonwhiteness" or only between former "white" masters and former "nonwhite" subjects. Now that the mantling power of white supremacy has been pulled away and political power redistributed among "nonwhites," long-submerged patterns of attitudes and behavior about skin color and other physical features have been reappearing in varying intensities along the entire color spectrum and in many different parts of the world. This is in some places in some part a legacy from the era of white domination, though not as great a part as some ex-colonial subjects have defensively claimed it to be. Submission to white power led people of many different kinds to internalize and accept as true many of the myths of white superiority. In some sections of virtually every society and culture over which white men made themselves masters during the last two or three hundred years, many nonwhites, especially among the elites of the colonial population, adopted the going "white" standards of beauty and value. This "yearning after whiteness" produced color-caste attitudes which placed whiteness or lightness at the top and blackness or darkness at the bottom. Although blacks in the Americas were perhaps the most deeply damaged by this process, they shared its deformities with people in every part of the world where white domination was practiced in its various styles by the colonial masters.

Among Filipinos, for example, I found an almost obsessive preoccupation with color and physical characteristics. It turned up in the ways individuals referred to almost every aspect of everyday family life, in connection with dating and mating, the raising of children, and it seemed to be a matter of note and mention at almost every point of contact between people of varying groups and kinds in the population. The most relevant words and a long string of vernacular equivalents or variations that cropped up with great frequency in interviews were: "fair-skinned," "dark-skinned," "high nose," "low nose," "chinky eyes." I would not presume from a limited set of exploratory interviews to try to say just where this preoccupation fits in the patterns of Filipino group identity, although it seemed to occupy a very central place. It is part of how Filipinos perceive their ethnic and cultural mixes—their Malay, Chinese, Spanish, and American layerings—and how these are expressed in their regionalisms, languages, social relations, religion, national consciousness, and political style. They clearly inherit their attitudes about skin color and physical features from every part of their past.

There are bits of evidence that suggest the currency of high value on light skin color among the brown-skinned Malay ancestors of the modern Filipinos. The Spanish, who ruled the Philippines for about three hundred years, created a relatively small *mestizo* or mixed-blood caste which, by the Spanish mode—quite different from that of other European colonialists—became the top elite of the local population, just under the Spaniards them-selves. The social value of looking like a Spaniard or a Spanish *mestizo* or *mestiza* remained the highest of all values on physical appearance among Filipinos through the half century of American rule, just as looking in any way Chinese—betraying some mix of parentage from Chinese immigrants of recent or remoter times—remained the lowest. Somewhere in between stood the product of part American parentage, a status sometimes valued for some of its physical attributes, like light skin, but held low in social terms because most such children were considered to have come from unions of American soldiers and the lower-class Filipina women who catered to them.

Characteristic American race-superiority attitudes of the time—the American years in the Philippines, 1900–45, were the vintage years in this respect—suffused the whole American presence in the Philippines, with its special mix of benevolence and contempt in the way it dealt with the "little brown brothers" who were supposed to make themselves over, as far as they could, in the American image. Like so many other peoples, the Filipinos are engaged in trying to redefine who and what they are. Many fac-tors will enter in this process, and while attitudes and feelings about physical characteristics may not prove to be the most im-portant of them, neither will they be the least. In recent years, some Filipino intellectuals have made self-conscious efforts to wean their society away from its version of that "yearning for whiteness" they feel they inherited from the colonial era. They like to tell their version of the story of how God, when he created man, took his first try out of the oven too soon, it remained a pasty white; left the second in too long, it came out a charred black; and did it just right the third time, producing a creature of a rich brown, the glowing color called in Tagalog by the name *kayumanggi*. In the making over of the Filipino group identity, they want brown to be beautiful too.

✦

The peoples of India were "niggers" to the British in the days of the Raj, and some color-caste attitudes among some Indians were no doubt shaped and surely reinforced by the common and familiar tendency of subjects to ape their masters. But such attitudes, especially as they relate to skin color, are pervasively present in the Indian culture itself and can be traced all the way back to versions of Indian prehistory that deal with the coming of the light-skinned conquerors, the "Aryas," and how they related to the dark-skinned inhabitants of the land, the "Dasyas."

These attitudes, identified with the shaping of the Hindu society over the millennia, persist today in the entwining of color with caste. The Sanskrit word for the large caste groups, *varna,* means color, and the word *caste,* from the Latin via the Portuguese, means purity connected with biological lineage, or something very close to and including color. In classical Hindu texts, there is an association of colors with the main caste groups—white with the Brahmans at the top, black with the Sudras at the bottom, red or bronze and yellow with the middle groups of Kshatriya and Vaisya. Although there is much denial that these assignments of color values bear directly on skin color as such, there is enough in the past and present actuality of Hindu society to make it plain that skin color is related in important ways to hierarchies of status in the Hindu system.

Although mountains of literature have been produced about Hindu caste, this aspect of it has not been overstudied. Some modern Indian writers argue heavily against the presence of color implications in the caste system without being able to make the fact of color caste in Indian society go away. Highly explicit color values are found in the elaborate criteria that figure in beauty standards and marriage preferences—as anyone can discover any week in any Indian newspaper's matrimonial advertisements—and other choices, relations, and attitudes along the spectrum that shades from the light-skinned northerners to the dark-skinned southerners.

These values, vivid in Indian life, have been reflected in some of the new relationships created by recent political change. Indian attitudes about color have obviously had much to do with relations between Indians and Africans in Africa. These might be seen, again, as a product of European-created circumstances in which Indians (particularly in Kenya, Uganda, and South Africa) occupied the position of middlemen-traders sandwiched between the ruling whites and the ruled blacks. They naturally identified themselves as far as they could with the dominant whites, keeping as detached as possible from the lowly blacks. Gandhi began his life's struggle in South Africa, but it was a struggle to win rights for the Indians there, not for the blacks.

In recent years, Indian-African antagonisms in Africa, rooted in their economic relations but hardly less so in their racial and cultural differences, erupted more than once into violence, mostly in the form of African attacks on Indians. Indians, for their part, belatedly began to seek common political ground and greater acceptance among Africans, both among those who gained their independence, as in Kenya and Uganda and other parts of East Africa, and among those who are still very far from doing so, as in South Africa. The new nationalist India, intent on winning and influencing African friends, began extending facilities, including scholarships, to African students for study in India. In India, unhappily, many of them quickly encountered the Indian color attitudes that hold the dark-skinned person in the least esteem and the black person in no esteem at all. This erupted embarrassingly into public view and into the international prints. As far back as 1955, a group of African students in New Delhi publicly complained that they had found "the prejudices of the Indians almost as bad as that of South African Europeans." These complaints touched off a flurry of mortified and deeply felt disclaimers and explanations from their Indian hosts.[11]

The case of India's eighty million ex-Untouchables illustrates on a massive scale what can be done in a culture with the concept of bodily pollution and uncleanness in some chosen class of victims. The matter of skin color also appears, although more ambiguously and irregularly, in this Hindu pattern. In some parts of India, Untouchables are commonly thought to be darker than most other Indians. This is reflected in some of the terms used by caste Hindus to describe Untouchables, the most mortifying ones employed in Kerala, for example, being *karumpan,* "black fellow," or *karumpi,* "black girl." Although more Untouchables may be darker than lighter in color, there are also black or near-black Brahmin or other caste Hindu southerners, and lighter brown Untouchable northerners. A popular folk rhyme dealing with personality attributes of different groups of people include the following lines: "Beware of a black colored Brahmin and the white colored Chamar [Untouchable leatherworker]; they can only be handled with shoe in hand"—meaning that they only understand a forceful or threatening attitude. The implication, according to one explanation, is that the transposed skin colors in these castes came about only through bastard birth and that bastards are always crooked and need punishment. The extent to which the line of pollution and Untouchability in India is also a color line is, like almost everything else in the Hindu setting, unclear and ambiguous.[12]

The Chinese too have strong feelings about physical characteristics, their own and others. Indeed, the Chinese are a very "physical" people; it is part of that earthy concreteness that is so strongly associated with the Chinese cultural style, and one of its expressions is a Chinese racial chauvinism that has always been in view at or near the surface of most Chinese relations with non-Chinese.

Belief in the superiority of the race of Han and the view of all non-Chinese as "barbarians" are well-known features of the standard Chinese self-image. They go back to the remotest antiquity. "I have heard of making Chinese out of barbarians," said the great sage Mencius nearly 2500 years ago, "but I have never heard of making barbarians out of Chinese." From those most ancient times, Chinese terms for non-Chinese of almost any kind were characteristically derogatory, and they almost always either referred to some physical characteristic or attributed to non-Chinese some beastlike character or nonhuman origin.

Virtually all non-Chinese were *kuei-tze,* "ghosts" or "devils," inhabitants of the nether world beyond and below China, where civilized human beings dwelled. Peoples around the fringes of ancient China were usually described by words representing animals —foxes, wildcats, wolves, apes, and varieties of insects. *Hsiung-nu,* the name for the "Huns" beyond northern China's borders, means literally something to do with slaves, but a history of the Wei period also tells us that the *Hsiung-nu* were the result of the union of a barbarian chieftain's daughter and an old wolf. "That is why," the *History of Wei* goes on to explain, "these people like to stretch their necks and utter long cries, like wolves howling." The Turks are similarly recorded as the outcome of a union between a female wolf and a young boy.

Skin color rarely appears among these descriptions, but it does figure sharply in passages about the *"kun-lun* slaves" brought to China by the wide-ranging Chinese traders from islands in the southern seas during the T'ang and Sung dynasties. Usually called "devil slaves" or "black devils," they were apparently seen more as beasts than as humans. In the nineteenth century, the "black devils" reappear in the shape of Indian troops brought in by the invading British. Chinese writers of the time describe the English as the "green-eyed devils"—like the fiercest and most evil of the dragons of the spirit world—and their "slave soldiers" as "black devils." "The white ones were cold and dull as the dead ashes of frogs," wrote a poet, "the black ones were ugly and dirty as coal."

How and when the Chinese were introduced to the European idea that they were members of the "yellow race" and how they received the news are all matters still apparently waiting a closer look at the relevant literature of the past century or two. Much waits to be found, as a letter written by a Chinese scholar in the closing years of the Manchu dynasty indicates: "Of the five colors, yellow is the color of the soil, and the soil is the core of the universe. Westerners identify Chinese as a yellow race. This im-

plies that from the beginning, when heaven and earth were created, the Chinese were given the central place. When Westerners
laugh at Chinese egotism, why can we not explain it by this rea-
soning?"

In the Chinese classical tradition—as in the Japanese that so
largely stemmed from it—the celebration of whiteness as a criter-
ion of feminine beauty is a familiar theme. A poet of the fourth
century B.C. celebrated a bevy of beauties for their "black-painted
eyebrows and white-powdered cheeks." Of Yang Kuei-fei, the
most celebrated beauty in Chinese history, the T'ang poet Po Chu-i
wrote: "So white her skin, so sweet her face / None could with
her compare." Hands and arms of "dazzling white" move grace-
fully through endless reams of ancient Chinese poetry. The most
common metaphor for feminine skin was white jade, and references to all the visible surfaces of jade-colored female skin abound
in poets' songs. Chinese folk songs are similarly filled with the
whiteness of generations of beloveds: "My sweatheart is like a
flower," sings one. "Please, do not let the sun burn her black."
In story after story, Chinese writers of this century were still
quivering at the "snow-white" or "pure white" necks and arms of
their heroines. There is some evidence that these standards have
prevailed not only among effete upper-class Chinese but among
rude villagers as well.[13]

Although Chinese racial and cultural chauvinism is a well-known
fact, its particulars have been little studied. It has always figured
in the long and complex history of Chinese relations with non-
Chinese peoples within China itself, continuing into the present
Communist era. Chinese overseas have intermarried freely with
many other kinds of people but not without creating certain strains
or areas of separateness between mixed Chinese and the unmixed,
a condition not difficult to discover in places like Hawaii and the
Philippines.

Some suggestion of the Chinese style in these matters turns up
in their vocabulary in conflict situations. In the conflict between
Chinese and Malays in Malaysia, for example, the racial issue—
and any expression of it bearing on skin color, in particular—is

quite marginal compared to the cultural, historical, economic, and political issues that lie between the two groups. But even so, the powerful and highly chauvinistic Chinese cultural self-image reinforces itself by views of others expressed, as Chinese feelings so often are, in physical terms. While the most common local Chinese term for Malays is probably *malai-kwai,* or "Malay devils," another common one is *bla-chan,* literally a "prawn paste," a way of referring to the Malays as "brown" with the additional suggestion of dark and unattractive. The Chinese term for Indians in Malaysia is *tousee-kwai, tousee* meaning a kind of black bean, the literal rendering thus becoming "black bean devils." This is like a Shanghai term for Indians, *hei-tan,* which means simply "black coal." The common Malay vernacular responds to the Chinese in kind, its word for the Chinese being *mata-sepek,* which means "slit-eyes."

Chinese racial attitudes have come into public or semipublic view only rarely, as they did in 1945 when Chiang Kai-shek's government in Chungking tried to keep black American troops from entering China over the Burma Road, which they had just done more than anybody else to reopen. In 1963, an African student in Peking described Communist Chinese mentors as filled with "the idea of the superiority of Yellow over Black."[14] On the larger scene of the Sino-Soviet conflict in recent years, the Chinese Communists made strenuous efforts to win friends among Asians, Africans, and Latin Americans by stressing the solidarity of nonwhites against whites. In public print, this has always been done by euphemism, the Chinese stressing the "European" character of the Russians in order to keep them out of all Asian or Afro-Asian enterprises. In their corridor politicking, they have been described as using the racial theme bluntly and crudely in their attempt to win friends for themselves and to alienate others from their Russian foes. There has been some impression but little information about the extent to which their own racial behavior has helped to defeat these Chinese efforts, especially among Africans.[15] Before the tentative reopening of relations with the United States that began in 1971, Chinese Communist propaganda in general bestowed on Americans all the beastlike features traditionally attributed to all barbarians. They were depicted as the offspring of wolves, like the *Hsiung-nu* of long ago; and like the early-arrived Portuguese explorers of four centuries ago, they were described as devourers of children.[16]

✦

Because the body is the most primordial of all features of basic group identity, extraordinarily powerful taboos and sanctions have been attached in many groups to exogamous unions or marriages that threaten their physical sameness; "purity" is the usual word, carrying with it that strong sense that there is contamination in the mixing of one physical stock with another. This is a familiar characteristic in one degree or another common to all cultures. The practice of Untouchability in the Hindu caste system came, some scholars have speculated, out of the effort of the "Aryan" invaders to punish and outlaw any mixing between themselves and the dark-skinned people whom they overran. Chinese abroad have often married non-Chinese, but never without incurring strong feelings in their families about mixing with "outsiders" and especially about the children of such unions. The Japanese, for their part, hardly needed Spencer's injunction to them a century ago: "Never intermarry!" Among Japanese generally, physical homogeneity is one of the most highly prized of all their attributes.*

---

* Some Japanese also felt that "yearning for whiteness," especially during the period of the American Occupation, when everything American, including American beauty standards, came to be ardently admired in some sections of Japanese society. The double eyelid operation became a popular fad among some Japanese women. Most Japanese, however, guarded themselves jealously against dilution. Their more deeply held attitudes were much more accurately shown in the lot of the GI-mixed children left behind by soldiers of the Occupation, painful enough for the white-mixed, many times more so for the black. A glimpse of this appeared in an interview with a young woman with two impeccably Japanese parents who remembers that as a small girl in the 1950s, her "big," i.e., somewhat less than almond-shaped eyes, a faint coppery tint in her black hair, and her slightly fairer-than-usual skin led schoolmates to taunt her as *ainoko,* a mixed child, an epithet accompanied by a burden of rejection and loathing that she has never been able to forget. There is an ironic ambiguity, I learned in some of my interviews, in the remark sometimes made by a Japanese about some-

Taboos and sanctions notwithstanding, large numbers of people in the world are products of mixed marriages or unions between members of physically quite different groups. Across color and other assorted lines of distinctiveness, they combine different sets of genes and body characteristics. When their features placed them at or near the two ends of the given physical spectrum, such individuals could often fade into the physically nearest parental group, if that is what they wanted or were allowed to do. This clearly has been happening for many generations at the margins of all kinds of groups. In some cases this has brought about a change in the common physical cast, or at least in the range of commonly accepted physical types, as among the more open and mobile segments of the highly diverse American society. This has taken place most largely, however, within certain physical limits: e.g., the North-South European, blond-brunette, rather than across any wider gaps.

Where physical differences have been greater, as across various color lines, such unions could and did take place, but in much smaller numbers and without bringing down the governing system of taboos and sanctions. The only way the children of such unions could mitigate these penalties was to become as much "like" the high-status group as they could. The only way they could escape them altogether was to "pass" and disappear altogether into the higher group. This could be done, obviously, only where the physical appearances of the groups involved were varied enough or similar enough to make this possible. It does happen all the time, even in caste India. But where plainly visible body differences are a critical fact in group differences, such passing becomes impossible. Even where all other conditions are or can be made equal, the physical characteristics themselves remain a barrier to status and belonging in the dominant group.

---

one: "He/She doesn't look Japanese." This is at one level a compliment, implying that his/her looks are "Western," but it is at the same time a peculiarly stabbing way of excluding that person as *different* and is meant that way too, to wound. Western beauty standards still largely dominate in films and television, and mannequins used in Japanese department stores only quite recently began to include some Japanese figures among the commonly used Western male and female models.

Until now, one common result for the children of such mixed unions has been automatic identification downward into the lower status group—that "one drop of Negro blood" made a person a Negro by the laws and customs of white-supremacy America. A common outcome was rejection by or withdrawal from both parental groups and creation of a "new" group, relegated to a special marginal inbetweenness, that often acquired its own legal, social, and group character: e.g., the Anglo-Indians in India, the "Coloreds" in South Africa, and other such Eurasian and Eurafrican groups created during the colonial era. Members of these groups took the full brunt of the obloquy and exclusion that was the fate of the "half-caste" on both sides of their lines of descent. In colonial times, such groups often moved under the patronage of the master race into some narrow place of their own, separate and above the subject masses below, in some colonies as minor bureaucrats, soldiers, policemen, jailers, or, as in British India, as skilled railroad labor. Most of them were left painfully, and often tragically, placeless when the colonial masters left and the new masters took over.[17] In the more recent and even more poignant case of the children fathered by American soldiers, black and white, in Japan, Korea, and Vietnam, their most common fate has been almost total rejection by all, isolation in orphanages ended in only a few cases by adoption by American families, or abandonment to whatever lives they could somehow manage to eke out at the furthermost margins of these societies.

In some instances in the colonial period, this mixed group became the top elite of the lower unmixed or less mixed mass, enjoying social and economic advantages from their greater closeness to the master race, as the so-called mulattoes or lighter-skinned Negroes did in the Americas and the Caribbean; or they eventually became the elite of the society as a whole, as the *mestizos* did in most of Latin America and the Philippines after the end of Spanish rule. This invariably took place on the basis of cultural assimilation to the higher status group, the adoption of its styles and its racial attitudes. Such groups usually sooner or later came under the counterattack of their own lower orders, as lighter-skinned Negroes did in America at the hands of Marcus Garvey and his call for "race purity" and again more recently in the tendency of some separationist blacks to identify black nationalism with "race purity" and integrationist ideas with "house niggerism," the "field hand" vs. the "house servant" syndrome carried down from the days of slavery.

In Mexico, some attempt was made by some intellectuals to give their revolution the color of an Indian reassertion, trying to re-establish pre-Columbian legitimacy against post-Columbian Spanish impositions. A handsome museum in Mexico City became a monument to their efforts, but there has been no change of great consequence in the way the Mexican caste system works. In the Philippines, in similar circles there was a certain shift from contempt to envy of the hitherto despised aboriginal hill peoples whose "purity" could be contrasted to the uncertain physical and cultural mixedness of the lowland Filipino Christians, but here too without thought of changing the established caste order in the society. For black Americans, the changes of these years have not yet broken down the established caste order in the larger society, but they have to a much greater extent wiped out the old color caste order among themselves.

✦

For black Americans, more clearly perhaps than for any other group, the element of color and physical characteristics lies at the very center of the cluster that makes up their basic group identity. It is the one element around which everything else in their lives has been made to revolve, the heart of the identity crisis that is with them every hour of every day and which they need more than anything else to resolve. For them, in the most literal sense, the changing patterns of group identity brought on by political change have meant coming to see themselves and to be seen in new ways.

In some measure, the same is also true for other physically different groups, especially other nonwhite minorities living in a predominantly white society. Almost any highly visible physical features can instantly trigger any system of exclusion or discrimination or other behavior which they inspire.* In the American society now, Chinese-Americans and Japanese-Americans suffer markedly less than they did a generation ago from any systematic discrimination, but they still suffer from the often galling experience of being taken on sight not as Americans but as Chinese or Japanese, always in any case as someone clearly *different* and instantly invoking, by their very faces, the stereotypes that still so largely govern how they are perceived by others. Members of darker-skinned groups may no longer be subject to the older forms of legally sanctioned exclusion in the public domain, but the experience of rejection has far from disappeared from their daily lives, whether in relation to other-hued members of their own groups—as among Puerto Ricans and other varieties of the "Spanish surname" or "Spanish-speaking groups"—other nonwhites, or the white population in general. In every case, physical characteristics remain a crucial element in group identity patterns as they move on through the current experience of political change. It is crucial, but it is not as centrally located in the design as it is for black Americans.

---

* Physical characteristics obviously are a key factor in the identity patterns of all individuals who have some physical features that mark them off from others in some notable and usually painful way. Besides women, whom we have already mentioned in this connection, and homosexuals, who are not always visible but some of whom now say that they want to be, there are others who have taken up current moods and styles of assertion and have tried to form groups based on distinctive physical attributes: thus the National Association to Aid Fat People to oppose "stigmatization of the overweight" and "open the eyes of people to the legitimacy of multiple body styles"; the Little People of America, who claim that the plight of people of extremely short stature "is the same as that of other minority groups except that discrimination is worse for us"; and, not without some seriousness, even an organization called Uglies Unlimited to combat job discrimination in favor of the good-looking. (United Press, October 5, 1973; *Boston Globe,* October 28, November 24, 1973; *The New York Times,* June 27, 1974.) In a word, their proposition is that fatness, shortness, ugliness can be beautiful too. These are all visible kinds of people with certain shared physical characteristics, but as in the case of women, they are far from forming the basis of a "group" and, with the possible exception of the "little people" or midgets, even farther from constituting, in and of themselves, the stuff of a basic group identity in the sense that we are dealing with it here.

The power and weight of the rhetorical and actual reassertion of *blackness*—including the term itself, *black*—has been so strong recently that it already may come as a surprise to some to discover that it has been under way in this form for barely ten years and that it represents a stunning turnaround from what were then still the prevailing attitudes among black Americans and had been for many generations. Like everything else in this experience, the reassertion was not actually "new," it was not the product of a "new" black militancy. Long before the great flood of language and literature on this matter loosed after the dams of segregation and other constraints broke in the 1960s, much had been said and written—if not heeded—about the question of Negroes and their blackness. The names of remarkable men spring out of a century of concern with this matter on the part of figures like Martin Delany, Frederick Douglass, W. E. B. Du Bois, James Weldon Johnson, and A. Philip Randolph. Some writers of the "Negro Renaissance" of the 1920s began to face it squarely, as in the poetry of Claude McKay and Langston Hughes, in Wallace Thurman's novel *The Blacker the Berry,* published in 1929. It came under intensive scholarly scrutiny by E. Franklin Frazier and others in the 1930s. A long and hard and lonely road had been traveled by many seekers for black self-respect before black finally did begin to become beautiful for a new generation of black Americans in the 1960s.[18]

How far and how deep this change goes will become apparent only with the passage of more time and with further experience. Still, even as it appears now on the visible and audible surfaces and in some limited studies,[19] it is plainly a remarkable fact, perhaps the most lastingly important fact of all the recent great turmoil in black American life. For nothing was more deeply rooted and more crippling than the self-rejection that dominated the black experience in America through so many generations. It was precisely around the characteristics of blackness of skin and Negroidness of feature that the white world built up its rationale for reducing the black human being to subhuman status. Around these characteristics too the black man built up his own ways of surviving, submitting, and resisting. He did all these things, and in all its aspects this mutual process was woven into the fabric of the American culture and the personality types it helped to create. In their acceptance of what the white world made of them, blacks rejected themselves. Over the many years, riding over the recurring appearance of rebels and rejecters who spoke for different responses, there was the flight from blackness, the flight from Negroidness itself, the flight from the African origins, the yearning for whiteness. Out of this self-rejection came the institution of color caste that raised "whiteness" to the highest value in all aspects of life, civilization, culture, religion, human worth. It became an intricate system of social, group, and personal relationships based directly on degrees of relative lightness and relative darkness of skin color and other degrees of physical Negroness: the shapes and kinds of features, hair, lips, and nose, "good" if they resembled the white's, "bad" if they did not. This was carried to the wide use of artificial means—hair straighteners and skin whiteners—in the effort to close the gap between the two.

To begin breaking down this whole structure within, as well as the walls of segregation without, has been the main business of black Americans engaged in these years in reshaping their group identity. Among all the assorted pluses and minuses attached to the holding of basic group identities, the most fundamental plus is probably the extent to which such identities enable the individual to accept himself with some measure of esteem. To the extent that they fail to do this, they inflict all the deep minuses of a negative identity. And it was such an identity, built primarily around the facts and features of skin color and physical characteristics, that blacks in America acquired over such a long time. Changing this around, transforming a negative into a positive identity, replacing self-rejection of the most literal kind with self-acceptance, has become the task of a whole new generation of black Americans coming up in politically and psychologically changed circumstances. It is probably the single strongest and most striking example we have of the power of the reach for self esteem in the reshaping of group identities that is so much a part of our current experience. James Baldwin long ago warned blacks that they were going to have to learn to get along "without the crutch of their blackness." They had to begin by accepting the blackness itself, both as a fact and as symbol, and, in the first place, accepting the word *black*. This brings us to the matter of the names we go by.

V

NAME

✦

In the works of the School of Names there are three fallacies:
the fallacy of corrupting names with names; the fallacy of
corrupting names with actualities; the fallacy of corrupting
actualities with names.

—HSUN TZU (CA. 250 B.C.)

NAME is surely the simplest, most literal, and most obvious of all
symbols of identity. But, like everything simple, it is complicated.
The quest for the meaning of naming goes back to the first framing
of thought, the beginning of language, the first holding of knowledge, and forward again to all the persisting riddles.

Naming, John Dewey reminded us, is knowing itself, "the distinctive central process of knowledge."[1] All philosophy has wrestled
with viewing knowledge as fast or fluid, petrified or plastic. It came,
from Heraclitus and the Chinese through to James and Dewey, to
the effort to capture the elusive actuality of things by seeing them in
constant motion, always being transformed, changing more rapidly
than the words, i.e., the names, used to describe them. Because of
the "many traditional, speculatively evolved applications of the
word 'name' . . . many of them still redolent of magic," Dewey
looked for greater precision in other terms—"designation," "cue,"
"characterization," "specification," "sign," "symbol"—hoping this
would help make it plainer that "we take names always as namings,
as living behaviors in an evolving world of men and things."[2] But

words and names used to represent "truth" acquire their own history. They impose themselves on the process and they usually grow, as James put it, "stiff with years of veteran service," not easily flexed or replaced.[3]

"One of the difficulties of the history of ideas," wrote Alfred Cobban, "is that names are more permanent than things. Institutions change, but the terms used to describe them remain the same."[4] The same difficulty bothered the Chinese philosophers who belonged some twenty-five centuries ago to what was called the "School of Names"—*Ming Chia*—so called because it was concerned with the distinctions to be made between "names" and "actualities." There were at least two tendencies, Fung Yu-lan tells us, one "emphasizing the relativity of actual things and the other the absoluteness of names." Debate over "rectification of names" went on for several centuries, revolving essentially around the argument that "things in actual fact should be made to accord with the implication attached to them by names. Like the three corrupting fallacies noted by Hsün Tzŭ, this is a problem still very much with us in a time when many names are being "rectified" to accord with "actualities" that are being differently seen.

The same holds true for the magic power that has always been attributed to names. One of these Chinese ancients said that he "wished to . . . correct the relations between names and actualities, so as thus to transform the whole world." In the William James version, "the universe has always appeared to the natural mind as a kind of enigma, of which the key must be sought in the shape of some illuminating word or name. That word names the universe's principle, and to possess it is, after a fashion, to possess the universe itself."[5] Hence the taboos on names that have appeared in every culture. It was forbidden to Jews to write or utter the name of Yahweh; the founder of the mystical Hasidic sect in eighteenth-century Europe called himself "Baal Shem Tov," or "Master of the Name." In old China, as in many other societies, it was forbidden to use the personal name of reigning monarchs. In the Indian epics, no one ever addresses anyone of higher rank by his personal name or uses the personal pronoun when addressing him. In cultures of every kind, names of deities, rulers, and even of ordinary people have carried with them powers of magic and incantation, to inflict or avert harm, to solve mysteries, to meet needs, whether grandly universal or obscurely personal. In the beginning was the word. Immediately thereafter, it seems, was the word tabooed.[6]

But if it is the magic of knowledge you are seeking, the word by itself will not do, James cautions. "If you follow the pragmatic method, you cannot look on any such word as closing your quest. You must bring out of each word its practical cash value, set it at work within the stream of your experience. It appears less as a solution, then, and more particularly as an indication of the ways in which existing realities may be changed."[7]

In the stream of our current experience, the cash value of names has been fluctuating with great and unusual violence. Names keep turning up in one way or another in all the ongoing rediscoveries, revisions, remakings, and reassertions of group identities. The name of a country, of an individual, of a group, carries in it all the cargo of the past. A name will seldom itself be the heart of the matter of group identity, but it can often take us to where the heart can be found, leading us deep into the history, the relationships, and the emotions that lie at the center of any such affair.

Names of countries usually reflect some image out of the remote or recent past of a people, a place, an idea. "China," as we have remarked, means "central country" in the sense held by many peoples about their own lands, that this was where it all began for everyone everywhere. The name "Japan," meaning "the place where the sun rises," conveys much the same idea, and not at all metaphorically. "In my humble opinion," wrote a Japanese sage of the last century, "our sacred country is where the sun rises and the spirit of matter starts . . . the center of the world and the foundation of creation."[8] In the wake of some of Japan's more recent history, the great blow that defeat dealt to the Japanese self-image brought on some differences of view over the rendering of its name as "Nihon" or as "Nippon." Either form identifies it as the place from which the sun appears, but the one suggests a certain softness of spirit, the other a harsh muscularity.

Recent political change has brought name changes to many places. Under the pressure of their strained relations with their fellow Communist Chinese, the Russians have begun to erase Chinese names from the territory of eastern Siberia that was seized in 1860 from a feeble China by the expanding Czarist empire. Nine cities and towns and two hundred and fifty rivers and mountains that had retained their Chinese names for more than a century suddenly acquired brand-new Russian names in 1973, arousing great scorn and anger in Peking. "The renaming of places can in no way alter history," said Hsinhua, the Chinese press service.[9] In many other cases, however, altered history has led to much renaming. The political changes that turned ex-colonies into new states inspired the reappearance of some long-submerged country names—e.g., Vietnam, Ghana, Mali, Malawi, Zambia, Sri Lanka—as part of a re-identification with the distant past. The name "Zaire" for the old Belgian Congo is derived from "Nzadi," the old name of the great river that runs through that country. Its capital, Leopoldville, named after a Belgian king best known for the atrocities committed in the colony during his reign, became Kinshasa, said to be the name of the fishing village that once stood on the city's present site. In North and South Korea, different attitudes and usages and name choices involving the ancient name "Chosen" reflect strongly felt current views about some very old affairs. When Egypt joined others to become the "United Arab Republic," the name sat uneasily with many Egyptians who in the past would not ordinarily have allowed anyone to confuse them with Arabs; fortunately, from this point of view, the united republic did not remain united very long and Egypt became Egypt again. Or consider the quite unique example of "Pakistan," a purely synthetic name, made up as an acronym of the names of the main regions from which that remarkably synthetic state was carved—Punjab, Afghanistan, Kashmir, Sind, etc.—omitting any initial for Bengal. This omission was finally confirmed twenty-five years later by the severance of Bengal from

Pakistan and the emergence of a brand new Bengali state with the old name of the Bengali homeland, Bangladesh.

Other new states have kept their old given names. The name "India" comes from the name given to that land by the Greeks in ancient times, the people who then lived there having never had any common name to go by that might have otherwise served the purpose. The masters of the country had called themselves "Arya," meaning "one who is faithful to the religion of the clan," and others *mleccha,* meaning, as Hajime Nakamura slyly puts it, "barbarian or, loosely, Non-Aryan." There was no word in old India to include both Aryans and non-Aryans together.[10] Long after the Greeks had a word for it but long before a modern independent India would seek to establish "Indian" as the name of a new national identity for its people, the name "Indian" entered upon a lively existence of its own far, far from the land of India itself. It began about five centuries ago, when Europeans trying to reach the fabled wealth of the "Indies" kept on identifying as "Indians" (or "Indios" in Spanish) the people on all the other islands and places they did reach, as in the Americas and the Philippines. The Philippines was named by its conquerors after their king, Philip II of Spain. Since the Philippines became a republic on its own in 1946, there have been occasional suggestions that its name be changed—one proposed new name: "Maharlika," meaning "noble" or "dignified" in Tagalog. But the nationalist ardor that changed "Indios" into "Filipinos" after the fall of the Spanish did not extend to turning "Filipinos" into something else.

Individual or personal names also usually serve as badges of the basic group identity. To be sure, the personal name remains primarily the symbol of the single and unique person who bears it. Indeed, it establishes the fact of his existence. To be without a name is almost not to be. "Nameless fear" is worse than any other kind of fear. The penalty of namelessness imposed on bastardy in our culture is one of the heaviest short of death a group can lay. Names, like social norms, provide a minimum security, the bearings that every individual has to have around him or else be hopelessly lost. As Helen Lynd so acutely remarked: "The wood in *Through the Looking Glass* where no creature bears a name is a place of terror."[11] In most cultures, we not only have names, we also have "good" names or "bad" names. Good names are inherited, won, protected, besmirched, lost, and, worst of all, filched. Good or bad, we do everything we can to keep them on view after we are gone, on ancestral tablets or graven stone, anything that will keep our names there to stand for us as particular people as long as possible after we have disappeared.

Individual as they may be, however, these names are essentially group names too. Family surnames carry with them all the associations of the language and tradition from which they come. Given names are usually those of recent or remote forebears or the names of the group's saints or heroes. By his names, it can be said, ye shall instantly know everything you might want or need to know about someone you encounter. For the uttering of the name itself can and does serve as an instant signal for behavior based on group affiliation, producing its almost automatic response, open or closed, welcoming or rebuffing, including or excluding the stranger who up to that instant has done nothing else but tell you who he is—hence, in so many different settings, the familiar business of name changing by individuals who want to mitigate or conceal their inferior status or outsiderness. It is in effect the functional equivalent of skin-bleaching or hair-straightening by blacks or double-lid operations by Japanese women. The purpose is to be more "like" those more favored, to gain a more comfortable anonymity by sharing, at least in name, the identity of the dominant group.

In the ex-colonial world, the shift in power relations has brought about some reversal of this process. European given names were often acquired by colonial subjects by baptism, bestowal, or choice based on the need or wish to accommodate to the master culture. In one case, unique as far as I know, in the Philippines, where Christian given names had long been bestowed by baptism, Spanish surnames, taken column by column from a Madrid directory, were simply "given" to large numbers of people by a mid-nineteenth-century Spanish governor for the greater convenience of his tax collectors, eventually creating quite a mistaken impression of the number of children actually fathered by Spaniards in their colony. Filipinos still like and even cherish their Spanish names; but in other countries, the shedding of such acquired foreign names, like changing the names of countries, has been one of the easier, more obvious, and more demonstrative ways for ex-colonial subjects to reassert themselves and their own cultural identities. In newly named Zaire, President Joseph Desiré Mobutu not only changed his own Christian given names, as others were doing all over Africa, but in the name of Zairian "authenticity" he outlawed all such names altogether and fixed penalties for any priest who baptized a child with any but a Zairian name.

In Israel, many returning Jews, especially in the new state's early years, symbolized the shedding of their Diaspora past by adopting Hebrew names—often names out of the biblical tradition that stressed boldness and strength—to fit their new Israeli identities. For some blacks in the United States, the quest for a more prideful and self-accepting identity has involved not only the matter of changing their group name but also changing individual names, adopting African or—for reasons that invite examination and reflection—Arabic names. Perhaps boldest and harshest of all were those Black Muslims who shed what they regarded as slavemasters' surnames and substituted a plain "X," as though to proclaim that although they could no longer go by the names that the hated white world had given them, they did not yet know who they were.

The great shaking up of all groups and all relations between groups has brought on a shaking up of all the vocabularies of words and names, proper and improper, by which many groups were called or described. Least touched, it seems safe to say, is the lexicon of epithets, the vulgar, vernacular, or slang names that members of different groups have for others. The list in recent American English is familiar: nigger-coon-jig-wop-guinea-kike-yid-sheenie-mick-spick-chink-jap-honky-polack-wog-gook-dink-frog-limey-kraut,etc., most recently joined by "wasp," an ever-changing index to the ways in which people despise one another, forever being enriched by new additions as each generation makes its own revisions and contributions. Such names imbed themselves, sometimes get to be used banteringly, even affectionately, and sometimes, in a complicated semi-jocular or say-it-with-a-smile transference, are used by people about themselves. In no case, however, does the point of the name lose its poison. The feeling that aims it goes deep. The styles, frequencies, and time-and-place considerations in the public or private use of these vocabularies continue to vary with all the changing circumstances, but there is no basis for thinking that they might disappear any time soon.

There is some ratio in these usages bearing on the amount and kind of contact members of different groups have with one another. At greater distance and with sparser contact, such names or usages are more likely to reflect great ignorance, indifference, a less intimate level of distaste or deprecation. But among groups that live in any close proximity or who play any significant role in one another's universes, these vocabularies give the most direct and most pungent expression to the feelings that most members of most groups still most commonly have about others in these circumstances: distrust, fear, dislike, contempt, envy, hostility, hatred.

Many other words and names that are normally part of more polite discourse have also come to express this essential non-brotherhood of man. Education experts from a number of countries meeting in Paris under UN auspices a few years ago listed some of the words that they said provoked an "adverse reaction" in those about whom they were used. It included "tribe," "native," "savage," "primitive," "jungle," "pagan," "kaffir," "bushman," "backward," "underdeveloped,' "uncivilized," "vernacular," "colored," "race," and in testimony to the speed in which new name styles could assert themselves, also "Negro." The panel of experts advised the use of inoffensive substitutes, e.g., "developing" for "underdeveloped," "savanna" or "wooded savanna" for "jungle." They also advised, with an odd disregard for precise meaning, that in place of "native" the word "inhabitant" should be used. "Races" or "tribes," they proposed, should hereafter be called "population groups" or simply by their proper names.[12]

But all such proper names, the names that people call themselves or are called, also carry with them their own heavy store of affect and usage, of past and present history; and all of it comes to bear now, as changes come, on how people see themselves or are seen. Examples are almost without end. There are the new pools of meaning forming in Israel around the terms "Jew" and "Israeli," along with all the other lesser terminological ironies and curiosities that turn up so bountifully in that "new" nation where Jews from English-speaking countries became "Anglo-Saxons" and Jews from countries where they were never anything but "Jews" became "Poles," "Moroccans," "Yemenites," etc.[13] In South Africa, a complicated history is traceable in the passage of terms used by the European minority about the African majority in that country, from "kaffirs" (an Arabic word meaning "unbelievers") and "niggers" to "natives" to "nonwhites" and "non-Europeans" and currently to "Bantu." English-language newspapers in South Africa, liberal in these matters, at least as compared to the Afrikaner government, went through a small terminological crisis several years ago about which term to use. The *Rand Daily Mail,* which had abandoned all the official terms in favor of "African," decided to use the adjective "black" instead of "nonwhite." Capetown's Afrikaans paper, *Die Burger,* decided to stay with "nonwhite," or *nieblanke.* But even *Die Burger* felt a wisp of a breeze from more distant winds of change; the official name of the government's policy of rigid racial separation had also been going through terminological change in these years, from "apartheid" (meaning "apartness") to "parallel development" to "separate development" and most recently, with the establishment of separate territorial Bantustans, to "multinational development." In making its own decision about what to call all those Africans, *Die Burger* decided to stay with *nieblanke* but to use it hereafter with a capital "N."[14]

One can learn a great deal of the social and political history of the Philippines by tracing the passage from the term "Indio" to

"Filipino" as it is now commonly used. "Indio" in the Philippines, as in Spanish America, was a term of derogation and contempt. The name "Filipino," like "Mexicano" or "Chileno" or "Americano," originally meant a "pure" Spaniard born in the colony, and thus distinguished from the "Peninsulares," or the Spaniards born in Spain. In time, the colonial cousins began to be regarded in Spain as of lower caste, even with some suspicion that they were all in one way or another the products of mixed unions with Indios or, worse still in some parts of Spanish America, with the *negros,* or the blacks. This, at least in part, eventually helped to make rebels and revolutionists out of the Bolivars and others who overthrew Spanish rule in the Americas early in the nineteenth century. In the Philippines, those who led the rebellion against Spain in the 1890s never had accepted the term "Indio"—the peoples of the Philippines continued to call themselves by their regional names: Tagalog, Ilocano, Cebuano, Pampangeno, etc. They still commonly do. The rebellion against Spain brought with it the gradual adoption of the name "Filipino" to describe all the peoples of the islands. The nationalist victory over the Spanish was snatched away by the Americans, who took over rule of the islands themselves and put the nationalists down in a bloody little war after the defeat of Spain. The nationalists failed to win power, but they did get a new name out of it all: the first American governor-general, William Howard Taft, officially recognized them as "Filipinos." The term "Indio" has disappeared from the Philippines. In Latin America, both the term and its negative value survive. In North America, the people called "Indians" by everyone else continued for the most part to call themselves by their own various distinctive tribal names: Iroquois, Sioux, Comanche, Hopi, Navajo, etc. In the changing times of recent years, some groups have tried to organize politically on an all-Indian or Pan-Indian basis,[15] taking over finally and making their own the name "Indian" that had been imposed upon them by their conquerors.*

---

* In North Carolina in 1965, members of a community of Indian-Negro-white mixed origins, always previously lumped with Negroes for purposes of segregation under the white-supremacy system, won recognition as a

We are not done yet with the varieties of the "Indian" experience, for there remains India itself, where the idea that there might be a new national identity called "Indian" makes only slow headway against all the separate groups bearing separate names by which most people in India still identify themselves. Unique among them are the educated ex-Untouchables, who would dearly wish to shed their own group affiliations and their own group names and, if they only could, become "Indian" and be nothing else.

Except for the stark word "Untouchables," there never was any single name to cover this great mass of people, now numbering some eighty million. In the various Indian languages, they were known by many versions of words that mean "Untouchable" or "outcast" or variations thereof: "Pamchamas," "Atishudras," "Avarnas," "Antyajas," "Namashudras," etc. One also could come on "Pariahs," "Unseeables," and "Unapproachables." In British officialese, the term "Depressed Classes" began to be used late in the last century, and although vague—it was not certain what classes it covered—it remained the official name of Untouchables and others for many decades. In 1919, the first separate representation in a number of public bodies was given to members of the "Depressed Classes" and this included Untouchables along with quite a scatter of others, such as the remote and possibly aboriginal peoples still administratively described as "Tribes." It was not until 1932 that the term "Depressed Classes" was officially defined as meaning only the Untouchables. But at just about this time, "Depressed Classes" was replaced by "Scheduled Castes." This came about because the British government, already engaged in a number of programs for the benefit of this lowest group, was preparing to include it in the array of communal separate electorates (for Muslims, Christians, Anglo-Indians, etc.) through which it hoped both to appease and to weaken Indian nationalist pressure. Special

---

distinct "Indian" group by getting the state legislature to give them a name, the "Haliwas," made up of syllables of the counties, Halifax and Warren, where many of them live. *The New York Times,* August 3, 1972.

effort was made in the 1931 census and by a special committee to draw up a "schedule" of the "castes" entitled to benefit from these various special arrangements. At the Round Table Conference in London in 1931, held to discuss future political concessions by the British in India, B. R. Ambedkar, the Untouchable leader from Maharashtra—the most prominent leader yet to appear from this great mass of people—demanded a separate electorate for the Untouchables. He also demanded "a change of nomenclature." He proposed that the Untouchables be called "Protestant Hindus" or "Non-Conformist Hindus." What emerged instead, when the electoral award was made and eventually incorporated into the Government India Act of 1935, was the new official term "Scheduled Castes." This was when Gandhi, intent on keeping the Untouchables in the fold of his Congress Party, bestowed on them the brand-new name "Harijans."[16]

"Harijan" means "Children of God." Gandhi took it from a poem by a Gujarati sage. The name was intended, it was said, to give new dignity to the Untouchables and to impress on caste Hindus the need to admit them into the Hindu fold, at least by allowing them to enter Hindu temples. Gandhi's caste Hindu followers generally accepted the name, if not the idea that anything ought to change because of it. Among Untouchables, however, including those who followed the lead of Gandhi and the Congress party in politics, it remained an uncomfortable label. On one occasion in 1938, Ambedkar's group in the Bombay state assembly challenged the Congress majority on this issue. They demanded that the name "Harijan" as used in a bill before the house be changed to "Scheduled Castes." The chairman, a Congress caste Hindu, replied that he understood that the name was intended to give dignity to Untouchables and challenged Ambedkar to suggest a better name. "Ambedkar replied [recorded a biographer] that all he would say was that he was not in a position to suggest any better name." When the Congress majority voted them down on the subject of their own name, Ambedkar and his followers walked angrily out of the chamber. Untouchables in the Congress fold were hardly less uneasy over the term. A former member of Parliament and one-time member of Gandhi's own entourage explained in an interview:

We usually don't use the word "Harijan." In fact, most educated people don't like "Harijan." The word connotes Untouchability and I don't think anyone likes it. Before Gandhi introduced it we were simply known as the "Untouchables," or by particular group names, such as Mahar, Mala, Pulaya, and so on. But very few liked to be called "Harijan." Nobody took it in the right spirit. Gandhi wanted to remove the inferiority and give a sense of superiority. But people did not take it that way. It just meant getting another name instead of a caste name, but a name that meant the same thing: Untouchable.

A graduate student from Andhra described himself as a follower of Congress but said: "I do not like 'Harijan.' It means 'children of God.' Aren't all the other people children of God too? Why this particular name for us? I think it is very childish." One of Ambedkar's followers, a member of Parliament, gave a more strongly colored reason:

"Harijan" is a bad word introduced by Mahatma Gandhi. In Hindi it means a boy whose father's name is unknown, hence children of God. In the Hindu temples there were, as you know, the devadassi, the girls who took part in worship ceremonies and also served the priests. Sometimes they gave birth to children and these children were called "Harijan." That's why we don't like the name.

While this seemed to leave the unwieldy "Scheduled Castes" as the nearest thing to an accepted general name, Untouchables much more commonly referred to themselves, or thought of themselves, by their various "caste" or "community" names. But these too were a constant reminder of status. In the home village—still "home" even to most of those who had become city dwellers—the caste name itself was usually used by the caste Hindus as a derogatory expletive. Each group name itself—and there are hundreds of them in all their scattered and separate varieties across India—served as a term of contempt and shame whenever it was used by others and could not avoid carrying this weight with it whenever one used it to identify oneself. For older people who stayed in the village, this had been and largely remained the accepted state of things. For children, now going to school in mounting numbers under the new regime of independent India, it soon became a daily ordeal. For educated ex-Untouchables who went out into the world to go to more advanced schools or those who lived in cities and encountered these humiliations whenever they traveled out in any direction, it was the source of a constant harassment of spirit.

Although it was coming to be frowned upon by more cosmopolitan Indians and happened less often in the big cities, it was still common practice in India on casual encounter, as in a train, for one person to open conversation with another by asking: "And what community do you belong to?" If he replied truthfully, the traveling ex-Untouchable would still feel, almost like a physical impact, the sudden fall of silence in the crowded compartment, a pulling away from further contact, an end to the talk. "When I travel anywhere I am upset and discouraged by this," said an ex-Untouchable with an M.A. degree. "I have learned that if people you are traveling with know you are Scheduled Caste, they would never offer you water or a place to stay. . . . So I never declare my community or my name. Nobody among us does. We never talk about community, because the mentality of the people hasn't changed."

Some of the same weight is attached to personal names. Traditionally, an Untouchable had no surname but would be known by his given name followed, for purposes of any more detailed identification, by the given name of his father. In this tradition, moreover, Untouchables did not choose their children's names. This was the prerogative of the landlord or some other local caste Hindu dignitary. He would often choose whatever day of the week it happened to be. Thus if you were born on a Tuesday in a Hindi area, your name might be "Mangala." Often caste Hindus would give the name of some lowly object, also an unclean one, like "Panahi," which means simply "shoe," or they might bestow what were called "bad" names, e.g., a name meaning "a person who should be dragged." Now educated ex-Untouchables more usually do the naming themselves and, of course, they choose "good" names, frequently Sanskrit-sounding names taken from among those used by the touchable castes, not uncommonly the name of some god, hero, or benefactor. Among the ex-Untouchable students I interviewed in Bombay, several bore the name of "Gaikwar," family name of the

Maharajah of Baroda, who opened early opportunities for Untouchables in his realm, or "Shinde," the name of a caste Hindu reformer of two generations ago. But other names would be chosen mainly for their good upper-caste sound: "good" names like the recognizably Brahmin Pande, Mehta, or Parshad; a Banya name like Vakil or Patel; a Kshatriya name like Singh (which could be either a Sikh or a Rajput name); and their equivalents in other language areas. In this way, the choice of names often became part of an effort to blot out one's identity in order to "pass" as a member of some higher caste. But while for some the choosing of new names was a way of trying to erase the past, for others it had become a way of making demands on the future. One self-assured young man of thirty-six from Uttar Pradesh said: "I have four children: a boy of eight whom I named Ajai, which means a person who can never be defeated; a girl of five I have called Anula, after a famous Buddhist princess of Ceylon; a son of three I named Kennedy because he was born in 1960, Kennedy's year; and the youngest boy, only five months old, I have named Lincoln."

In the matter of name, as in so much else having to do with group identity, no example is more dramatic than that of black Americans and their choices of what names to go by. If their *blackness* itself has been at the heart of their crisis of self-definition, the word "black" has been the key to it through a long history. To trace how this word has been used is to trace the passage of black Americans from crippling self-rejection to the beginning of a liberating self-acceptance.

The new free use of the word "black" dates only from about 1966, less than ten years ago. This was perhaps the single most meaningful effect of the highly expressive and sometimes explosive spasm of black radicalism that rode the crest of the turmoil in the ghettos of American cities between 1965 and 1968. The slogan of the time that created the greatest public stir was probably *"Black Power!"* The slogan for which that time may be remembered, however, is more likely to be "Black Is Beautiful." In both its literal and its symbolic meanings, it became the password to a measure of self-acceptance by black Americans that generations of earlier leaders and tribunes of the people had sought in vain to achieve. If the name "black" was not wholly accepted by all "blacks"—many of whom did not and still do not see themselves as "black" at all—they all nevertheless had to come to terms with the new usage. This is a shift still being grindingly made, its extent, depth, and meaning still being shaped by ongoing experience. But it *is* being made. We did not get a black "revolution" out of the events of the 1960s, but we did get a "black" revolution. And that, as the history of the matter must make plain, is quite a revolution in itself. Helped by all the peculiar pressures and vulnerabilities of people and institutions in that time of great troubles, and particularly by the radicals' ready acess to the new electronic mass media, instantly seen and heard by all, the word "black" in a few years became the accepted word for public and personal use, replacing if not quite totally displacing "Negro."

This was all the more remarkable because for several generations before this, as many may have already forgotten and many more may never have known, the issue over the name to go by had been fought around the use of the term "Negro" and it had involved precisely the same values as counterposed to the word "colored." For "Negro" means "black," and those who rejected its use did so precisely for that reason, although the usual more conscious or explicit reason was that "Negro" was associated with slavery. There were always some radicals who opposed *both* "colored" and "Negro" and urged the use of "African" or even "black," but the real issue for the greater number was the flight from blackness and all the complex feelings it involved. The seekers after self-respect who favored and used "Negro" during all this time did so because they wanted to be bolder, clearer, and firmer about who and what they were. It testifies to the curious chemistry of language and the tangle of meanings that get enfolded with words that the name "Negro," meaning "black," had to be loaded finally with the weight of all the submissiveness of the past before being discarded to make way for the reappearance of the word "black" itself as the accepted group name.

This came about partly under the stimulus of the euphoria created for a time by the re-emergence of independent African states in the 1960s and the achievement of a new standing for black Africans in the world. The effect was that along with "black," the name "African"—long rejected as the symbol of black origins—also regained its standing, especially as it appeared in "Afro-American" used as an acceptance and an affirmation of those origins.

When you begin to trace the matter back—and it goes back nearly two hundred years—you find that the usages have varied and that preferences and arguments have swelled and swirled around a whole collection of labels: "blacks," "Africans," "negroes" with the small "n," "Negroes" with the capital "N," "Coloreds," "Colored People," "Colored Americans," "People of Color," "Ethiopians," "Racemen," "Negrosaxons," "African Americans," "Africo-Americans," "Afro-Americans," "Aframericans," "American Negroes," "Negro Americans." Even a brief look into these differences is the beginning of discovery of some of the real inwardness of the black identity problem in America.

During the years 1945–65, the years of the civil rights revolution and the beginning of the great shift in the status of the group in the society, the most commonly accepted usage had finally become "Negro." The long battle fought to get newspapers to print the word with a capital "N" had been won only as late as the 1930s. The term "colored" continued to be used almost as widely in print and in speech and in many quarters was still regarded as the more polite form. The name "Negro" continued under challenge from various directions. Among those who wanted no part of being either "Negro" or "black," the avoidance pattern sometimes went so far as to produce the not uncommon use of the term "group" or "group man" as a form of self-reference, whites being called "the majority group" or simply "the other group." At the other end of the spectrum were the small fringe groups of black nationalists, among whom the Black Muslims became the largest and most visible group during this period. They used the terms "black" or "black men." The Muslims also expressed their sense of non-identity, however, as we have already noted, by their abandonment of surnames. They also came out of a tradition of Islamic cults that also in their way reflected a flight not just from the term "Negro" but from Negroness too. One of the groups that preceded the Black Muslims in this tradition had begun by calling on their followers to "refuse longer to be called Negroes, or black folk or colored people or Ethiopians but to be called 'Asiatics' or 'Moors' or 'Moorish-Americans.' "[17]

The slave traders called their African cargo "Negroes" or simply "blacks." Early in the slave trade, the word "Negro" apparently came to be used more or less synonymously with "slave." Indeed, a South Carolina court held in 1819 that the word "Negro" had the fixed meaning of "a slave." This has been a frequent reason given for objection to the use of the word "Negro." It has been seen as "a badge of shame" hopelessly freighted with its "slave origin and its consequent degradation." Closely associated with this idea and even more commonly given as a reason for not liking the word is the slippage of "Negro" into "nigger," the term that carries in it all the obloquy and contempt and rejection that whites have inflicted on blacks in all this time.

Different usages began with the free Negroes who had come up out of the slave system by various means and had begun to group and assert themselves at the time of the American Revolution and the establishment of the new Republic. The 1790 census noted 59,000 free Negroes in the population, and although they were still called "Negroes" by whites, they wanted no part of the word that meant "slaves." Their way of distinguishing themselves from the slaves was to resume calling themselves "African." This was the name they attached to the new institutions they created for themselves at this time, e.g., the African Baptist Church, formed in Savannah in 1779, the first African Lodge of Masons (1787), the Free African Society (1787), the African Methodist Episcopal Church (1796), and others. The first schools established for their children were called "Free African Schools" in New York and elsewhere.

By 1830, when free Negroes met together in their urgent common interest, the adjective "African" had been replaced by "Colored." In Philadelphia that year, they formed the Convention of Colored Citizens of America, and in general had come to refer to themselves as "colored people" or "people of color." At least two sets of circumstances seem to be essential parts of the explanation for this change in terminology. The first is that in the intervening time an effort had been launched to get free Negroes to migrate back to Africa. This was the program of the American Colonization Society, led by some well-intentioned whites but inspired mainly by slaveowners worried about the subversive potential of free Negroes living beyond their control. The overwhelming majority of free Negroes, especially in the Northern cities, wanted no part of any such migration, especially under such auspices. There were some free Negroes who despaired of ever being able to live decently in America and who looked back to Africa as an alternative, but these remained in the minority. It seems reasonable to suggest that the label "African" was abandoned, at least by Northern free Negroes, because they were intent upon remaining Americans and rejected the schemes to send them as "Africans" back to Africa.

The choice of the term "people of color" or "colored people" to replace "African" suggests the second set of circumstances clearly involved in this change. The term "African" had been used mainly by free Negroes in the North, most of whom had gained their freedom in the early years of the Republic. The clusters of free Negroes in the South, especially those in Charleston, South Carolina, and New Orleans, came out of a much older process. The first differentiation among the slaves was that made between the field hands and the house servants, and from among the latter came the issue of unions between white masters and slave women, often treated as a second family, given their freedom, means, and education. It was the descendants of such groups who developed their own special caste position (which included slaveholding of their own) and whose most visible mark of caste was their lighter color. This community in Charlestown in 1790 formed not an "African" association, but the "Brown" Fellowship Society, "which admitted only brown men of good character who paid an admission fee of fifty dollars." In New Orleans, the even older and more aristocratic mixed descendants of the older French and Spanish settlers became a distinct group in the population and were called the *gens de couleur*. It is from this term and from this group, carrying with it all the connotations of higher caste associated with nonblackness and mixed ancestry, that the vague and essentially nondescriptive term "colored" or "people of color" was derived. With its adoption by the Northern free Negroes in place of "African" during the decade before 1830, it became the term of preferred and polite usage.

Although this term became one of general use, it never stood alone or uncontradicted. At the very beginning, in the 1840s and 1850s, when some of the most militant free leaders, despairing of ever gaining a decent status in America, became advocates of migration to Africa, some effort was made to revive the use of the term "African." In 1880, T. Thomas Fortune, editor of the *New York Age,* proposed the term "Afro-American" as a way of getting away from "Negro" and its vulgar equivalents. It is interesting to note, in view of the new sense in which this term has now gained currency, that Fortune's argument for it was in effect also an argument in favor of getting away from blackness, or at least from African blackness. He wanted this new term to describe the "new" race, which was, he wrote, "much nearer the American than the African type." It was adopted as the name of a newspaper, *The Baltimore Afro-American,* but never gained wide usage. It became instead the term preferred by strongly nationalist or even "race-minded" groups and individuals, remaining little heard and little used until it began to gain its wider currency in recent years.

But the argument, largely centering on the continued use of "Negro," went on and on, acquiring peculiar force around the years of the turn of the century. Booker T. Washington advocated the use of "Negro" and rejecters of the word charged this to his general posture of submission. Then along came W. E. B. Du Bois, no submitter, who not only espoused "Negro" but used "black" also and stressed color almost obsessively in his own special struggle for the reassertion of Negro identity. It did not matter, he pointed out, whether they were called "African" or "Ethiopian" or "colored," but what mattered was who and what you were and where you stood in the society. This was the view advocated by many other leaders over the years, although the N.A.A.C.P., founded in 1909 by Du Bois and others, followed the preferred usage among middle- and upper-class Negroes and used "colored."

Most of the later-middle-aged or older members of the present adult generation of black Americans grew up in the universe of color caste that largely shaped many of their own most deeply held attitudes and also their choices of what name to go by. In this universe, "black" was a word of rejection, shame, anger, violence, vituperation, disgust. It was an insulting word, a fighting word. Prefixed to any name or obscenity, it multiplied the assault many times over. Prefixed to "African" it was for many the ultimate derogation. It carried with it all the weight of association with "primitive," "savage," "evil" that the white world had pressed on blacks during the long time of their subjection. It was everything from which a person had to escape to join the nonprimitive, nonsavage, nonevil, non-African white world.

It has to be said also, however, that this was not altogether a flight from self; it was part of a profound confusion about what that *self* really was. For large numbers, the euphemism "colored" reflected a deeply rooted ambivalence over their own physically mixed origins: by the best available estimates, in this generation more than 70 percent of all black Americans have some degree of white ancestry.[18] There were many who had a strong sense that they were in fact no longer "black" or "African," but physically as well as culturally something else, as Thomas Fortune had said, something more "American." When Marcus Garvey in the 1920s assailed the leaders of Negro Americans of that day for their lack of "race purity," he brought on himself the fierce counterassault of men like W. E. B. Du Bois, A. Philip Randolph, and James Weldon Johnson, truly giant figures in the history of the struggle of black Americans to achieve a self-respecting place in American society. They helped bring Garvey down, but they also came out of that struggle with a profoundly deepened sense of how damaging the whole color caste system had been for the life experience and the outlook for Negroes in America. During all his great years as editor of *Crisis,* Du Bois kept pushing the word "black" at his strongly resisting readers.

This was the generation and this was the leadership that won the civil rights struggle in these decades. The breaking down of the system of legal segregation and discrimination was led from the beginning and finally won by the National Association for the Advancement of *Colored* People, headed by Roy Wilkins. Martin Luther King, who mobilized the freedom movement that made this great shift effective, had come up as a younger man who used "colored" but later came to use "Negro." Just as their lifelong efforts to free their people from bondage came to a climax, men like King, Wilkins, and many others found themselves targets of attack by younger people whose new militancy they had made possible. It was a complicated mix of things that produced this sequence—the victory in the fight against segregation coincided with a loss of faith in the prospects of any effective integration—but the symbolic shift appeared in the change of name. The people who had finally won the same rights before the law in America that everyone else had long enjoyed and who had begun to regain a self-respecting view of themselves were being called not "colored," or "Negro," but "black."

VI

LANGUAGE

And they said, Go to, let us build us a city, and a tower, whose top may reach unto heaven . . . And the Lord said, Behold, the people is one, and they have all one language; and this they begin to do: and now nothing will be restrained from them which they have imagined to do. Go to, let us go down, and there confound their language, that they may not understand one another's speech. So the Lord scattered them abroad from thence upon the face of all the earth . . . Therefore is the name of it called Babel; because the Lord did there confound the language of all the earth . . .

—GENESIS, 11:4–9

THE CADENCES of the mother tongue are among the earliest sounds a child hears. He begins to hear what the psychoanalyst Paul Schilder has called "the melody of speech" long before he can distinguish any of its words. It conveys to him some of the first sensations, emotions, and meanings that he begins to experience, that is, to learn. Long before he can speak words, he comes to understand them; and not long thereafter, with speech, he makes the words his own. Thus he begins to acquire a language, the most distinctive of all human attributes. The language he learns becomes one of the means—some would say the single most decisive means —by which he discovers himself, his family, his kind, his culture, his view of the world.

Much of how this happens is still a mystery, only dimly known or guessed at, much about it still argued or still arguable. Some modern students of language believe they have learned more about it than we know about any other aspect of human behavior above the purely biological level. Whether it is much or little, this knowledge has been but slowly wrested from the confusion and general mutual uncomprehendingness that began, we are told, on that far day when a jealously defensive Yahweh struck down with the plague of tongues those presumptuous tower-building men of Shinar, called Babel. There are now said to be at least four thousand languages, or many more depending on how you count them, each one playing its particular role in the lives of the people who speak it. How language is acquired by the individual—whether it is learned from experience or is shaped by some innate capacity of the human mind or out of some combination of these processes—continues to be studied and debated. But it is acquired, and our concern with it here picks it up near the very beginning of every individual's life, at the edge of that moving sea of meanings into which we are plunged long before we know, in any conscious way, what is happening to us.

That first learned language is, to begin with, the *mother's* tongue, with all that conveys and contributes to the forming of the self and the development of the individual personality. It opens into every aspect of life. "Each of the manifold uses of language has its special importance for the discovery of identity," notes Helen Lynd; "the very acquisition of speech is a major factor in helping a child to know who he is." And Erikson: "Speech not only commits [the child] to the kind of voice he has and to the mode of speech he develops; it also *defines him* [italics in original] as one responded to by those around him with changed diction and attention. They in turn expect henceforth to be understood by him with fewer explanations or gestures. Furthermore, a spoken word is a *pact:* there is an irrevocably committing aspect to an utterance remembered by others. . . . This intrinsic relationship of speech, not only to the world of communicable fact but also to the social value of verbal commitment and uttered truth, is strategic among the experiences which support (or fail to support) a sound ego development."[1]

"The world of communicable facts" is the world as it is seen by the family, the group, the culture in which the child enters. It is the world as named and described in the group's language, the tongue in which the child learns what the world is and how it came to be, the words and tones in which the group describes itself, spins its tales of the past, sings its songs of joy or sorrow, celebrates the beauties of its land, the greatness of its heroes, the power of its myths. It is the language in which he learns, absorbs, repeats, and passes on all the group's given truths, its system of beliefs, its answers to the mysteries of creation, life and death, its ethics, aesthetics, and its conventional wisdom. The mother's tongue serves to connect the child to a whole universe of others now living or long dead. It thus extends to all who share or have shared this tongue, as Herbert Kelman has put it, "some of the emotional intensity and irreducible quality" attached to "those primordial bonds that tie the child to his mother and immediate kin."[2]

The matter of language-and-reality has preoccupied philosophers for several thousand years. The matter of language-and-culture has in more modern times engaged scholars of many disciplines. Most recently, under the pressure of accelerated social and political change, linguists, anthropologists, psychologists, and even political scientists have been led to wrestle with some of its more stubborn confusions. As summed up especially for the benefit of political scientists by the linguist Dell Hymes, the issues of long standing in this discussion have largely had to do with differences of view or of emphasis between the so-called Cartesian tradition, stressing the universal cognitive patterns in all languages, and the Herderian, after Johann Gottfried Herder, the eighteenth-century German poet and philosopher, who stressed the distinctive cognitive patterns in the structures of different languages. It has been an argument over what languages have in common and what distinguishes them in particular, and especially over the decisiveness of the role of language, the extent to which it shapes or is shaped by the culture it expresses. Herder, whose conceptions of *Volks-geist* and *Nationalgeist* fertilized the growth of modern European nationalism, saw language as "the most distinctive element in a Volk's cultural heritage." It is what awakens and sustains a community's sense of its separate existence and "differentiates it from the rest of humanity." It is "the embodiment of a Volk's inner being, its inner Kraft (strength), without which it ceases to exist." After Herder, Wilhelm von Humboldt is credited with beginning, early in the nineteenth century, "the tradition of seeking clues to national character in specific types of linguistic feature."[3]

In our own time, this Herderian view has been most commonly seen as the forebear of what is known as the Sapir-Whorf hypothesis. These two American scholars strongly argued the view that language is not merely an instrument for communicating experience but actually defines it. The key quotes are from Edward Sapir in 1929:

Human beings do not live in the objective world alone, nor alone in the world of social activity as ordinarily understood, but are very much at the mercy of the particular language which has become the medium of expression for their society . . . The fact of the matter is that the "real world" is to a large extent unconsciously built up on the language habits of the group. No two languages are ever sufficiently similar to be considered as representing the same social reality. The worlds in which different societies live are distinct worlds, not merely the same world with different labels attached.[4]

and from Benjamin Lee Whorf in 1958:

Language is not merely a reproducing instrument for voicing ideas but rather is itself the shaper of ideas, the program and guide for the individual's mental activity, for his analysis of impressions, for his synthesis of his mental stock in trade . . . We dissect nature along lines laid down by our native language . . . the world is present in a kaleidoscopic flux of impressions which has to be organized by our minds— and this means largely by the linguistic system in our minds. We cut nature up, organize it into concepts, and ascribe significances as we do largely because we are parties to an agreement that holds throughout our speech community and is codified in the patterns of our language.[5]

Taken as a chicken-and-egg or cart-and-horse issue, the Sapir-Whorf view of the governing role of language in culture has been subjected to much scholarly scrutiny and challenge. As an opposite view, others have argued that language is but a "minor agency" or, more moderately, that life fashions language, not language life.[6] More commonly shared are the varieties of the middle view that language is always one of a cluster of factors, that there is an interplay among these factors that is never uniform. Dell Hymes observes that "language is never the only means through which members of a society acquire their habits of thought, and the degree to which it is the means varies."[7] Others have suggested that to make inferences from linguistic to nonlinguistic data is rarely convincing, that complex as it may be, language is much less complex than the whole fabric of the life of a community of which language is but one part, and that it is possible to go much too far in ignoring universals that do appear in human existence and culture.[8]

Given the difficulty of drawing nonlinguistic inferences from linguistic data, and the absence of any convincing yardsticks for measuring differences from community to community, the linguist Charles Hockett makes the point that when one looks at correlations that *can* be made, they are almost always trivial or obvious, e.g., the highly differentiated Eskimo vocabulary for snow, the relatively sparse vocabulary in Arabic about the weather, etc. "The more important the matter involved," he notes, "the harder it is to pin down." In scientific or technological or generally in "practical" matters, inherited linguistic patterns have been adjustable with relative ease. New vocabularies are devised, words borrowed, subsystems—e.g., mathematics—serve to ease the passage or often, as in the case of some social scientific jargons, to complicate it. It is quite another matter when we come, in Hockett's words, to "such goings-on as story-telling, religion, and philosophizing."

Literature on such subjects is, he suggests, "largely impervious" to translation.[9]

If not quite impervious, it is clearly much more resistant. The hard and precise language of science is much less hard and precise, to be sure, in the age of Einstein than it appeared to be in the age of Newton, a transfer in time and perception that many so-called hard scientists have made much more readily than a great many "soft" or so-called social scientists, even until now. Still, the "hard" facts of life do get reasonably precise treatment in most languages in which, as they become relevant to the affairs of that society, they are welcomed. On the other hand, the "soft" stuff of human existence—emotions, morality, art, religion—is expressed in blurry and ambiguous ways at best in every language. There are some human experiences, indeed, for which some would argue, as Helen Lynd does for example in the case of *shame,* there are no adequate words at all, no "signs" in the sense of fixed terms with firm meanings, but only "symbols" in the Jungian sense, "the best possible formulation of a relatively unknown thing." Language can actually cut off levels of experience because there are no names for them or because they are labelled only with vague or plastic words to which each person or group gives varied meanings. Lynd cites for examples a study of the uses of "honest" in *Othello* and "fool" in *The Praise of Folly* and "sense" in *Measure for Measure* to show how far from precise or truthful we can be when we fail to take into account the ambiguity, complexity, and surplus meanings attached to such words.[10] Here is where "fashions of speaking" become "fashions of perceiving,"[11] and of these there is no end, creating obscurity and confusion in any one language, not to speak of what can happen in translation from one language to another.*

---

* Such translations, however, sometimes illustrate how indelible the imprint of culture can be. In *Ways of Thinking of Eastern Peoples—India, Tibet, Japan* (revised English translation, edited by Philip P. Wiener, Honolulu, 1964), Hajime Nakamura details what happened to the Indian Buddhist sutras as they made their journey of a thousand years across Asia and shows, by examining the translations from one language to another, how each one gave to these scriptures its own distinctive cultural cast. What

Yet such translation must almost constantly take place, not only between countries and cultures but within them. The final and perhaps most decisive challenge to the Herder-Sapir-Whorf idea of language-and-culture seems to be the argument that its underlying assumption of one-language-one-culture is hardly borne out anywhere anymore. It is true that in western Europe the shaping of single languages out of groups of dialects did indeed figure centrally in the creation of nationality and nationhood, but it is not easy to summon up more contemporary parallels. On the contrary, as Dell Hymes flatly says: "There never is effectively but one language." Multilingualism is obviously prevalent over most of the world, and even more common is the fact of diversity of use within a single language. To questions about the role of language in culture, Hymes persuasively concludes that "no universal answer is to be given. Because the role of language is not everywhere the same nor ever the whole story, the question changes from one of the place of language in culture to one of the place of speech codes in societies."[12]

As in culture, so in the basic group identity it creates; however "kingly" it might be, to use Whorf's phrase for it, language rarely rules the whole domain. As he acknowledged, it was "in some sense a superficial embroidery upon deeper processes of consciousness. . . . I mean 'superficial' in the sense that all processes of chemistry, for example, can be said to be superficial upon the deeper layer of physical existence."[13] To be sure, everything a

---

struck me most forcibly was the degree to which many of the characteristics he brings into view across a gap of one to two thousand years resemble some of the most familiar images and stereotypes which are current among us now, including many I examined myself in some detail in *Scratches On Our Minds* (now *Images of Asia*), as they appeared in the minds of Americans in recent years. Thus, for one example, the abundance of abstract nouns in Sanskrit in contrast to the concreteness of Chinese, "abundant with words expressing bodies and shapes." In contrast to both, Nakamura quotes an eighteenth-century Japanese scholar as saying that the Japanese language "is fond of using concise and pithy expressions." In a long conversation I had with Nakamura several years ago about these matters, he turned aside, with amused surprise, the thought that he could possibly have imposed on these ancient texts any fresher impressions of his own about these contrasting cultural styles; the old texts, he said, spoke for themselves.

person first sees when he looks through his culture's window on the world bears names in the mother tongue of the group into which he is born. "Users of different grammars are," indeed, "pointed by their grammars toward different types of observations and different evaluations." This defines much or even most of what a person absorbs and experiences and this gives shape to what he is and what he becomes. To identify a person as being by origin a speaker of German or of Hausa or of Chinese is to assume much about him from this single fact alone. Much, but far from all, for among the elements that make up the basic group identity, language is but one, and its weight, value, and importance in relation to the other elements vary greatly in varying situations.

Examples of this are almost without number. Attempts to revive old tongues among the Irish and the Welsh have been much less successful than the survival of the strong sense of Irish and Welsh separateness. Command of the revived Hebrew language may have become essential for anyone who defines his basic group identity as "Israeli," but it was not for centuries and is not now at all essential in the identity cluster that makes a "Jew." Some American Indians, it has been pointed out, have held on to pieces of territory and let their ancestral languages go; others have held on to the languages and lost the land. Joshua Fishman cites, among many other examples, studies that show that second- and third-generation Americans have retained "ethnic group loyalty" long after losing the ethnic language (like those Germans who "maintained their self-identification as Germans in the midst of Polish or Ukrainian majorities long after completely giving up their German mother tongue," or, one might add, like the "Baba" Chinese in Malaya who lost the language long ago but never lost their identity as Chinese) and others like some American ethnic groups who hold on to the language long after losing anything describable as functional ethnic group loyalty.[14]

Pierre Van Den Berghe has pointed out that in South Africa all members of the Afrikaner *Volk* are Afrikaner-speakers, but that all Afrikaner-speakers—e.g., many of the Colored, or persons of mixed Afrikaner-black descent—are most emphatically not members of the *Volk*. Indeed, in this setting where color and physical characteristics play such a commanding role, a non-Afrikaner-speaker *can* belong to the Afrikaner Nationalist Party—as "quite a number of German and a few English-speaking whites do"—whereas an Afrikaner-speaking Colored cannot.[15]

Karl Deutsch identifies language as one of the major "building blocks of nationality," at the heart of the communications system, which is the main source of the "complementarity" that makes "a people." At the same time, he stresses that it is never language alone but always a cluster of characteristics that brings about the complemented result. He cites the experience of the Swiss, who, he suggests, "may speak four different languages and still act as one people," each Swiss having enough learned habits, symbols, memories, and other patterns in common with all the others to enable him "to communicate more effectively with other Swiss than with speakers of his own language who belong to other peoples."[16] Even in Switzerland, however, some language tensions have come into view, and although the example is a small one, it is a peculiarly telling example of how a language can serve as the forward point of the interests of one group of its speakers and be quite subordinate to other interests held by another group speaking the same language. Thus the French-speaking Catholic minority in the Swiss Jura has been pressing for the creation of a separate canton of its own, apart from the German-speaking majority, whereas "the francophones who share Protestantism with the German Béarnais are either indifferent or, in part, hostile to the demand for a separate canton."[17]

Language, in sum, is crucial to the way any individual sees the world; but it not only shapes, it is also shaped by what is seen. Language is a critical element in the making of every individual's basic group identity, but, to repeat, only as one of a cluster of critical elements that can arrange themselves in a host of different combinations. It plays its role in highly varied ways, a variety now spectacularly on view in every corner of the world where groups, tribes, nations, and cultures are trying to sort themselves out in new patterns of self-identification and relation to one another. In the new politics of retribalization and fragmentation that is currently such a large part of this process, the issues are often marked most clearly by conflicts over language, which serves as the most obvious and handiest sign of political, social, or group boundaries, overlying many other more deeply laid concerns. As a symbolic or triggering cause, language places high among the many reasons people have been confronting and killing one another in mounting numbers in so many parts of the globe in recent years.

Language issues of one kind or another appear now in the politics of "old" Europe and America and "new" postcolonial Asia and Africa. Old language loyalties (like Basque, Catalan, Breton, Welsh) reappear in varying intensities in countries made up of one or nearly one piece linguistically (such as Spain, France, Britain), and a new language dispute even turns up in the one-language culture of Norway. New pressures for varieties of bilingualism turn up out of the seams of racial and ethnic division opening in the English-speaking culture of the United States. Old bilingualisms generate new levels of hostility and confrontation, as in Belgium and Canada. New language strains appear even in multilingual Switzerland and again, as of old, around the edges of old irredentisms along the frontiers of Italy and Austria.

Such issues have assumed their sharpest forms in the postcolonial world, made up for the most part of countries with dozens, scores, even hundreds of distinct language communities (e.g., India, Nigeria, Philippines). In Europe, long centuries of linguistic evolution led eventually to the forming of nations made up of relatively homogeneous language communities. In the colonial world—Latin America, southern Asia, Africa—colonies were forcibly put together of conglomerated and agglomerated populations speaking many tongues. At the upper levels of these societies, the language of the colonial master became the key to education, status, prestige, power, advancement, development, modernization. In postcolonial India and Africa, members of the ruling groups from different regions and countries speak to one another in the ex-metropolitan lingua franca, English or French, not in any of their local tongues. At lower social and economic levels, the requirements of the slave trade and the colonial experience produced widely used pidgin or patois or Creole tongues that drew on the power-prestige languages of the masters and on varieties of local languages and dialects, as in East Africa, the Caribbean, along the China coast, and in the lands and islands of Southeast Asia. One of these newly created languages grew into Swahili, heavily derived from Arabic, now the lingua franca of much of East Africa and the adopted national language of Tanzania; another became the pidgin English-Melanesian that some believe may become the national language of the Australian half of New Guinea, even as the new Indonesian masters of old Dutch New Guinea seek to make their language the current one in their territory.

A language, a famous linguist once said, "is a dialect with an army and a navy." With the collapse of the old colonial power system, the forming of new nations in the old colonial boundaries, and the new push and pull for power among the various population groups, the question now was who had the army and the navy, in both the literal and the cultural sense. As symbol and as substance, language issues rose to bedevil the nation-building process everywhere: how to handle the multiplicity of languages, what to choose as a national language, whether to continue to use the ex-colonial master's language, advance the use of some one or two of the country's own languages, or even to create a new one. In many cases, as in parts of India, there are strong emotional-cultural attachments to mother tongues, readily generated into political cleavages and leading to murderous violence, often on specifically linguistic issues. Some studies purport to show that elsewhere, as in parts of Africa, insistence on the primacy of particular single languages is much less strong, partly because in so many countries no single language group is clearly dominant either in numbers of speakers or in prestige. In these cases, perhaps wishfully, some believe there is a better chance for what Joshua Fishman has tried to call "nationism"—a harder-headed state-oriented practical approach to nation-building—in place of the much more emotional ethnic-oriented mother-tongue bonds of Mazzini-type or European-style nationalism. Other students of the matter seem to believe that language divisions, both in themselves and in what they come to stand for, will persist and sharpen rather than decline and disappear.

The variety and complexity of the language aspects of current politics are well illustrated in the attempts that have been made by some scholars to draw up typologies that are meant to describe the situation in some reasonably coherent fashion. The difficulty of doing this is a language problem in itself, especially when it is done by linguists, the tangled and tortured actualities producing tangled and tortured terminologies.[18] In a much more usable way, Dankwart Rustow, a political scientist, has grouped types of language situations by the history and politics of the way different states were formed at different times.[19] He produces a broad and often unavoidably crude but a lucid and workable sequence in which he locates:

(a) Postimperial states, meaning large traditional states that have kept their geographic identity into the modern period, e.g., Japan, which also remained linguistically homogeneous, and Russia and China, both of which under Communist rule follow the old imperial policy of political and linguistic dominance of variegated populations by an all-powerful center.

(b) Postdynastic states of western Europe, which largely grew out of or developed into linguistically homogeneous nations, with notable exceptions in Belgium, Finland, and Switzerland, the latter becoming a model of that rare political accomplishment, a viable multilingual nation-state.

(c) Linguistic states of central and eastern Europe and the Middle East, in which the multivaried shapes and styles of history, politics, and nationality emerging out of the Hapsburg, Russian, and Ottoman empires are included. Here the principle of "linguistic nationality" found the going hard, whether in the characteristic multilingual fragmentation of most of this vast area on the European side, or in the relative homogeneity achieved by the spread of Arabic over its large domain.

(d) Countries of overseas immigration, with the varying linguistic experiences of the United States, Australia, New Zealand, Argentina, Brazil, Canada, and Israel providing the main examples.

(e) Postcolonial states of Asia, Africa, and Latin America in which, Rustow remarks, "the principle of linguistic nationality has fared far worse" than in all the other areas and categories. Here the large blocs of a hundred million Spanish speakers and seventy million Arabic speakers are divided, often bitterly and violently, among a large number of states. In the rest of the postcolonial world, only relatively few intermediate-sized language communities and large numbers of small to tiny groups make up the great bulk of the new nations formed out of the fallen empires. More than half the new states created after 1945 have no linguistic majority, and among those that do, ironically, there are bitter political divisions, as in Korea and Vietnam. In Africa, paradoxically again, the few relatively large linguistic groups, like the Hausa speakers, are divided among several countries.

Rustow goes on to sort out a number of characteristic language situations where a distinct language is predominant throughout the country, as in western Europe, Japan, Turkey; where a single language dominates in a number of neighboring countries, as in Spanish-speaking America; where among a variety of closely related languages one serves as the official language, as in Indonesia; where among a variety of unrelated languages only one has a substantial literary tradition, as in Morocco or Peru; where a number of unrelated languages have no literary tradition, as in tropical Africa; where unrelated languages have their individual literary traditions, as in India or Malaysia. From this crowded list of varieties, Rustow draws the plain general conclusion that language is never a single controlling factor and is never static. The Herder-Mazzini

romantics "assumed that language is the most indelible characteristic of peoples," whereas in fact it "is a variable, dependent on
political factors." Here too, it seems to me, the actuality blurs such
sharp divisions: language is variable in some aspects, powerfully
indelible in others.

✦

Immensely varied language effects have come, then, out of all the
different kinds of political experience over time. They appear
always folded in with other elements of identity. They have come
as a consequence of the rising and falling of empires and other
power systems, of the massive shifts of cultural impact and influence, the huge forced or free movement of people across seas and
continents over the centuries, the push and pressure and press of
trade, industry, enslavement, conquest, communication, war, and
revolution. To trace the single element of language in the basic
identity cluster held by any individual or group of individuals, one
would have to begin with the surviving—that is, the indelible—
traces of the mother tongue and then go on to the added layers
expressed in, or formed by, other languages acquired in each setting of time and circumstance.

The spread of European power, the colonial experience, and the
great migrations during the last three or four hundred years created
such layered effects in the lives of vast numbers, bringing about
what is probably the greatest mixing of peoples and tongues to take
place since they were scattered apart by the Great Divider at Babel.
The products of this experience fill all our recent history and crowd
the contemporary scene, with the heavy European stamp on people
in the Americas, Asia, and Africa much more widely pressed than
the Hellenic and Roman marks left on the peoples of a much
smaller world long ago. Out of this has come our vast patchwork
design of connected and contending cultures; of shared and con-
flicting systems of ideas, beliefs, and values; all the great jagged
irregularities of uneven development of societies, economies, technologies separating and uniting different peoples and different parts
of the world.

Hence whatever pluses may be made of this history: the belief that through all this movement has come enlargement of knowledge and with it some enhancement of human existence. But hence too all the crippled cultures, the besieged traditionalists, the deracinated modernists, the deformed wielders and victims of power: all the cost and confusion, the alienation and anomie, produced by what is called the modernizing process. In painful flight from all these consequences now, many people of many kinds surge to what refuge they can find or retrieve from the ruins of their many Houses of Muumbi. This includes for many the languages they spoke or their fathers and mothers spoke when they still lived there. Trying to retrieve the "variables" and identify the "indelibles" of this experience is like trying to see all this history as though it were a film that can be reversed, when it is actually live action going on all around us, some of it in view, much of it still unseen and unheard.

All these dramas take place on a stage crowded with players talking to one another mostly in obscure riddles, like characters in a Pinter play. In this cast, the Nehru-like between-two-cultures type is a familiar and usually pathetic or poignant figure[20] who moves, as Nehru did, far and deep into the alien culture to which he can never quite belong and is driven or drawn back to the other to which he can never quite return. Often this is a matter of pieces of different worlds into which individuals divide themselves, dividing indeed by the language spoken in its different parts. This could be and to some extent is part of the process of creating a more universal culture, as, for example, in science, but for the individual it has been more frequently an experience deeply ribbed and tangled in complicated emotional and psychological conflicts. There are those Africans, for example, represented by the black Frenchman Leopold Senghor, or the African English-speakers Julius Nyrere had in mind when he said that "at one time it was a compliment rather than an insult to call a man . . . a 'Black European.' " Citing this remark, Ali Mazrui has argued that the British colonial African's adoption of English was actually an expression of cultural nationalism because the African was proving how wrong the European was to think that the African was mentally inferior.[21] Or Mazrui, again, depicting an African heaven in which all the African languages continue to be spoken but are simultaneously translated for all listeners into their preferred tongues, not by any electronic machinery but by an act of will. Mazrui portrays, as a witness at a remarkable heavenly trial, a poor Ibo cobbler who had been murdered by Hausa rioters and who, under the terror of that memory, chose vainly to try to conceal his Ibo identity by speaking not in his own tongue but in halting English.[22]

Similar problems and ambiguities are attached, reports another African language specialist, to the development and use of Swahili in East Africa. Arab slavers had been around for much longer than the Europeans, but the Arabic origins and associations of this language were eagerly and pridefully appropriated as a way of acquiring higher status; for many of the same reasons, Arab forms, names, origins, and religious beliefs were adopted by a number of cults that rose among American blacks. More recently, the Arab connection in East African affairs has shifted in value from a borrowed plus to an ambivalent minus. In Zanzibar, for example, where black Africans took power from the hands of their former Arab rulers, it became the fashion to shift emphasis from the Arabic to the Bantu origins of Swahili words in order to "stress the African rather than the Arab character of the language." Tanzania's decision to make Swahili its national language, this writer says, was more "a decision of intention than of fulfillment," for while Swahili in general served as the common medium of ordinary speech among speakers of many other tribal tongues, English continued to be used at all higher levels of national activity.

This has led some East African intellectuals to fear that "having English as a medium of thought and Swahili as a medium of the masses" opens the prospect of class divisions deepened along linguistic lines. Said one African scholar: "By passively accepting English as the medium of intellectual activity, we are unwittingly placing a barrier to the intellectual development of our people. We are unconsciously inflicting the same malady that the great bulk of the so-called intellectual elite of East Africa suffers from—namely of being almost completely incapacitated to undertake any serious thinking in our own languages. This kind of mental and spiritual stagnation is a direct but long-lasting effect of colonialism."[23]

The same strong issues appear in a different setting in Peru, where the issue of using Spanish or the Indian Quechua and Aymara languages in the Peruvian educational system has been much debated. In one such discussion, a Quechuan scholar pleaded for the teaching of literacy in the Indian mother tongue "so that the individual child will not learn an inferiority complex along with his Spanish," an experience heavily documented in studies of the Peruvian school experience. A priest replies: "This business of saying that the Castilian language is a foreign language is false. [It] is completely our own, it has survived for more than four centuries among us." A Quechua-speaker replies that Quechuans who want to follow European ways take up an apprenticeship in the Spanish language and culture, "and once they have learned 500 or 600 words, they bury Quechua within themselves and do not wish to speak it any more; they exchange a language of limitless possibilities for a restricted language which constricts their minds and diminishes them as humans instead of exalting them."[24]

The Philippines is a country in which by some counts about eighty languages are spoken. There are eleven principal languages, each with more than a million speakers. Tagalog, spoken in a large part of the major island of Luzon, is the language of about one third of the total population. English, according to census figures, is spoken by as many. A version of Tagalog, called "Pilipino," has been proposed as the national language. It is still far from widely used, although the mass media, especially films, have been extending the spread of Tagalog, many of whose words, along with Spanish and English and Chinese words, have been absorbed into many of the regional languages.

Some of the Filipino experience is reflected in the view of a well-known Filipino writer who had always written in English. Under

the nationalist impacts of his later years, he told me, he began trying to write in his mother tongue, Tagalog, and found himself experiencing a shift of cultural personality, which he summed up as
the transfer from "active" English to "passive" Tagalog, a difference, he found, that cast different light and different meaning on
every sentence he wrote. In the Filipino school system, Spanish was
still regarded, in a ritualistic sort of way, as a prestige language
that was required study for all, but rarely acquired as a language
for actual use. English was studied by everyone from the first or
third grade on, but acquired, he said, with something less than 50
percent effectiveness by the great majority; a test of university fresh-
men in 1963 based on American placement standards for compre-
hension and inference rated them most generally at sixth-grade
level. The basic language of his students, he said, was "mix-mix,"
a combination of Tagalog and English similar to what has in other
places been called "Spanglish" or "Franglish" or, in India, "Hin-
glish." In Filipino political life when it used to be free and open,
politicians would speak publicly in English, informally in Tagalog
or their local tongue, and most of the time in some kind of "mix-
mix."

Despite various well-intentioned programs, he said, neither Tagalog nor the other Filipino languages are being studied or enriched in
any systematic way, and English remains at best a partially acquired
language. He said: "Mix-mix—'halu-halo' we call it—*is* the language," as indeed it has been at one early stage or another of most
of the languages we now speak. But now even for the best-educated,
the difference between English and the mother tongue remains one
of depth of expression. Another highly placed intellectual with an
impeccable command of English said: "Tagalog expresses the tones
of feelings of everyday life, which English cannot do. English is
academic and abstract, a way of manipulating ideas. But for the
vivid, dramatic, emotional parts of my life, Tagalog serves in a way
English cannot. When I make love, it's in Tagalog. We communicate best in Tagalog. Persuading my children to do something, I do
it best in Tagalog. When I want to register the most, I do it in
Tagalog."

Another figure who comes to mind is the middle-aging father of a family of American Jewish immigrants I met in Israel. His father had been an immigrant from Russia who lived in Brooklyn. "I remember," he said, "how ashamed I used to feel when I heard my old man speak his broken English, and I really made sure that my English wouldn't sound like that. But here I am now in the same position with *my* kids. I wonder how they feel when they hear me speak my broken Hebrew. And it's all turned around because they're the ones that speak English with an accent!"[25] The language *he* commanded, learned on the streets and docks of his native heath where he'd worked from boyhood until his middle years, was pure Brooklynese.*

The feeling of inadequacy in the use of a language marks one of the many points where variabilities and indelibilities are not easily separated. Unlike the immigrant or the immigrant's son who wants and needs to be like those to whom he has come as a stranger, the Frenchman who thinks his own is the queen of all languages does not suffer from speaking other tongues with a French accent; he only suffers from hearing others speak French with non-French accents, or even on hearing other Frenchmen whose accent is not Parisian. On the other hand, the immigrant carries with him his own indelible attachment to the language he knows as he knows no other. I think of the example of an Argentinian Jew who left Argentina as a youth and acquired relative fluency in several other languages in the course of building his personal and professional life in other countries for the next twenty-five years, speaking them all, however, with an accent that is unmistakably Spanish, and writing them with something less, he always feels, than impeccable accuracy. "Can you imagine what it means," he once asked me, "never, really *never,* to be at home in the language you are using?"

---

* A dying if not already dead language, according to a mourning writer in *The New York Times,* August 16, 1972. "Brooklynese died for lack of native speakers. . . . In streets where Brooklynites once argued in unmistakable accents, the liquid sound of Black English and the musical intonation patterns of Spanish are now heard. . . . The only surviving speakers of that lovely dialect are television comedians and a small number of elderly citizens. When they pass, Brooklynese will be one with the ages."

He occasionally revisits Argentina, where except for surviving members of his family he has virtually no pleasant associations or attachments, but where he now finds the experience of visiting unaccountably pleasurable. The pleasure, it soon appeared, came partly from regaining physical touch with some of the scenes of his childhood, but mainly from his ability to speak and hear the one language of which he felt fully and unaccentedly in command, not just Spanish but Argentinian Spanish, and not just Argentinian Spanish but Argentinian Spanish as it is spoken in Buenos Aires. Here, if only momentarily, the indelibles displaced all the political and religious and other variables that shaped the element of language and everything else that has gone into the making of this man's basic group identity.

In Malaysia a deep cultural cleft lies between all Chinese and the Malays, and almost as deeply between those Chinese who were educated in the Chinese-language schools and those who came up in the English-medium schools in the late colonial or immediate postcolonial period.

The Chinese-educated Chinese, always by far the larger part of the Chinese population until now, used to be taught in Chinese schools built and paid for by the Chinese themselves. In these schools, the children of generations of Chinese in Malaya learned to "see" the world with China at its center. They studied Chinese language, history, geography, literature. In the lifetime of the present adult generation, they successfully established *kuo-yu,* the so-called Mandarin national language of China, as the common tongue of educated Chinese in the South Seas, although each regional group preserved its own dialect at home. The older Chinese-educated continued to regard China as their homeland and some version of Chinese traditional behavior as central to their way of life. During the colonial period and up to 1949, this was for the most part an unquestioned and unambiguous attachment. After 1949, there was considerable ambivalence and some conflict between the generations of old and young Chinese-educated as to which "China" they had in mind.

The English-educated were those who moved at a very early age —usually from primary first grade—into the English stream, entering missionary schools or government schools set up to help produce English-educated office workers and minor bureaucrats for European business and government needs. Prudence and foresight in many Chinese families dictated sending at least one child of the family, sometimes several, into this important stream. By the time Malayan independence came in 1957, an estimated one quarter of the Chinese population was English-educated. These individuals acquired English as their principal language and the only one in which they discovered the world beyond their homes. Somewhere during their time in secondary school, they found themselves "thinking" in English. They no longer had enough Chinese to deal with all the new matter in their heads that had nothing to do with China at all.

Some had never known any Chinese; some so-called Baba families from much older immigrations had dropped Chinese for Malay or English many generations before. More commonly, Chinese children could still use the dialect learned at home—Hokkien, Hakka, or Cantonese—which remained good for the limited talk of personal family affairs, the kitchen, and the market, but useless for the subjects opened to them in school. These had to do with the "West" or the colonial British version thereof: history of the British Empire, literature from Shakespeare to Tennyson ("and not one step further!" said one product of the system) in the form of two or three plays laboriously read in class and a poem or two memorized. (One Chinese intellectual told me how it was not until he was sent to China for higher education—it was in 1947—that he learned for the first time of the existence of Russian, French, and American literature.) But whatever enrichment they were able to acquire thereafter, it was in English, via books, press, films, just as for the Chinese-educated it was in Chinese, also via books, press, films. The result was the acquisition of two wholly different universes. As one unhappy "Baba" put it, the main difference between the two was that for the one, China was still the more important place in the world, for the other it was not.

After 1957, both groups had to cope with the pressure of the Malay rulers of the newly independent country to impose Malay as the national language of the new "Malaysia," in which the Chinese found themselves precariously located as second-class citizens. This became the source of friction and collision. In Singapore, a Chinese city which became an independent state by itself in 1965, a new experiment was launched in the form of a four-language-track educational system in which the major medium of instruction could be selected: Chinese, Malay, English, or, for the 10 percent Indian minority, Tamil. Only the curriculum was to be exactly the same in every case, aimed at creating not little Chinese, Malays, Englishmen, or Tamils, but something new, "Singaporeans." How that experiment has been working out is another one of the many subjects waiting for authors.

In Malaysia generally, meanwhile, the issue of language has continued to be both an element in the fragile new politics and a complicated problem in the educational system and, indeed, throughout the society. The Chinese, whether Chinese-educated or English-educated, have to adapt to a language and a cultural/intellectual tradition that they find difficult to regard as equal or even comparable to their own. One Chinese intellectual, who felt a great stake in the new Malaysia partly because he felt so strongly opposed to the new regime in China, slapped his forehead and said with great passion: "I am doing my best, my damnedest, to convince myself: we must and will all become *Malaysians*. But in my heart, I don't know how not to be *Chinese!*" A completely Anglicized Baba who did not want his little daughter "to be left out as I was" was sending her to a special tutor to be taught not Malay but Chinese.

VII

HISTORY AND ORIGINS

✦

Within a few generations the culture, the attitudes, the beliefs,
the ways of living, the aspirations of a people undergo so many
changes that were a present member transported back through
these generations, he would seem to be among an alien folk.
But since there is no break in the historical solidarity, the belief in oneness withstands all the impacts of change. Anchored
in the assurance of the immortality of the community and
sustained by the beliefs and traditions of its culture, the individual members share an inner environment that blankets
them . . .

—R. M. MACIVER

EVERY GOD'S CHILD has a past. It comes with being born, and
there is no way of being born without acquiring one. The cells and
tissues of the small new body, including those that make up the
tiny new brain, are composed of the stuff of no one knows how
many biological remembrances of things past. So may be much of
what goes into the shaping of the mind, spirit, and personality of
the new person who has just come into being. The matter is still
heavily argued, but whatever of the past does not come genetically
does come genealogically. The connection to the past, hardly less
than umbilical itself, is made at almost the same instant the actual
cord between baby and mother is cut. It appears in the names,
signs, symbols, and legends engraved on the tablets immediately
hung around the little neck of the newborn or stitched into the cover

wrapped around him to replace as best it can the irreplaceable warmth of the womb he has just left. Before he can "know" it, the baby is tagged with labels and enveloped in the past he has inherited. Before he can "hear" it, he is told the story of his origins, where he came from, and given some idea of where he is going, the "facts" about the world he has entered, the "history" of those who have gone before him, the "myths" to believe about what it all means. Complete with explanations and instructions, the package contains everything he is deemed to need for the shaping, making, and even ending the new life he has just begun. Whatever he may do about them later, at the beginning the new baby needs these continuities and connections in the same way that his body needs his mother's milk. Plentiful or sparse, strong or weak, complicated or simple, sweet or bitter, pure or adulterated, for better or for worse, he begins to take them all in during the very first moments after he is born.

In one form or another, this introduction to the past has taken place at the beginning of every human being's life from most archaic times until now. It occurs implicitly and explicitly in every ritual, every ceremony, every observance of the event of birth in every culture we know anything about. Some, like Christian baptism or Jewish circumcision and rite of entering the covenant, wait a few days. Some, as in ancient Polynesia, waited not at all, singers gathering outside the house where a new prince was being born to chant the story of his origins so that it might be heard as he was actually being born. Among the Osage Indians, when a child is born, a "man who has talked with the Gods" is summoned. "When he reaches the new mother's house, he recites the history of the creation of the Universe and the terrestrial animals to the newborn infant. Not until this is done is the baby given the breast." When the time comes for it to drink water, he comes again and recites the Creation once more, ending this time with the story of the origin of water. The same again, with solid foods, when he tells how grains and other foods came to be. "It would be hard to find," adds Mircea Eliade, "a more eloquent example of the belief that each new birth represents a symbolic recapitulation of the cosmogony and of the tribe's mythical history. The object of this recapitulation is to introduce the newborn child into the sacramental reality of the World and culture and thus validate the new existence by announcing that it conforms with the mythical paradigms. But this is not all. The newborn child is also made a witness to a series of 'beginnings.' And one cannot 'begin' anything unless one knows its 'origin,' how it come into being."[1]

Almost all myths in all mythologies are "origin myths." Words like "In the beginning" open every account we know by which human beings have tried to explain their world and how it came to be. In their endless variety and sameness, all human cultures make of every new birth an occasion to repeat and reinforce their beliefs about their origins and begin initiating the new member into their particular versions and ways of explaining what it is all about. By reciting these myths and these "histories" and re-enacting and re-living them again and again, notes Eliade, "one reconstitutes that fabulous time and hence in some sort becomes 'contemporary' with . . . the Gods or Heroes" who made it. By "living" the myths, one emerges from profane chronological time and enters "a sacred Time at once primordial and indefinitely recoverable."[2] The shared past enters into the making of every individual life in every culture, whether in archaic times or in our own. It does so whether it appears in the guise of "myths" that deal with what has been imagined about "sacred" time, or as "history" that purports to relate the "facts" of "real" or chronological time. It is incorporated at all levels into what has been called "group mind," "collective memory," "historic memory," Durkheim's "collective representations" or Jung's "racial unconscious" or "archetypes."

This location in Time, fixing links to past-and-future, is clearly the deepest and most pressing of all the needs served by what every person acquires somehow from his antecedents, from some version of the shared collective experience linked to his own personal history and origins. It assures him, as he profoundly needs to be assured, that he comes from somewhere and is going somewhere, that when he dies, it is not the end, that he is not alone. He is connected to others alive and dead by all the threads that connect what they share through parentage, family, kin, extending in time to a shared ancestry, shared antecedents, shared beliefs, imagined or historic experience. These must be kept alive and continuous, hence ancestor cults and worship, filial and family codes, the common obsession with descent and posterity, hence too the religion, art, literature, myths or "history" that define who each one of us is. These linkages help make tolerable the individual existence that is otherwise intolerably bounded by its own fragile aloneness, its own birth, and its own death. The element of the shared past, of his own history and origins is deeply imbedded in every individual's personal identity; it is part of the basic group identity with which each personal identity is inseparably molded.[3]

✦

To begin considering how the past has been used and abused is to confront in a way the whole human story. A principal function of the past is to legitimize the present, and in the view of the British historian J. H. Plumb this has primarily been a matter of sanctioning power and authority. Plumb points out that this is why from earliest times rulers and ruling classes invariably traced their begats and their right to rule back to royal and even divine authority. As the Sumerians, Egyptians, Greeks, and Romans did, so did the Tudor monarchs and their courts whose chroniclers busily traced their lineage "back to the Conquest . . . to the mythical Lud . . . to David, the House of Jesse, right back to Adam himself" and back to "Edward the Confessor, Charlemagne, the Roman consuls, and even the Trojans, to say nothing of Noah and his Ark."[4] The genealogical need appears with each new group's push upward to status and power, Plumb notes, citing the fad for ancestors that swept the newly rich American bourgeoisie of the 1880s and the 1890s, when the New York Public Library built up its massive genealogical service, the Scottish clans underwent a strong revival, and the tartan industry a profitable rebirth. Americans put their own special value on humble beginnings and origins without, however, yielding up their fascination for intimations of nobility in the past. This could be a matter of some real or fancied remoter lineage in the old country or of status attached to *when* they arrived in the new country or both. The *Mayflower* and all the later Mayflowers played similar roles in all the later immigrant groups that came in their turn to make up the American society. As each one "arrived" in American life, there was almost sure to be a fresh surge of interest among its members in who and what their forebears had been, where they had come from, and when.[5]

Great mobility has made this kind of information hard for ordinary people to come by, although in many groups and cultures people do their best to leave their own traces behind, to keep some memory of them alive into the following generations. They inscribe themselves on gravestones, ancestral tablets, in parish ledgers; they leave their faces in pictures—the invention of photography provided an almost indefinite extension of existence for great masses of people whose lives are preserved now in mountains of family albums—their stories as told by old folks or preserved in heirlooms or possessions handed down generation after generation. American mobility stretched these bonds quite thin but never did remove the need for them. It is forever being renewed in elegiac celebrations by those who do know who some of their forebears were[6] and by others who do not. Many of the latter are deeply driven now to search out their antecedents, not to sanction any new or assumed authority but out of the need to cease being nameless, parentless, a person without a past, as among some young American blacks for whom the new emergence in the 1960s spurred a quest for individual family histories in the records of slavery and in the memories of old people in African villages.[7]

The individual's need for a personal past cannot often be satisfied further back than a generation or two, especially in the American society. Personal genealogies, so soon lost, can be much more successfully retained or regained in the "history" of the group with which the individual is identified, a kind of history which, as Fritz Stern has noted, usually serves "as a kind of collective and flattering genealogy."[8] The search for this kind of a usable past goes on by all kinds of means in all kinds of places, in archeological diggings not only in China, Africa, Israel, or in the pre-Columbian ruins of

Central America, but in the back yards and attics of the United States as well. It goes on in the libraries, museums, and archives where scholars of a hundred different new and old nationalities are now busily disinterring, re-examining, rewriting, dressing up the old myths of their many Pasts in the brighter raiment of new national Histories.

In his *Death of the Past,* Plumb proposes a distinction between "Past" and "History," the Past seen as a "created ideology with a purpose designed to control individuals or motivate societies or inspire classes" to serve the purposes of bolstering those in power. This kind of contrived Past is dying, Plumb thinks, because the postindustrial world no longer needs its sanctions—the prober of the solar system no longer needs Apollo as a god, only as a name for his spaceships. Now, at last, comes History, a veritable Knight of Rigorous Truth, whose mission in behalf of the multitudes shall be "to cleanse the story of mankind from those deceiving visions of a purposeful past" which only served the needs of the few. Such "visions," Plumb thinks, now appear only to survivors cast away on "islands of conviction in a surging sea of doubt."[9] Historians shall undo the lies of those few and bring truth to the many and it shall set them free.*

Like most promised millenarian outcomes, this one too appears to be subject to indefinite postponement, however beguiling the prospect of phalanxed historians overcoming the forces of darkness. It is difficult, looking around at the current actualities, not to see that Plumb's "islands" are continental in size, that the "deceiving visions" still grip most if not all the people in the world— including the world in which historians dwell, have their minds shaped, and do their work. The Past remains very much alive,

---

* For another view of these "visions" vs. "History": "History has the cruel reality of a nightmare, and the grandeur of man consists in his making beautiful and lasting works out of the real substance of that nightmare. Or, to put it another way, it consists of transforming the nightmare into vision: in freeing ourselves from the shapeless horror of reality—if only for an instant—by means of creation." Octavio Paz, *Labyrinth of Solitude,* New York, 1961, p. 104. The often-borrowed line from Joyce reads: "History," Stephen said, "is a nightmare from which I am trying to awake."

whether as fantasy, fiction, or fact, whether it appears out of the mists of "sacred" time or the smogs of "chronological" time, whether it is recorded in holy writ or as "history." Hindus and Muslims, Catholics and Protestants, all varieties of Believers and Non-believers, all kinds of the "We" and "They" continue to revile and kill one another out of the memories provided by both kinds of time and with the sanctions of both kinds of writ.[10] In all wars —ancient, recent, ongoing—combatants customarily invoke both gods and ancestors, and it has not mattered much whether either or both were real or imagined. If the Past is "dead," it dances, a lively corpse indeed, on new graves everywhere almost every day in whatever kind of time. Every "new" collision in some way re-enacts seemingly irrepressible conflicts rooted in some more or less distant past. "Past epochs never vanish completely," to quote again from Octavio Paz, "and blood still drips from their wounds, even the most ancient."[11]

The past keeps on being dug up, reappearing like a Hindu holy man from his pit, alive if not quite well, always new if not shining, always the same, or if not quite the same, then same enough. The power and continuity of the universal attachment to "beginnings" and "origins" awesomely illustrate how much more in human experience has remained the same than has changed. All the marvels of progress notwithstanding, human beings continue marshaled in their groups, bonded by their shared beliefs and fears, and they go on re-enacting and reliving their pasts today even as their most archaic ancestors did. They do so not only in their holy places where the blood of renewal is usually symbolic* but in the arenas of power where the blood is usually real. Whatever in human affairs may be "new," it is never wholly so under the sun: the past is

---

* I say "usually" remembering a moment of discovery during my own youthful "beginnings." Looking down at a great bloodstain on the stone floor next to the imbedded marker in the floor of the Church of the Nativity in Bethlehem, and learning that at this spot, believed by believers to be the site of the manger, on Holy Night the year before, a priest of one order had taken a heavy candlestick and brained a priest of a rival order in a contest over who had the right to stand at that holiest place at the holiest moment in the Christian year.

wrapped into every present problem or crisis of identity forced on people everywhere by the pressures of political change. The legacies of history and origin are inescapably and most inclusively part of every re-examination and every redefinition that people of so many kinds are now making about who they are and how they relate to others.

✦

In every case, this experience calls for new ways of dealing with the past. The new Great Powers of this era, America and Russia, grapple with the great unfinished business of internal self-definition, the multiplying difficulties of the time producing their different varieties of official decay and popular disaffection and nostalgia: Solzhenitsyn finds *his* House of Muumbi in a preindustrial Russian rural idyll-dream, Americans keep scratching around looking for theirs. While these two Great Powers struggle to fit their twentieth-century-style power into their nineteenth-century-style way of playing world politics, the ex-imperialists of Europe have had to grow more accustomed to their shrunken status and their more restricted territories; in Britain relegating the images and figures and attitudes of their days of greatness to their libraries, galleries, and museums, or nostalgia on TV (e.g., *The Forsythe Saga; Upstairs, Downstairs,* both set in the turn-of-century heyday of British world dominance); or, as in the case of France, keeping them alive for a few years in the waxlike figure of a de Gaulle or in continuing dreams of mastery again, if only over western Europe.[12]

On the other hand, among all the hitherto ruled, dominated, and demeaned peoples of the world, the recovery of local political power, however limited, opened the way to recovery of self-esteem by rediscovering and re-establishing their own sources of pride in the past. Their need becomes to erase its minuses, rediscover or, if need be, to recreate its pluses, to regain, to reassert, to celebrate once more a prideful association with all that went before, all the way back to the beginnings. Thus Jawaharlal Nehru, whose book *Discovery of India,* written in a British prison in India between 1942 and 1945, is itself a memorable example of this experience, noted that all colonial middle classes among whom nationalist movements arose "wanted some cultural roots to cling to, something that gave them assurance of their own worth, something that would reduce the sense of frustration and humiliation that foreign conquest and rule had produced. In every country with a growing nationalism, there is this search . . . this tendency to go back to the past."[13]

The reach is for the beginnings, the search is for greatness, if not "big" greatness, then at least little greatness, if not one's own greatness, then at least reflected greatness, especially a greatness reflected long ago. In Romania, a land, as its name suggests, identified with Rome, ardent Romanians have long identified themselves with the Dacians, a people conquered long ago by Trajan's Rome. They added Roman virtues, including Latin as the basis for their language, to their own great attainments of valor, the arts, and all the learned skills. It was for being "Roman," not for standing up to Rome, that the ancient Dacians are claimed and celebrated by modern Romanians. Still, to be "Roman" is not to be "Russian," and the celebration of this heritage by poets, playwrights, artists, and scholars was abruptly halted when Romania came under the control of Stalin's Russia in 1945. As soon as Romania came part of the way out from under Russian control with the beginnings of de-Stalinization under Khrushchev in 1961, the celebration of the Dacian heritage was resumed at a vigorous rate in all the faculties, publishing houses, media, and popular arts of the country.[14]

A less modest example is offered by Turkey, whose nationalist revival in the waning years of the Ottoman Empire early in this century was accompanied by the rediscovery and reinstatement of pre-Islamic, pre-Ottoman, pre-Persian symbols of the distinctive Turkish past. The young Turks who took over old Turkey also provided a notable modern replay of the universal myth-making by which peoples have immemorially located themselves at the beginnings of all human existence. It was formally proclaimed in 1935, by authority of Ataturk, nationalist leader of the new Turkey, that it was a Turk, facing the sun at civilization's dawn somewhere in Central Asia, who uttered the first word ever spoken by a human being—the Turkish word for "bright"—thus inaugurating all language, all culture. From these Turkish beginnings civilization then spread north into Russia, west into Europe, east to India and Indonesia, and south into the Arab world.[15] It obviously required strong potions to cure whatever it was that ailed the long-declining sick man of Europe.*

While some try to build self-esteem by evoking a past of imagined greatness, others have to try to do so by wiping out a past of real lowliness. Such is the case, in Nehru's own India, of the emergent ex-Untouchables and of their less well-known counterparts in Japan, the outcasts or *burakumin*. These are people who want to erase their history and forget their origins. Once unwilling to keep on accepting the status imposed upon them by their past, they want done with that past forever. Except for an occasional bard, holy man, or romantic hero, there is nothing in the past but their subjection, nothing they wish to retain, much less pass on to their children. Their subjection is tied to their origins. They cannot escape the one without banishing the other; for members of these groups to acquire some more satisfactory identity, the groups themselves have to disappear.

Ironically enough, they have already disappeared, legally. In Japan, the status of outcast was abolished by imperial edict in 1871. In India, Untouchability was explicitly abolished by the new Indian constitution of 1949, largely written by B. R. Ambedkar, the Untouchable leader from Maharashtra. In both countries, however, their nonexistence is legal fiction, their continued existence

---

* The Turks could not only create prehistoric history, they could also uncreate some quite recent historic history. At their insistence, all references to the Turkish massacres of Armenians in the 1920s were deleted from the report of the Sub-Commission on Prevention of Discrimination and Protection of Minorities of the United Nations Commission on Human Rights, meeting at New York, March 6, 1974. Cf. *The New York Times,* March 7, 1974, and *Armenian Reporter,* New York, March 14, 1974. The Russian and Chinese Communists remain, however, the world's leading practitioners of the art/craft of transforming events into nonevents, persons into nonpersons, and vice versa.

social fact, with very little sign that any effective change is taking place except at a most painfully slow pace. The past does not evaporate on command, not even in Japan and particularly not in India.

As I have reported elsewhere in some detail,[16] emergent Untouchables in India have historically tried to escape their lot by abandoning Hinduism. In much earlier times, many became Muslims and Christians. More recently, some have become Buddhists. But caste practices and caste attitudes have pursued them no matter what religion they embraced. Others have tried to *pass* as caste Hindus. As I have already noted, the absence of peculiarly identifiable physical characteristics makes this possible for some individuals. Indeed over generations of time some Untouchable groups have been able to inch slowly across the line into the gardens of Hindu touchability. But for individuals who make this attempt now, the way proves hard. In the face of powerfully persisting caste practices in connection with birth, marriage, and death, they usually find the deception all but impossible to maintain. In Japan similarly, this path to disappearance has been heavily blocked by the strong survival of the system under which personal and family records remain inseparably attached to every individual and follow him through every important event in his life.

By far the greater numbers of these outcasts in both countries still live on in stoic acceptance of the fate the past has inflicted upon them. But it is precisely through the onset of political change, education, and a reach for the first rung up the social-economic ladder that many begin to feel shame and anger where their fathers and grandfathers had known only passive submission. In both countries, more radical political solutions failing them, they would be glad to melt into the masses around them, in India to become caste Hindus like all other caste Hindus or, most wishfully, just *Indians;* in Japan to blend into the otherwise undifferentiated mass of ordinary Japanese. In both countries, however, they are emerging into societies not yet ready or willing to receive them on some new and more tolerable footing. In supermodernizing, swiftly changing Japan, this remains one of the many examples of the power of archaic survivals in an otherwise dynamic society. In India, where change in the imbedded institutions and practices of the caste system has barely begun or still not begun at all, it is clear that the ex-Untouchable is not about to escape his history or blot out his origins, not yet, not for a long time to come.

✦

Emerging from a status barely higher than that of Untouchables in India, American blacks now seek not to erase their past but to rediscover it. They are going back to it to re-establish those sources of pride and self-acceptance so largely lost to them during the long period of their submergence. This has to do with their past as Americans and also with that part of their history and origins that lies more remotely in Africa.

There are, to be sure, great differences between Afro-Americans and Indian Untouchables. The "long" history of submergence of black men is several hundred years long; the "long" history of Untouchability in India is several thousand years long, its origins shrouded in the prehistory of ancient India. The subjection of Untouchables in the Hindu system carries with it, from the dimmest times to this day, the sanction of an overpowering religious tradition. The subjection of black men by Europe and America was sanctioned only by the power and rapacity of white men who had to violate or make a travesty of their own religious beliefs to rationalize their actions. In America, the maintenance of slavery and all the subsequent forms of subjection of blacks took place in flagrant contradiction of the American political credo embodied in the Constitution. Untouchables in the Hindu system had never been anything but outcasts back into time beyond memory or record. Black men of Africa and the African Diaspora come out of a continent and a history that was very much their own until some four hundred years ago when Arab and European slave traders and invaders began the process that took so many of them into foreign slavery and only late in the last century brought their lands, as well as the Arab Maghreb and Egypt, under European rule or control.

I have suggested earlier that the black American's view of his African origins lies deeply imbedded in the core of his deepest sense of himself. It has to do centrally and crucially with his physical being, his color and features, his blackness and Negroidness and the value placed on these by the overridingly dominant white world and internalized at great depths for a long period of time by blacks themselves. This is what made the core of the black American group identity. This is what led to the flight from blackness, the flight from Africanness, the yearning after whiteness, the reach for other histories, other origins. And this is precisely what is being swept away now by the changes that have begun to take place, by the breakdown of the white supremacy system in the American society, and especially by the strong current of black self-reassertion that has been part of it.

This has brought recognition at last and a swift broadening in the society at large of the strong tradition of historical work created by a handful of black American scholars over more than a century, a span that includes the writings of George Washington Williams, W. E. B. Du Bois, Carter Woodson, Rayford Logan, and John Hope Franklin.[17] The work of these and other men laid the foundation for the present extensive revision of old texts and writing of new ones. The present school generation is getting a fresh view of a history that along with slavery and subjection also included a long procession of black martyrs and heroes, tribunes and artists and writers, going back as far as the history of the American republic itself. The old past is being newly re-examined. History is being rewritten and revised, by both black and white writers, and new balances of perception and self-perception are being struck. This new literature, especially that part of it prepared for use in schools, has begun to replace or at least to confront the works of white historians who for generations told and retold the American story as it suited *their* various class, regional, or racial biases. With a few notable exceptions, such works served in the past to create and reinforce the characteristic patterns of white superiority and black self-rejection and self-debasement that had dominated the scene for such a long time. Sharply contradicting Carlyle's maxim—"Happy are the people whose annals are blank in history books"—black Americans are clearly not going to be content until their pages of history are filled in some more satisfying way for them and they have altered the common knowledge of the nation of which they are part.[18]

The problem of blank pages remains more acute in the matter of the remoter past of black Americans in Africa. The political change that began to take place in Africa in the 1950s began to alter some of the patterns of ideas and feelings among black Americans about themselves and about their African origins. But in this relationship there are great complexities, depths of emotion, and experience that have only begun to be stirred in these years; it is going to take a much longer time to find new shapes that they may hold in time to come. I have attempted elsewhere to report in some detail on what I found to be some of the essences of the beginnings of change in this matter.[19] In addition to everything else, Africa represented for the black American what appeared to be the terrible emptiness of his past. The white world long pictured Africa in the oft-quoted phrase of the 1911 *Encyclopaedia Britannica,* as the "continent without a history" and of black men as standing apart, left behind in a primeval past, untouching and untouched by the swifter-flowing mainstream of developing human civilization. This was the notion of nothingness or nonbeing or invisibility that long dominated the white man's view of the black man and became the black man's view of himself during the centuries of white domination. Some passages of this kind, to illustrate, from early James Baldwin:

When I followed the line of my past I did not find myself in Europe but in Africa. And this meant that in some subtle way, in a really profound way, I brought to Shakespeare, Bach, Rembrandt, to the stones of Paris, to the cathedral at Chartres, and to the Empire State Building, a special attitude. These were not really my creations, they did not contain my history. I might search them in vain forever for any reflection of myself. . . . Joyce is right about history being a nightmare. . . . People are trapped in history and history is trapped in them.

Or further, about people in a Swiss village:

Out of their hymns come Beethoven and Bach. Go back a few centuries and they are in their full glory—but I am in Africa, watching the conquerors arrive.[20]

Resistance to this image of their remoter origins began to assert itself among American blacks a long time ago. The record of it will be found in the slender but continuous succession of works that stretch from those of Martin R. Delany and others before the Civil War through Alexander Crummell followed by W. E. B. Du Bois at the turn of the century, and in the output of the Association for the Study of Negro Life and History, founded in 1915, and especially of its director, Carter Woodson, and others since. With a few notable exceptions, Africans did not join in this effort until more recently. Most African movements of self-reassertion began much later than those in America but came to their climaxes much more swiftly, at least in political terms. Beginning in the 1950s, European colonial governments disappeared and new African states came into being with great and sudden speed. The change of names in some countries reflected the impulse to identify with the more distant African past and, indeed, amid all the inevitable confusions and instabilities of the new politics, fresh African efforts had already begun to discover a history long lost or unknown. The African historian Kenneth Dike, then head of Ibadan College in Nigeria, said in 1957:

If the African has no past heritage and no future except by imitation of the European ways . . . then the Gold Coast (Ghana) is destined to fail. But if the instinctive belief of the African in his traditions is justified, the ultimate emergence of West African states as independent modern states cannot be doubted. . . . Every nation builds its future on its past; so the African must not only have faith in his own existence, but must also satisfy himself by scientific inquiry that it exists.[21]

In Africa, as in the rest of the postcolonial world, this task of rediscovery awaits the work of a new generation of historians.

Whether "scientifically" or otherwise, they will at least be looking at the subject matter from their own points of view, being located, as the Indonesian writer Soedjatmoko has said, "at an indigenous vantage point from which to view the unfolding of the history of each of these nations . . . as opposed to the Europe-centric view" of those who wrote on these subjects previously.[22] In almost every case, this has to involve resurrecting and recoloring a past which has until now existed more as "myth" than as "history," establishing new versions, sifting new archeological or other evidence, offering new interpretations, all the essential things historians do from generation to generation as the changing need and spirit of their times move them. There will be a lively display of assorted ethnocentric motes and beams as new looks are taken at what went before and more eyes see in more different ways what is there. In one guise or another, a different Past will be summoned out of its hidden places to attend the present. For this reappearance, as in so many other cases in our time,* it will have to be dressed up in new clothes, have its face lifted, its warts removed, its features altered, by scholarly plastic surgery if need be. In this, as in so much else, the newly emergent national historians will be able to turn to their Western exemplars to learn how to proceed: the calling up of loyal historians to serve new national colors is an old European and American practice. New generations of Asian and African historians have libraries full of models to show them how any set of passionate beliefs can be decked out in the trappings of dispassionate scholarship.[23]

If some need to erase the past and some to discover it, others need to resolve it. Two examples, different as they are, are the Filipinos and the Japanese.

The group identity patterns that turn up most visibly on the open surfaces of Filipino life are those having to do with the re-

---

* "They too—the Chinese, the Hindus, the Arabs . . . carry about them, in rags, a still living past." Octavio Paz, op. cit., p. 65.

gional identities—Tagalog, Visayan, etc.—I have already mentioned in connection with their languages. These are still the most
meaningful and significant identities most Filipinos have. There
are other underlying feelings less directly expressed among Filipinos about their various ethnic mixes, about having Chinese or
Spanish antecedents, about being darker- or lighter-skinned or having this or that kind of eyes or nose. These are so strong that,
as I have indicated, one is moved to wonder whether this preoccupation with physical characteristics is not the key to the inner
chamber of the Filipino group identity itself.

In suggesting that Filipinos seek to *resolve* their past, I am referring again to those layerings of Filipino history, the Malay,
Spanish, and American legacies, among which some Filipinos look
for an identity that they can feel is distinctively their own. Their
problem arises from the troubling fear of some of these seachers
—writers, scholars, politicians, some radical youth leaders whom
I interviewed—that they are a people who have always taken on
and worn the features of others, that nothing authentically Filipino is there. This did not include, curiously enough, any awareness of the ambiguities attached to the origins of the name
"Filipino" itself, which I found to be not a matter of common
knowledge at all—I happened on it myself quite accidentally during a discussion with a Filipino writer working on nineteenth-
century materials—and therefore of no concern, not even to intellectuals concerned with Filipino "identity." They generally took
the name, if not the identity, for granted.

But they had begun, some of them, to look with new eyes at
their remote "Malay" past. The peoples of the Philippines come
from the same "Malay" or other aboriginal stock that peopled
most of Southeast Asia in the prehistoric past. In the Philippines,
this ancient stock and whatever survives of its culture has been best
preserved among the mountain peoples. Until recent years, these
hillsmen had been looked upon by the Christian Filipino low-
landers as pagan, primitive, and savage. For a time in the 1960s,
they began to be seen by some as older, purer brothers, untainted
by Chinese or Spanish infusions or by any of the multiple bor-

rowings of foreign ways and creeds. Partly out of this new attitude, a government Commission on Integration was created to restore to the mountain peoples their rights and dignities as citizens of the Republic, although no one connected with it was sure whether their aim should be to assimilate or pluralize the many differences. At the same time, there grew a certain cult of romantic glorification of the tribal arts, dance troupes dancing their dances, scholars collecting their artifacts, artists carving and painting their rough-hewn lines and bright colors. This new view of the remoter past, developed largely in a rather narrow milieu of intellectuals and artists, also made its way for a time into the realm of high policy, the idea of the "common Malay stock" becoming a major theme in the rhetoric surrounding the abortive "Maphilindo" pact which linked the Philippines, Indonesia, and Malaya for a few weeks in the summer of 1963. This romance did not last long either abroad or at home, but some of its memories have lingered on.

As I quickly gathered in the course of my interviews, the resurrection of the "Malay" past had certain drawbacks as a source of self-esteem. The hill tribesmen in the mountains of Luzon and other islands of the Philippines represented a certain heroic survival of a history with a heavy cast of submission in it. The Malay peoples of southeastern Asia were won more completely than any other anywhere in Asia by invading alien religions, Islam in Malaya and Indonesia and the southern Philippines, and Roman Catholicism in the rest of the Philippines. The new arrivals found some Hindu underpinnings, brought long before from the outside, which had been superimposed on the animism of the indigenous cultures. Some of these survived more or less intact, as in Hindu Bali, but both Hindu and animist backgrounds showed through mainly in the style in which the new dominant beliefs came to be held and practiced in these countries. Whatever may be the meaning of this greater permeability, it did not seem to be remarkably helpful to contemporary Filipinos looking for distinctiveness, even for greatness, in their more distant Malay origins.

The varieties of other Filipino inheritances show up in current affairs in their own dialectic fashion. The half-century fusion of American-style education and political democracy has produced breakdown and takeover by a petty dictator, Latin American style. For four hundred years archaic Spanish reaction and sixteenth-century-style Catholicism had put their heavy mark on Filipino culture and personality, standing solidly in the way of effective revision of the social and economic system they had created. When Ferdinand Marcos overthrew the democratic political system of the Philippines in 1972, his American mentors gave him their full support and the American-oriented Filipino middle class appeared to be glad to submit. Marcos did not make the trains run on time—there aren't many trains in the Philippines—but he did stop crime in the streets. Two years later, it was being reported from the Philippines that the principal resistance to the new system of authoritarian rule was coming from priests of the Catholic Church, who picked up the banner of civil liberties and democratic rights which Marcos had so easily struck down. If, as reported,[24] this resistance was coming in no small part from American and American-trained priests, it made the paradox all the more paradoxical.

The Japanese, for their part, have less trouble looking for past greatness; their problem is rather to know in what way, if any, they are great *now*. As we have already seen, there is nothing in the least ambiguous about Japan's name; it is the source of the sun, the beginning of all beginnings. Imperial Japan claimed for its emperor 2500 years of lineal descent from ancestors who until the defeat of 1945 were identified as divine. The myths of Japanese history play a large and obvious part in Japanese self-esteem, formally and explicitly among members of the present older generation and more implicitly among the younger, even among the radical young.*

---

* As a fellow inquirer of mine during one question-asking journey acutely remarked: "Those aspects of the Japanese past that are valued and admired by young people in Japan now are called 'Japanese' and 'traditional,' while those that are disliked become 'feudalistic' and not distinctively Japanese

For all their persistent uncertainties and insecurities, Japanese can and do seem to enjoy the sensations to be gained from feeling that they are a people with a long recorded history, with traditions of greatness, beauty, industriousness, and martial prowess. All this and more was incorporated into the nationalist tradition shaped in the Meiji era a century ago and crushed but not destroyed by defeat in war in 1945. It reappears now as Japanese struggle to define and redefine who and what they are and where they fit in the affairs of the world.[25] It turns up fitfully in the romantic swagger of popular samurai films, materializes in the life-and-death swagger of a Yukio Mishima, the novelist who committed ritual suicide to summon bemused Japanese back to their great traditions. It is evoked in the suddenly arresting and confusing reappearances of old soldiers re-emerging from caves on Guam and the Philippines to remind troubled Japanese, if only for a few days or weeks, that there was a time when all could be certain about their values.

Transmuted in one form or another, this tradition is funneled into the pride Japanese manage to take in some of their more current achievements. The uniqueness of the Japanese past, the power of the "tradition" is almost always included, I found during many interviews and conversations in Japan, as an essential part of what it means to be *Japanese*. The difficulty begins only when Japanese try to define what that uniqueness is. As among the Filipinos, this becomes a problem of identifying what they have acquired from others and what they can call their own.

Two often-used phrases vividly illustrate this matter: *wakon kansai,* "Japanese spirit and Chinese skill/learning/knowledge," refers to the great absorption of Chinese ideas, language, and arts that was undertaken in the seventh century under the leadership of Prince Shotoku, providing the main underpinning and the style of so much of Japanese culture as it developed thereafter; *wakon*

at all. In the same way, what they like or embrace in the present culture they call 'modern,' while anything about it they don't like becomes 'Westernized' or 'Americanized' or just plain 'capitalistic.' Cf. Deborah S. Isaacs, "A Research Report on Some Young People in Changing Japan," unpublished ms., December 1963.

yosai, "Japanese spirit and Western skill/learning/knowledge," applies to what happened in the Meiji period after 1868, when Japan, with that same remarkable deliberateness and enterprise, began its massive borrowing and absorption of Western modes and styles in industrial and all other new technologies, including the military, and embarked on the process of Westernization that transformed the country and the society and brought Japan as a major actor onto the stage of modern world history. It is clear enough what *kansai* was and what *yosai* was and is; the question that keeps rising and demanding some new answer becomes: What is *wakon?* What is the "Japanese spirit" that shaped these historic experiences?

To this question, one recurring answer among many is that *wakon* is the borrowing itself, or more specifically the capacity to borrow, the style of borrowing, not just the adoption but the adaptation of what is borrowed. "This is the essence of the Japanese uniqueness," explained Dr. Takeo Doi, noted psychoanalyst and author of one of the best-known of the great number of books on *Japaneseness* that began filling Japanese bookshelves in the early 1970s. "We became connoisseurs of world civilization. We borrow, we like it, we get self-esteem from it. We retain our own spirit by hiding in what we borrow something latent of our own."[26] In the same exchange, Kazuko Tsurumi said: "We speak of Japanese culture, not civilization. We speak of Chinese civilization, Indian civilization but of Japanese culture. We are uncertain of ourselves. But we are also very proud, proud of our sensitivity to new things. The Chinese are not sensitive, not curious. We really are, and we are proud of it."[27] In these conversations, the search for the essence of *Japaneseness* became a game of metaphors: was *wakon* like an onion, each savory layer peeling away, ending finally in nothing, or like an artichoke, each leaf with its taste of substance, all pulled away and disclosing finally, under a bristling protective cover, a soft, strong, hidden heart all its own?

Japanese self-preoccupation, always present in some muted way, suddenly became a very public affair, almost a fad, in the early 1970s. A series of events—the American reopening with

China prominent among them—abruptly undercut popular euphoria about the dazzling achievements of Japan's "economic miracle" of the 1950s and 1960s. The world energy crisis abruptly threatened to undercut that miracle itself. These "shocks" brought into open public self-scrutiny the private insecurity that had long been part of the Japanese cultural style and has accompanied the whole remarkable course of Japan's modern development. In the ongoing effort to resolve the elements of their past and the needs of their present, Japanese at many different levels are asking themselves: If it be true that the *wakon,* or Japanese uniqueness, *is* the capacity to borrow judiciously and adapt distinctively from other cultures, and that the history of the Japanese nation over time has been created by its use of ancient Chinese arts and modern Western technologies, then *what now?* Having sampled in spectacular fashion the blind alleys of the one and the disasters of the other, what is there in the present postindustrial world for Japan to borrow and adapt *now?* Or, for sheer lack of borrowable advantages, will Japan have to create its next national reincarnation out of something strictly Japanese, and thereby produce something finally new under that old rising sun? At the end of his sensitive review of this long course of Japanese self-scrutiny, Hiroshi Wagatsuma concludes: "There seems, however, no clear answer as yet to the century-old question as to the true nature of the culture that the Japanese can be proud of, and that they must cultivate and develop as something uniquely theirs."

✦

Unlike people who carry the burden of having a history of which they are ashamed or of seeming to have no history at all, or having a history that leaves them with an uneasy feeling of emptiness at the core, Jews are people who have had almost nothing but their history to identify them as Jews and to serve them as a basis for survival. Their religion, based on Mosaic law and its later Talmudic interpretations and on a tradition that consists mainly of their beliefs about their origins as a people, has been the main carrier of this sustenance. One of the smallest groups of people on earth—now fewer than twenty million out of a world of nearly four billions—the Jews have one of the longest continuous histories, some four thousand years, and have maintained a peculiarly visible and influential presence through much of it.

During this long time, Jews lost most of the other normally shared features of a single people, including—as anyone looking about him on a street in Jerusalem or Tel Aviv can readily see—even such common physical characteristics as they might ever have had at any time in the past. Even their religion, their single most common holding, was split into varieties or degrees of observance of the ancient Law and took on, like their physical appearance, a great number of different local colors and variations. Being a "Jew" came to mean, as far as any universal or common definition could go, being a person linked to a certain history involving that ancient Law, the idea of a single God, and the conviction of having been chosen to do that God's business on earth. This was a history of origins, moreover, that was intimately meshed into the origins of Western, or what has been called "Judeo-Christian," civilization as a whole. At various times and places in the ancient past and in the centuries of the Diaspora, many Jews "disappeared" as individuals and sometimes in whole groups.* Many more suffered and survived every possible variety of persecution and exclusion and all the forms of self-hatred and self-rejection that afflict all despised and subordinated groups. But the essential Jewish identity framed and defined by the tradition of Jewish history proved able to sustain the greater number of Jews through

---

* One of the more remarkable examples of the disappearance of Jews through assimilation took place in China, where a group of Jews settled in the tenth century and preserved their distinctive separateness, especially in Kaifeng in Honan, until the mid-nineteenth century, when they finally faded away altogether, into the Confucian literati class and into the general population. Cf. William C. White, *Chinese Jews,* Toronto, 1942. In "Jewish Assimilation: The Case of the Chinese Jews" (unpublished ms., Northwest Christian College, Eugene, Ore., 1972) Song Nai Rhee shows how the Kaifeng Jews identified the Jewish tradition with Confucianism and indicates how, in the absence of any repression or exclusion, the one body of ideas absorbed the other as the Chinese society gradually absorbed its assimilated Jews.

this long period of time in their unique apartness and their capacity over the centuries to withstand the hostility that reached its culmination in the Hitlerian holocaust.[28]

The re-establishment of Israel as a Jewish state after an interval of some two thousand years was an attempt by surviving Jews not only to find ground on which to defend themselves against extermination but also to establish a political framework once more for the Jewish separateness, to establish a national sum for their many parts. It was perhaps the most dramatic of all the current examples of the interaction of political change and group identity, for in Israel, where Jews gathered from all over the world, the question of questions, besides survival, became: *Who and what is a Jew?* This question is wrapped up in a great swirl of cloudy confusion, unhelped by any light at night, and involves in some way for every Jew every aspect of the group identity complex out of which the new Israeli identity was to be formed. Of these, none is more centrally fixed or more emotionally charged than the matter of history and origins.

In Israel this involves at one extreme the view that the last prideful chapter of Jewish history ended when the last Jewish resistance ended at Masada in A.D. 73 and that the Diaspora that followed was a long dark age in which the Jew became a creature of weakness and shame. In this view, even in its more moderate forms, truly prideful Jewish history was resumed only in 1948, when the State of Israel was recreated by fighting Jews and made it possible for all Jews to become Israelis again; of this, Masada itself became a symbol offering more than one image of the conceivable future.[29] In the flow of these attitudes and feelings about the past, different pools of meaning began to form in Israel around the terms "Jew" and "Israeli," especially among the Israeli-born sabra youth. To be an Israeli meant not to be the "Jew" whom the Gentile world held in contempt for so long, essentially the Jew as represented in the whole stock of anti-Semitic stereotypes built up around the Diaspora Jew, most particularly around the East European Jew. Being in Zion meant ceasing to be the pale and puny and money-trading "Jew" and becoming a tan and muscular and strong soil-tilling Israeli, no longer cringing and defenseless, no longer a homeless Yiddish-speaking wanderer unwanted and persecuted everywhere, but a Hebrew-speaking citizen of one's own ancient land, reclaimed by force of one's own arms and prowess and stoutly held by the same means. By cutting across two thousand years of Jewish history and picking up the threads of that glorious past broken so long ago, the new Israelis were re-establishing the primary role of the national-historic tradition in the Jewish identity. It displaced the religion, certainly the formally practiced religion, to which the Zionists traditionally gave small place or no place at all, whether as socialists who reject religion in general or as Zionists who saw most of postbiblical Judaism as part of the unwanted baggage of the Diaspora.

The Jews who came to Israel after 1948 from different parts of the world held a wide range of varying views of these matters —the role of formal religion and the place of the traditionally orthodox religious establishment in Israel is one of the most contended and contentious in the new state—but in general they, and more especially their children born in Israel, tended to become part of the process of becoming primarily Israeli nationals with the new attitudes and images of newly confident self-asserted power that went with that role, especially after the victory of the Israeli armed forces over the Arabs in the Six-Day War of 1967. Among the many shocks that came with the barely averted disaster of the Arab-initiated war in October 1973 and the severe international isolation in which Israel found itself was one reported by the Israeli journalist Amos Elon, who quoted a young Israeli soldier back from the Suez front as saying: *"For the first time in my life I felt like a Jew."*[30]

The same experience brought a new major turning also in the consciousness of Jews outside of Israel, especially in the United States, where the effective integration of Jews as Americans had come after 1945 to seem not only possible but on the verge of being realized. I shall be dealing again with the current patterns of Jewish group identity when I come to consider the element of nationality, where I think the subject mainly lies. But let me say here, where it is also so vividly relevant, that American Jews came in these decades to the conviction that they would successfully remain Americans in America, making American history part of their own history and their own part of America's. They were becoming a distinctive group enjoying what it was that united them as *Jews*—their history and their religion—while sharing with all others their nationality and their common holdings as *Americans*. But the security of the state of Israel, as a symbol of the end of Jewish exile and marginality for all Jews, had to be built into this expectation. The fears for its security, and therefore for the security of all Jews, raised and then dramatically allayed in 1967, rose again in enormously sharpened form around the events and sequels of the Yom Kippur War of 1973. All the ghosts of Jewish history, thought to have been laid in America after 1945 and in Israel after 1967, reappeared at Jewish shoulders. Whether in America or in Israel, it seemed, Jews were still going to have to construct their future out of the stuff of their past, with all the greatness of its travails and all the travails of its greatness.

✦

The Chinese are also the possessors of a Great Past, indeed, in what is often a not-very-humble opinion common among them, the Greatest of all Pasts. In contrast to the Jews, who were dispersed in fragments all over the world and became marginal wanderers enclaved in other lands and cultures, the Chinese, except for a scatter of migrants who spread through the South Seas, remained in their continental-sized land. The Jews enjoyed only a relatively brief period of imperial power in the tiny territory they ruled in biblical times; for much the larger part of their long history they have been cast down and powerless. The Chinese empire had extended periods of great power rising and falling in dynasties lasting for centuries at a time. They fell prey to some foreign conquerors, Mongol, Manchu, but never until the Western incursions of the nineteenth century did these challenge the primacy of the Chinese culture. The Jews spent some two thousand years of subordination, debasement, persecution, ending in a great holocaust in which half their number died; the Chinese suffered weakness and humiliation for barely a century at the mercy of the Europeans and later the Japanese. During this time, the rulers of China ate the bitterness of impotence, defeat, failure, and dependency in the treaty port era and went through their own version of the experience of feeling inferior to Western power and technology. To put an end to this weakness and to reassert Chinese pride and power became the goal of all the politics of reform and revolution of this period, from the abortive Taiping rebellion of the mid-nineteenth century to the success of the Communist revolution of the mid-twentieth. The nationalism of modern China has taken on some of the trappings of shifting ideologies of Western origin but draws its strength far more decisively from the driving need to re-establish the greatness of the more distant Chinese past.

This underlying self-image places the Chinese at the opposite end of the spectrum from India's Untouchables. Indeed, they tend to see themselves as without peer, above all other peoples on earth, far above, for example, the Japanese, whose tradition they see as junior and derivative from the Chinese in all its important beginnings. It has been said that the Chinese, perhaps uniquely, have no "creation myth," strictly speaking. The inference presumably is that the Chinese could never imagine a time when they were not there. The progenital figures in the Chinese world at the dawn of time were the Sage Kings of the Golden Age, already ruling kingdoms, the Hsia and the Shang, from which everything thereafter, e.g., in Confucius' time, was already a decline.[31]

This view of China's Great Past was not only self-sustainingly held by Chinese through their periods of humiliation by foreign powers, but has also been shared by many Westerners from the time of Marco Polo down to the present. As I have shown in some detail elsewhere,[32] this Chinese self-image has been unadmiringly seen by some as insupportable arrogance and chauvinistic egotism and admiringly by others as a valid and enviable legacy. In individual Chinese, many varied forms of this self-awareness have been especially mixed, in overseas Chinese for example, since the Communist regime began successfully reasserting Chinese power and importance and arousing respect and fear in the rest of the world.

The Chinese Communists and Mao Tse-tung himself have been eclectic to a degree in how they have used the Chinese past. Chinese factional polemics have been conducted almost entirely, it sometimes seems, through the use of more or less obscure historical allusions. For various shifting current political purposes, they have transformed old villains into new heroes, like Ts'ao Ts'ao, the great malefactor and tyrant of the famous *Romance of Three Kingdoms,* and Genghis Khan, the great Mongol leader of hordes, or old heroes into new villains, like Confucius. "In current Chinese Communist fashions," a noted China specialist could write in 1961, "Confucius seems to be 'in' this year." At this writing (1974), the old sage is very much "out," having become the principal named target of a countrywide attack on otherwise unnamed opponents of Mao's regime.[33] But whatever the zigs and zags of Chinese Communist polemics and historiography, the view of China's greatness remains constant and constantly inspiring.

Stuart Schram has called attention to what he has oddly called "an astonishing continuity of thought" in Mao Tse-tung's own writings on this theme, from earliest days to his most recent. Quite unastonishingly, Mao has been consistent, as youth and as aged superleader, on the subject of the great glory of the Han people, on the great age and ageless greatness of the Chinese people, "its great thinkers, scientists, inventors, statesmen, and strategists . . . its rich store of classical works." Mao repeats the familiar list of Chinese "firsts:" the compass, paper-making, block-printing, movable type, gunpowder. He recites the familiar salute to China "with a recorded history of 5,000 years . . . one of the oldest civilized countries in the world," its people "famous for its endurance and industriousness . . . a people with a glorious revolutionary tradition and a splendid historical heritage." The Chinese, proclaimed Mao as he stood at the threshold of newly conquered power, "have always been a great, courageous, industrious people. It was only in modern times that they have fallen behind. . . . Our nation will never again be an insulted nation. We have stood up."[34]

For one example of how the Great Past serves its function in the Chinese group identity, let me cite finally the tiny vignette of a Chinese-American high school boy, brought up in a Boston suburb with the characteristic greater accent on his American rather than his Chinese origins, who ran into sneering bigotry for the first time, he said—it was in 1970—at the hands of a fellow student. This drove him to explore, also for the first time, just what it meant to be Chinese. He did not have to look far or consider much detail to make two powerfully reassuring discoveries. "I learned that China was old, very old, had a long, long history," he said, "and that it was *great,* very *great;* it made me feel that China was my homeland, my real homeland, it made me feel good."

VIII

RELIGION

Tzu Lu asked about the worship of ghosts and spirits. Confucius said: "We don't know yet how to serve men, how can we know about serving the spirits?" What about death, was the next question. Confucius said: "We don't know yet about life, how can we know about death?" Fan Ch'ih asked about wisdom. Confucius said: "Devote yourself to the proper demands of the people, respect the ghosts and spirits but keep them at a distance—this may be called wisdom."

— FROM THE *Analects,* XI : 1 1 , VI : 2 0

THE HOLDINGS that come to every person out of the past include what is called "religion." It comes under many names and takes many forms, but religion essentially has to do with belief in a god or gods, in some kind of supernatural power that governs the world and controls the destinies of all who live in it. Some such set of beliefs, with attached law, rites, and practices, has been part of every known human culture from the most distant past until now.

In certain key respects, religion is an intensely individual matter. It provides the means by which the religious person or even the nominal believer satisfies some otherwise unappeasable needs. But even as an individual matter, religion is for the most part a shared experience. It is one of the holdings that links every human being to others. This applies even to the mystics and saints, who may be unique persons but who usually derive both the form and the substance of their particular religious experiences from the distinctive traditions out of which they come. Gautama Buddha, Francis of Assisi, the Baal Shem Tov, and Gandhi may all have had something in common, but no one would mistake one for the other or successfully insist that their similarities were greater than their differences.

Indeed, the word itself, "religion," is most commonly defined as coming from the Latin *ligare,* "to bind, to tie, to fasten"; the same root figures in words like "ligament" or "obligation," meaning a connection, a *bond.* A suggested alternative Latin root is *relegere,* "to read over and over, to collect, to gather," i.e., the received wisdom or *tradition.* Out of the thickets of much scholarly and religious discussion of these word origins, these characteristics emerge unscratched and remarkably well preserved: whatever else it might also be, religion is a *bond.* It is a bond to God or some equivalent, to vows, to a community of fellow believers, to some order of rites and practices, to a shared body of beliefs, laws, and doctrines. It is a *bond* to an inherited *tradition* derived from ancient wisdom and teachings gathered over time, preserved orally or in scripture, handed down and read and interpreted over and over again by successive generations of believing heirs.

These two ideas, of a bond and a tradition, appear with impressive consistency in the etymology of the words used in many cultures and languages for "religion," meaning a system of beliefs and observances. The Sanskrit word *dharma,* usually taken in this sense, also means law, doctrine, duty, order, temple ritual, propriety, caste obligations, the organized totality of things, the cosmic order, and more. But the root at the heart of this word, *dhar,* means "to hold, to carry, to bear," i.e., to *bind,* to *tie,* to *fasten.* The same syllable appears in Old Persian *data,* meaning "law," and reappears from this source in Aramaic and Hebrew as *dath,* meaning "law." In modern Hebrew, the word for "religious," in the sense of strictly observant of laws, rites, and rituals, is *dati,* while the word for the less observant but still accepting believer is *messorati,* meaning "traditional," or subscribing to the *messorat,* or the tradition. The Indonesian word usually given for "religion" is *agama,* from a Sanskrit word meaning "text." The Greek word identified by the *Oxford Classical Dictionary* as coming closest to "religion" is *hosios,* meaning "usage or custom," becoming "that which is lawful and proper with regard to holy things or traditional morality."

The Arabic equivalent is *din,* also originally from the Persian, the noun form of a verb that means "to conduct oneself properly, to follow traditional usage." The noun itself denotes conformity, propriety, obedience, usages, customs, standard behavior. The name "Islam" itself comes from *aslama,* "to submit, to surrender oneself wholly, to give oneself in total commitment" to a commanding God and "to recognize it as binding upon oneself." The word *Muslim* means "one who submits," who accepts this bond with Allah. In Chinese the word used for "religion" is *tsung-chiao,* which would be literally rendered as "taught principles," but *tsung* is the same root used in *tsu-tsung,* meaning ancestors, and the root itself means "connection," or what you are bond to, and *chiao* means "teaching," or what has been learned.[1]

These examples, one gathers, can be multiplied nearly everywhere in both hemispheres and between both poles, the common characteristics of "bond" and "tradition" reappearing in different words, just as, in Emerson's vivid phrase, "the ocean receives different names on the several shores it washes."

Against this sameness of design in the meaning of the word "religion" one has to lay at once the great variety in the experience of it. If we heed William James, we have to avoid falling into the notion that it may have some single essence rather than the "many characters" that he reminded us could be important in it.* All reli-

---

* Since I have begun here by trying to identify at least what the word "religion" essentially consists of, let me also quote the whole cautionary passage from James: "Most books on the philosophy of religion try to begin with a precise definition of what its essence consists of . . . the very fact that they are so very many and so different from one another is enough to prove that the word 'religion' cannot stand for any single principle or essence, but is rather a collective name. The theorizing mind tends always to the over-simplification of its materials. This is the root of all the absolutism and one-sided dogmatism by which both philosophy and religion have been infested. Let us not fall immediately into a one-sided view of our subject,

gion may include a bond to a tradition bearing on belief in a god
or some supernatural force, but as universal experience and a vast
art and literature attest, the uses of religion are indeed without
number and the ways of experiencing, describing, analyzing it
without end. My purpose in dealing with this large subject here
obviously has to be limited and modest. It is simply to locate religion in its role as one of the primary elements of basic group
identity. I will attempt, with quick, respectful, and grateful backward looks at the insights of men with such names as James, Frazer,
Marx, Freud, Weber, Eliade, and others, to summarize the functions that religion performs, for individuals and for groups, indicat-
ing thereby why and how it is so universal and so primordial a part
of the common human experience, bonding human beings into
groups and by the same token setting groups against one another.
I will then go on to suggest by particular examples the disorderly
variety of ways in which religion figures in case after case of group
identity patterns as they now come under the impacts of political
change.

As one of the primary elements of basic group identity, then, in
some of its many mutually nonexclusive guises, consider religion:
— a powerful personal-individual-emotional-subjective experience
— a powerful institutional-social-historical-objective actuality
— a way of dealing with the awesome forces of nature, or pro-
pitiating, cajoling, blaming, accepting, appeasing, praising the con-
trollers of the uncontrollable, religion as the "art of winning the
favor of the Gods"
— a provider of a set of explanations for the inexplicable, answers for the unanswerable, a way of incorporating the incor-
poreal, knowing the unknowable, defining good and evil, right and
wrong, solving the mysteries of life and death and time; in Weber's
emphasis, religion as a source of meaning

---

but let us rather admit freely at the outset that we may very likely find no
one essence, but many characters which may alternately be equally important in religion." *The Varieties of Religious Experience* (1902), New York,
1925, p. 26.

— a way of ordering the vagaries of misfortune and good fortune, of identifying the guilts for which suffering is a punishment and making them bearable, and providing—Weber again—"the theodicy of good fortune for those who are fortunate"

— a supplier of significance for the insignificant, occupying itself "with personal destinies and keeping us in contact with the only absolute realities we know" (James)

— a source of solace, a refuge from pain, fear, confusion, panic; embracing, healing, consoling, reassuring—God as mother

— a source of authority, of commanding law to be obeyed, God as executor of punishment, even vengeance, upon the wayward and the sinning, the only sometimes-forgiving model of hard uprightness, unbendingness, inevitability—God as father

— or, more explicitly in Freudian terms, "a dramatization on a cosmic plane of the emotions, fears, and longings" stemming from each person's own relations with his/her father and mother (Ernest Jones)

— as sanction and upholder of temporal authority, providing the halo of divine origin for earthly rulers, defining and defending norms, public morality and obligations, a bulwark against anarchy/ evil, the indispensable bonding cement in the social order, God as "symbol of society" (Durkheim)

— as tool of power, blesser of the banners of conquerors and consolers of the conquered, upholsterer for the seats of the mighty, cushion maker for the weak, a system for keeping masters undisturbed in their mastery and subjects "well-conducted and united" (Machiavelli), or religion as "the opium of the people" (Marx)

— or, contrastingly, religion as source of challenge to authority, as in the Chinese idea of the transferable Mandate of Heaven, and in the many millenarian revolutionary movements that joined religion and politics in holy and sanguinary assaults on power in many different societies over many centuries.[2]

In all but very rare varieties of religious experience, the individual and social aspects of the matter interlock. It is the great power of

religious belief and affiliation for the individual that has under-
pinned the great power of religion in the social and political history
of every society. It has served as both a stabilizing and a mobilizing force in the pursuit of mixed religious and nonreligious ends by
those in power. Indeed, the meshing of religious and political beliefs
and institutions is a characteristic common to almost all cultures.

It is sometimes suggested that there are fundamental differences
in this respect between "Western" and "Eastern" cultures, but in
this as in so many other matters there is obviously no total "West"
and no total "East" and it would be hard to say where the one ends
and the other begins. The suggestion is that in the "East," religious
belief and practice permeate everyone's daily life and govern the
whole shape of the society, as in the Hindu caste system, as well as
occupying special institutional places in the political system, as the
Buddhist priesthood establishments do in countries like Sri Lanka,
Burma, and Thailand. In the Islamic countries, often lumped for
these purposes with the "East," society in theory is a total system
based on the Koran and leaving no room for any separation of the
religious and the secular in the conduct of both individual and state
affairs. In fact, of course, practices differ widely among the many
Muslim or predominantly Muslim states that now exist in Asia and
Africa.[3]

In Christian Europe, not only politics but all political theory was,
to borrow R. H. Tawney's description, cast strictly in the theologi-
cal mold from the Middle Ages to the middle of the seventeenth
century. It was only then, amid the beginnings of capitalism and
modern nationalism, that the age of religious wars "virtually
ended" and the "age of the wars of economic nationalism" began,
and the Enlightened idea began to take hold that religion was a
private more than a public matter. The State, first in England, then
in America and France, ceased to derive its formal sanction from
religion and located it instead "in nature," in varieties of the idea
of a social contract among individuals who came together to protect themselves and their property—especially their property—
without benefit of any "supernatural commission" or other form of
divine authority.[4] Even so, the old relationships persisted in Cath-

olic Europe and its American colonies, and in much of Protestant Europe, including England, where the power of the church of Rome was first broken but where it was replaced by England's own Established Church, to say nothing of New England, where seekers after religious freedom for themselves took quite some time before they granted it to others. The anti-parochial ideas of the Enlightenment gained ground but far from prevailed. Religious differences were centrally involved in the ethnic divisions that have long played such a key role in American politics, especially at state and local levels. The further development of nineteenth-century nationalism in Europe and in Spain's colonies abroad was strongly anti-clerical in its thrust if not in many of its outcomes, the old conflicts and old relationships persisting with considerable strength into our own time. The old church–state issues still play major roles in the politics of Italy, Spain, and Portugal; and in Ulster, the ghosts of the old religious wars find new graves every day around which to dance.

✦

In all its many mixes of individual/subjective and collective/objective experience, religion has bonded people together in their many groups and cultures. By the same token, however, it has also deeply and violently divided these groups from one another.

Religion has supplied to the members of each such group the strong cement of traditionally shared beliefs about the meaning of their existence. It has helped them, to borrow good words again from William James, to meet the conditions of their lives with stoic resignation or passionate happiness, according to their needs. As a strong super-superego, it has had an ennobling effect at the most and a restraining effect at the least. Even those who, like the Calvinists, built their beliefs around original sin, the idea that a doomed depravity was the natural condition of man, counted on their religion to keep a rein on some of the consequences. Religion has surely kept some people at some time in some places from acting on their worst impulses, natural or otherwise, a small favor for which we all must have some reason to be grateful.

But the bond between and among fellow believers was one thing, the encounter between differing sets of believers was quite another, and such differences have been as universal as religion itself. For whatever the force of any one group's belief in the universal truth and application of its own particular myths, doctrines, and practices, these have obviously differed deeply and sharply from group to group. The belief in the existence of supernatural force of some kind may be common to all religion, but hardly anything else is.* The differences have been great, and when they have confronted one another, they have not ordinarily done so in any mutually tolerant spirit, as they did once upon a time in old China, and as many hoped they could in the new democratic societies created by the revolutions in Europe and America that came out of the Enlightenment. In the new modernizing and mainly Protestant countries, and in anti-clerical France, church and state were more or less successfully separated and freedom of worship and belief extended as a right to all. This, again, was no small feat, considering the unreasonableness of trying to deal with these matters in a reasonable way. But this system of tolerance for diversity in the public sphere did not extend very far into the private encounter of these differences in individual and community life. Here the more normal we-they rule of group existence more commonly prevailed. On some scale from mild to strong and in some association with other differences—such as race, nationality, class—the resulting patterns were not merely of separateness but of rejection, exclusion, discrimination, hostility, hatred. The accumulated evidence suggests that the more strongly religious beliefs and affiliations are held, the greater the hostility toward other religious beliefs and those who hold them. This stares out at us from all we know of history and

---

* "In the name of religion what deed has not been done? For the sake of religion men have earnestly affirmed and contradicted almost every idea and form of conduct. In the long history of religion appear chastity and sacred prostitution, feasting and fasting, intoxication and prohibition, dancing and sobriety, human sacrifice and the saving of human life . . . superstition and education, poverty and wealthy endowments, prayer wheels and silent worship, gods and demons, one God and many gods . . . How can such diametrical oppositions all be religious?" Paul Johnson, quoted in *International Encyclopedia of the Social Sciences,* 13:417.

contemporary experience; it is obvious enough to have been con-firmed and reconfirmed by modern social scientific inquirers.[5] It appears not only in the big and bloody events of our history, but all around us every day in its more ordinary guises in which its vio-lence is more commonly psychological than physical. It is the normal way in which people relate across the separateness of their differences in which each clings to or is bound by his sense of his own group's uniqueness.

In this respect, there *are* some significant differences, at least philosophically, among some of the major religious systems. In the Hindu and Buddhist traditions and in the Chinese religions, there is a certain professed inclusiveness, a recognition that there has to be more than one path to God, more than any one way to meet the needs that gods are meant to meet. This does not mean that the great gallery of "Eastern" gods have not been called upon to ride with all kinds of slaughter-bent armies over time, but only that there has been nothing doctrinally exclusive about their re-spective godlinesses. This obviously did not prevent the philosophi-cally inclusive system of Hinduism from creating the most compart-mentalized and socially exclusive system ever known, a Great One-ness on high, multiple and rigid separatenesses below. The great binding force of its doctrines and beliefs caused those bound by it to submit to its constraints for many centuries, a condition that continues for millions to this day. It is possible to view this as a realization of the peaceful life, but if so, hardly any religious system we know of has better exemplified the view that religion's principal function is to keep the animals quiet in the zoo of the social order.

On the other hand, this notable passivity within the bounds of Hindu caste did not keep Hindus from hurling themselves into massively violent collisions with Muslims when the occasion arose. Through an old and many-layered complex of religious-political conflicts, Hindu-Muslim hostility came to a climax of great mutual slaughters during the partition of India at the time of independence in 1946–47, when about a million were killed and five million more fled across the new religiously demarcated borders to find safety. These events, along with Hitler's slaughter of Europe's Jews, are the major examples in this century of violence generated to a decisive degree out of religious differences.

It remains true, however, that the idea of exclusiveness had a much larger part in the forming of the Jewish-Christian and Islamic traditions. The ancient Hebrews came to believe that there was only one God and that he had chosen the Jews to be his people. The early Christian fathers distinguished between "true" and "false" religion. Islam divided humanity not merely between believers and nonbelievers but between believers and *rejecters,* between those who submitted to God's command and those who defied it. Hence, then, the great separations of the chosen from the unchosen, the saved from the damned, the believers from the infidels, the pure from the impure, the children of the true gods from the victims of the false. Hence, then, the need, the duty, indeed the divine command to slay the Amalekites, to stone the sinner, to put heretics to the torch, nonbelievers to the sword. From these passions, from the wounds of these severances, great streams of blood have flowed through the courses of much human history.

A lot of this killing and dying has been done, of course, for other than religious reasons. It is not often easy to sort out the religious from the nonreligious drives in all the religiously connected violence that has taken place over time. Religion has often served as the thrusting point, the sharp edge, the mobilizing spur, the badge and the bulwark of the solidarity that people have needed when they confronted each other to kill or die, whether it was over religion itself or religion entwined with more earthly interests having to do with security, pelf, power. Thus the great world-conquering sweep of Islam, the Crusades, the Inquisition, Europe's Religious Wars, the Cross coming to America with the Conquistadors, the spreaders of the Gospel accompanying, indeed sometimes leading with sword in hand, the spreaders of European empire, trade, and power in the Americas, Asia, and Africa. Whatever the mixes of holy and unholy causes in the calculations and passions of those who created such events, at least two common features come plainly into view: (1) all concerned on all sides in these affairs have usually sought the blessings of their respective gods (or often, as in

Christian Europe, the same God), and (2) however cynical the leaders might ever have been, their followers generally believed they had these blessings and killed or died because they held certain creeds to be true, practiced certain rites, or—perhaps most commonly—lacking faith or piety or both, simply wore the badges of belonging or not belonging to this or that religious persuasion, like so many of the Protestants and Catholics who have killed or been killed so wantonly in Northern Ireland in recent years.

✦

There is one thing we can say with certainty as we scan the group identity conflicts that crowd our contemporary scene: in one degree or another, religion figures in them all. Usually it appears enmeshed with other factors of great weight—race, land, nationality, history, power—too much so to enable us to be precise about its place in the whole except in the roughest way: peripheral, secondary, central. I have already mentioned two cases—the Hindu-Muslim collisions in India and the Protestant-Catholic conflict in Ulster—where religion itself seems close to being a centerpiece of the whole design of the affair. But even in these instances, it obviously appears as but one aspect of the whole culture past brought freshly into view by swiftly changing political circumstances. Much has been written in both these cases to show how other factors interweave with the religious to form the new pattern of events.[6] Still, it is clearly the religious identity, even when it is only an identifying badge, that has determined the living or dying of so many who often wanted no part themselves of the battle for power raging around them.

A third case in which religion clearly plays a central role is that of the Roman Catholic Church itself, the world's largest and most powerful religious institution, until only yesterday the modern world's strongest symbol of conservative religiosity. Under the pressures of changing power relations and social conditions around the world, it too has been undergoing a wrenching process of renovation and change. After Pope John XXIII opened the way to new initiatives within the Church itself, beginning with Vatican Council II, 1962–65, the remarkably monolithic structure of the institution began to come apart, with profound effect upon its belief system, its holy orders and clergy, its ritual, and its organization. The controlled order of the past has given way to constant strain and recurring crises in every aspect of Church life, giving rise to radical pentecostal movements, a "counterreformation," even threatened rebellions and schisms. As its monolithism cracked and its authority diminished, the Church, like other great systems in more temporal spheres of power, began to suffer a loss of that cemented coherence that had kept its great mass of believers so unquestioningly bound to it for such a long time in so many different lands and cultures.[7]

The Roman Catholic Church is itself a political institution of great power. Its role in the politics of many countries has generally been governed by quite worldly considerations and strong authority-supporting biases in most public affairs. Hence the many morally ambiguous positions it long held in relation to secular power, including, and perhaps especially, recent regimes like those of Salazar, Franco, Mussolini, and Hitler and a much larger number of their more obscure colonial and postcolonial counterparts in Asia and Latin America. In these settings, along with its good works, the Church more often than not served the classic function of keeping the masses of its believers in a submissively soporific condition.* As at the time of the Reformation, this identification with conservative or oppressive power had its part in the eventual onset of the more recent disaffection and pressure for change within the Church itself. Leaders of the reform movement have appeared among cardinals and bishops, and politically radical priests and nuns have become familiar figures in political turmoil on every continent in

---

* Of the Church's role in colonial Mexico, Octavio Paz writes: "The religious life—a source of great creativity in an earlier epoch—became mere inert participation for the vast majority. For the minority, wavering between faith and curiosity, it became a sort of ingenious game, and, finally, silence and sleep. Or to state it another way, Catholicism was a refuge for the great mass of Indians. The Conquest had left them orphans, and they escaped this condition by returning to the maternal womb. Colonial religion was a return to prenatal life, passive, neutral, and self-satisfied. The small minority who wanted to emerge into the fresh air of the world were either smothered into silence or forced to retreat." *Labyrinth of Solitude,* p. 167.

recent decades. Still, interlocked as they are with the pressures for political change, the issues at the heart of the crisis in the Catholic Church remain, in a central and nuclear way, religious issues. For millions of people who depended on the Church precisely because it spoke for the firm certainties that sustained them and provided the strongest anchor they had for their sense of themselves, the crisis in the Church opened a group identity crisis of great depth and unpredictable outcomes.

There are two other cases of a different sort in which religion occupies a peculiarly central place in the political change process: the Netherlands and Lebanon. In both countries, formal and informal political and governmental structures were created to accommodate different religious groups in the population. In both countries now, the current pressures for political change are testing the fragility of these arrangements. The groups involved—Protestants, Catholics, and others in the Netherlands, and Maronite Christians and Muslims in Lebanon—have been losing whatever sense of relative stability these systems had created for them.

In the Netherlands, the Dutch Reformed Church and the state had shared a special relationship ever since Dutch Protestants won their freedom from the Catholic Spanish in the seventeenth century. In response to liberalizing pressures two centuries later, the special position of the Reformed Church gave way to a plural system. Parallel sets of cradle-to-grave institutions were created to cater separately to the communities of Protestants, Catholics, and others (including dissident Protestants, Jews, freethinkers, etc.) in every department of life—political, social, education, trade union, press, and latterly, radio and television. Each was perceived as a *zuil,* or "pillar," standing separately while helping, along with others, "to hold up the pediment of the nation."[8] In recent years, the distribution of power among the political parties that governed the country for these constituencies began to show strain as the inner coherence of each component part began to erode. This was particularly true of the Catholic Church, which went through a particularly radical transformation in the 1960s. The relatively stable balance or coherence of the system as a whole gave way again to a chronic instability. The Netherlands experience, little studied abroad, it seems, plainly has lessons to teach all who may be seeking in times to come to build new political systems to meet the demands of group separateness.

The state of Lebanon, which came into existence only in 1945, rules a land in which for many centuries shifting populations of Maronite Christians,* Shiite and Sunni Muslims, and Druses had co-existed and contended with one another, in ancient empires, under Ottoman rule, and finally under the French. The new state was launched with a constitution designed to give each group some safeguarded representation in the government. It was supplemented by an informal arrangement under which it was understood that a Maronite Christian would be president, a Sunni Muslim premier, and a Shiite Muslim speaker of the parliament, with political and government posts distributed proportionately to all groups in the population. This system survived precariously, threatened by more or less constant communal tensions and intermittent armed conflict. It suffered even more under unresolved differences among Lebanese over issues of their history and origins and cultural identities, Lebanese Christians identifying their past as Phoenician, Lebanese Muslims linking their cultural identity to Arabism and Islam. This has caused problems in Lebanese politics over the pressures of Pan-Arabism and regional Arab nationalism. The Lebanese come under peculiar pressure in this respect from the Muslim nationalists in neighboring Syria who regard Lebanon as a province of "Greater Syria," an expanse that they see as taking in the entire region bordered by Egypt, the Arabian peninsula, Iran, and Turkey. In the conflict over Israel, Lebanon tried for a long time to maintain a certain isolated position of its own, but by 1974 this had become painfully difficult. The pressure of the increasingly insistent Sunni Muslims, now seeing themselves as dominant in the country,

---

* A distinctive indigenous Christian sect dating from the seventh century, under its own patriarch and with a special relationship to the Pope in Rome.

and of the Palestinian guerrillas occupying the southern part of the country bordering on Israel began to erode whatever political stability the system had managed to maintain. The Maronite-Muslim agreement over distribution of posts in the government began to break down. After barely thirty years, another plural political system based on a scheme to accommodate differing religious groups was coming apart.[9]

Religion occupies a peculiarly central place in the experience of still another quite different group of people, the Untouchables of Hindu India. The element of history and origins, I have said, lies at the core of the group identity crisis of the emerging ex-Untouchables, but this history is obviously not separable from the religion that shaped it. Hinduism decreed their outcastness and untouchability. Because they accepted its beliefs and sanctions, they submitted to this condition for more generations than can be remembered. Millions of them still do so. Only the great compelling power of the Hindu belief system accounts for this uniquely massive and enduring history of submission. It was a submission, moreover, which because of its religious sanction carried with it its own sense of propriety and even—hard though it might be to see it through any other cultural lens—a certain dignity, a conviction of the rightness of remaining in what Jagjivam Ram, an ex-Untouchable who became a member of the Indian cabinet, once called their "psychological cages."

For more on this matter, I have to refer the reader again to what I have written elsewhere[10] but will illustrate here with one memorable vignette described to me by a Brahmin writer who remembered an old Untouchable who stood outside the gate of his family home one year when he came back from school, a boy all fired up with enthusiasm for India's emancipation from its dead past. "Come in!" the boy urged the old man, "come into the house!" The man looked down at him with a stern eye. *"You* may have given up your religion, young master," he said, "but *we* have not given up *ours*."

For most of the years of his life, the Untouchable leader B. R.

Ambedkar believed that Untouchables could be liberated only if the Hindu caste system were totally abolished. This was, rather vaguely, part of Nehru's vision for a free India, but it was never Gandhi's. Ambedkar did achieve the constitutional "abolition" of Untouchability when India won its independence; all Untouchables became ex-Untouchables by law. But they remained Untouchables in fact. The Indian society moved not toward abolition of the caste system but only in painfully tiny steps toward its reform. Despairing in his last years of any effective change in the Hindu society, Ambedkar finally called upon his followers to follow him out of the Hindu fold altogether. He chose Buddhism as their new religious home and was joined, shortly before his death in 1956, by several hundred thousand of his fellow Mahars in a public act of conversion. Of the great mass of eighty million ex-Untouchables, only some two million in all have taken this course since then; like Untouchables who many generations earlier had abandoned Hinduism for Islam or Christianity as a way out of their plight, the new converts found that their Untouchability pursued them into their new temples even as it had excluded them from their old ones. The great mass of ex-Untouchables still lives on in India in unchanged relations to caste Hindus and presumably still believing in the creed which declares this to be their inescapable fate. Some numbers of migrants to the cities are experiencing limited measures of change in their lives, while a tiny fringe of political militants continues to seek some quicker and more radical way of breaking out of the psychological and social cages in which they still must dwell.

It is difficult enough to identify with any assurance those cases of current group identity conflict in which religion can be said to play the central role. It is all the more so to try to distinguish in any precise way among all the other more peripheral or marginal roles it plays in so many other situations now everywhere in the world. Religion always appears as part of a complex of things and is one of the cross pressures that come to bear in every instance.

In the United States, black Christians come into severe conflict with their white fellow Christians over their status as blacks, not only in the society at large but within their own Protestant or Catholic Christian fellowships. In India, Hindus and Muslims commit carnage on each other but also break into groups and factions among themselves, clashing just as violently over differences of other kinds. Most of the Muslim states belong to various Islamic combinations—e.g., the Arab League, the Islamic Conference of Foreign Ministers—but political, economic, and military interests take ready priority over the common bond of Islam. The Muslim world is as divided and differentiated as the Christian. Christians, probably more than most, have set aside their common religious professions to engage in distinctly non-Christian practices against one another; perhaps the gap between unworldly profession and worldly practice only seems greater for Christians because of the excessively unworldly character of a gospel that preaches love for one's fellow man. In any case, it is clear that as an influence on behavior, especially political behavior, religion ranges from strongest of all to weakest of all, from the most to the least compelling: the differences are determined by the circumstances in each instance.

Never alone, then, always important but rarely in itself decisive, religion figures in some peripheral or marginal way in dozens of recent or still ongoing conflicts in all parts of the world where groups are now contending for place or power in so many different societies. Characteristically, religion defines some part of the differences that divide these groups and generate the conflicts between them. Religion serves to mobilize opposing political and military forces and to command popular support or submission in the cause. Often it serves simply to identify the contestants. Some examples:

— The civil war in the Sudan was fought between the dominant Arabized Muslims of the north and the Christian or "pagan" black southerners.

— The civil war in Chad was fought by Arab-supported Muslim guerrillas from the north against the predominantly more Christian and "pagan" and blacker south.

— In Nigeria, the Biafran civil war of 1969–70 was touched off when black Muslim Hausas in the north massacred thousands of mostly Catholic black Ibos—the war itself was fought over a complex of regional, tribal, economic issues.

— The irrepressible conflict in Cyprus lies between Orthodox Christian Greeks and Muslim Turks.

— In the Israeli-Arab conflict, religious differences suffuse the complex history out of which the encounter takes place; as the holy city for Jews, Christians, and Muslims, Jerusalem symbolizes the central, though not governing, role that religion plays in the ongoing struggle for place and power.

— In Sri Lanka, the unresolved communal tension lies between the Buddhist Sinhalese majority and the Hindu Tamil minority.

— In Burma, intermittent civil war goes on between the dominant Buddhist Burmese and the Christian Karens and others—Chins, Kachins, Shans, etc.—who have other faiths of their own.

— Buddhist Thailand has to deal in its southern border provinces with a Muslim separatist movement.

— In Malaysia, the politically dominant Malays maintain Islam as the state religion, their Muslim culture and practice intensifying their differences with the large non-Muslim Chinese minority.

— In the predominantly Catholic Philippines, the majority gives special minority status to the "pagan" hill tribes and wages war against the radical Muslim Moro minority in the far south, which seeks to control the territory it has always considered to be its own, and carries on its armed struggle with the help of nearby Muslim Malaysia.

Lest these examples leave the impression that conflicts of this kind involve only members of different major religious groups, it probably ought to be noted that when they do not have followers of a different religion to contend with, religionists of almost every variety have no trouble developing acute conflicts among themselves: e.g., Sunni Muslims and Shiite Muslims, as in Iraq, and between other Muslim sectarian groups elsewhere;[11] between Protestants and Catholics, violently in Ulster but virulently still in many other places; and similarly between and among Protestant sects and denominations and among varieties of anti-religious, non-religious, religious, and ultrareligious Jews in Israel and elsewhere.

In postcolonial Africa, as some of these examples suggest, religion is playing an especially visible role. In the cases mentioned, conflict over the reshaping of identities and politics in some of the new states escalated to the point of civil war. Elsewhere, however, similar struggles continue by other means. In the colonial period, the Christianity brought to Africa by the colonizers took hold in some unexpected and—to the colonizers—dismaying ways. Thousands of independent African Christian churches sprang up in various parts of the continent.[12] Some were millennial in character and in their own way initiated the resistance to the established colonial order that only later took the form of nationalist political movements. In the postcolonial period, the insistence of some of these groups of believers upon giving their loyalty to nothing less than the Kingdom of God brought them into conflict with new national regimes that had clearly ushered in something less than the millennium when they came to the seats of power. African Catholic churches, on the other hand, which usually functioned earlier as part of the colonial establishment, have also come into conflict with some of the new national regimes in replays of the classic church-state confrontation over spheres of authority. In Zaire, for example, which became about one third Catholic while it was the Belgian Congo, Colonel Mobutu, head of the Zaire government and a Catholic, came into head-on collision with the black cardinal at the head of the Church in Zaire, Joseph Malula. Mobuto declared Zaire to be a "secular state." Cardinal Malula, struggling to hold on to the Church's domain, especially in the country's educational system, resisted as strongly as he dared Mobutu's "Africanizing" encroachments.

Elsewhere in Africa, a major role is being played in the new politics of several countries by the confrontation of contending religions: the varieties of traditional African beliefs, Christianity, and Islam. They confront one another as belief systems, as institutions, and as agencies of rival foreign influences; the struggle among them is for the most part bluntly and explicitly political. Christianity, the religion of the lately dispossessed white European master, has reportedly been losing ground in the postcolonial years to Islam, partly on the strength of Islam's claim to be more indigenous and more hospitable than white Christianity to all races of men. In a shrewd mix of religious-political calculation, Nasser in his day made Cairo the center of a major effort to win African support for his version of Pan-Islamism and for the Arab cause against Israel. This effort ultimately scored important political successes, as indicated by the breaking off of relations with Israel by almost all African states at the time of the October war in 1973. In much the same context, but in a more fanatically religious spirit, the same goals have been pushed by Colonel Qaddafi, the fundamentalist Muslim leader of Libya. In March 1974, he told a Pan-African youth conference held in his country that Christianity had been "used in black Africa to obtain the annihilation of African man." He announced a vigorous proselytizing campaign to be run and financed from Libya and called for a "holy war" to expel Christianity from the African continent.

This Muslim offense meets a Christian defense that invokes the historic role of Arabs as invaders, enslavers, and destroyers in black Africa long before the white man came. In a reply to Qaddafi published in an Italian Catholic journal in June 1974, the black Archbishop of Abidjan summoned up the past of Muslim depredations in Africa, from the destruction of black empires in the eleventh century under the pretext of "holy war" to the conquest of the Sudan and decimation of its non-Muslim black population in the 1960s. Arabs, he wrote, enslaved black Africans "long before the Europeans arrived in Africa and continued after they had given it up"—a reference to charges of persistently surviving slavery in several Arab countries. "All of us," he went on, "Muslims and Christians, ought to be humble in the face of history." It was dangerous for the Muslims to invoke the principle of African "authenticity," he added. "It so happens that some apostles of African authenticity reject both Islam and Christianity as foreign religions that have corrupted the traditional culture."

Christian sources claim that there are 100 million Christians in Africa, about half of them Catholic, and about 140 million Muslims, including the population of Arab North Africa. These figures, estimates at best, leave uncertain just how many black Africans are neither Christian nor Muslim but remain faithful to their traditional religions. The survival and revival of these religions has become a cardinal goal of some African nationalists in many of the new African states as part of the reassertion of their own home-grown African group identities.[13]

In the African diaspora in the Americas, religion fills a large part of the story of how blacks submitted to oppression and how they fought to liberate themselves from it. There is no function served by religion that has not figured strongly in the black experience. Christian churches served blacks in American life in almost every conceivable way: as outlet, refuge, solace, tranquilizer; as preserver of dignity, spirit, humanity in dehumanizing circumstances; as channel to education and mobility; as catalyzer of resistance and struggle, provider of leaders and centers of organization—and all this in total separation from white Christian churches where the same doctrine of the brotherhood of man was preached.

Unsurprisingly, then, the most enduring and successful black Christian churches have been evangelical in character. For more than three centuries, black people in America had more to be saved from than any other kind of people, and there seemed more chance of being saved later on in heaven than ever on the American earth. The millenarian salvationist hopes and dreams of evangelical Christianity spoke more deeply and passionately to black needs than to any others in the society. These needs also summoned up varieties of cults, some retaining the Christian evangelical form, others breaking out of the Christian web altogether, seeking not only to escape Negroness itself and the pressures of the life white society imposed but to shed entirely the identity that white Christianity had imposed upon blacks. Some blacks, in tiny groups, have identified themselves as Hebrews, the true descendants of the lost tribes of

Israel: one such sect of a few hundred members now lives in Israel, to which it claims to be the only legitimate heir. Much more frequently, this escape was accomplished by adopting some form of Islamic belief and rites. Cults of this kind have a long history among blacks in American life. Perhaps the best known in recent decades that remained Christian was that of Father Divine. The most visible of the Muslim-style groups was the movement known as the "Black Muslims," whose leader was a prophet named Elijah Mohammad but whose most charismatic figure became nationally known as Malcolm X. The Black Muslims stood not only for withdrawal of blacks from the Christian fold but from the white society altogether. In the 1920s, Marcus Garvey created his own African Orthodox Church, whose followers worshiped a black God, a black Madonna, and a black Christ. But all these movements, Christian, neo-Christian, Muslim, or other, remained marginal and small. By far the great majority of American blacks remained faithful to their evangelical Christian churches and by far the largest and most successful of the great freedom movements that finally brought down much of the white supremacy system in the United States was the deeply religious evangelical drive led by the Baptist minister Martin Luther King, Jr.[14]

As in the case of Martin Luther King, evangelical religion can serve a group's strong thrust into the political arena; it also offers people a way of withdrawing from it. Religion as a refuge, as an individual and subjective experience, becomes more than ever a provider of personal solutions in a time of trouble and confusion. In this form too it provides an example of another kind of how religion figures in the present interaction of group identities and political change.

For if ever people were in need, they are now, in need of solace, of relief from pain and uncertainty, of answers to riddles, explanations for the inexplicable. In a world of nearly four billion people, there is plainly more need to escape from insignificance than there was when it was a less populated place. In an existence where science and reason seem to have done so poorly, faith and emotion promise to do better, especially if they supply some relieving comfort on earth now and an assured place in heaven later on. When what is known breaks down, it is time again to embrace the unknown, as great numbers embraced the Orphic mysteries in Hellenic times, as ghetto-bound European Jews in deep despair seized upon the liberating joys and somber pains of Hasidism in the eighteenth century, as great masses of desperately needy people have embraced mystical or millennial movements in so many places over the centuries. In our own time, Enlightenment-style understanding having failed to produce any durable peace of any kind among men, a great many people are turning again to the various ways of gaining the peace that is beyond understanding.

The proposition is that life cannot be lived on earth by man standing on his own two feet alone. Confused enough, fearful enough, threatened enough, every man, even the most Enlightened, will find his way back to his knees and to his God. The conventionally wise phrase for this in World War II days was "There are no atheists in the foxholes." Now we all live in foxholes, and the effect appears, notably in the United States but also in Europe, in the spurting growth and spread of varieties of evangelical religion. One of the most conspicuous, if not necessarily the most significant, examples was provided by the young and mostly middle-class Americans who turned in small but not negligible numbers from the frustrated confusions of the political activism of the 1960s to the relieving passions of revivalist religion in the 1970s. Such were the Jesus Movement and the Campus Crusade for Christ, which appeared on college campuses from which political groups had so abruptly disappeared. Smaller numbers gravitated to more extreme cults like the Children of God, some of whose devotees trickled out of the country to wander the world. Still others quit their inherited religious environments altogether and embraced more exotic "Eastern" cults, like Hare Krishna, or joined in the worshipful pursuits of sundry other Indian gurus. Some of these were able to attract devotees to their ashrams in India. Others, one a round-faced boy of sixteen, came from India to walk those gold-paved American cities themselves when they found they could fill sports palaces with thousands of more or less hysterical listeners, not all of them young, ready to believe—and pay for—the gospel brought to them from such distant places.[15] More important and presumably more durable was the revitalization and new growth of Protestant evangelical denominations and the appearance of a new pentecostal movement among American Catholics, which carried Church and worship reform to lengths which dismayed older-fashioned keepers of that faith. These movements all had at least one feature in common: they all stressed more intensely personal participation in worship and a return to the most literal versions of belief in personal contact with God and the achievement of personal salvation. They grew directly at the expense of the more rationalistic, more liberal, social-activist church groups that had dominated the American religious scene in the previous decades.[16]

These developments among Christians were paralleled among some Jews in the United States for whom a return to "Jewishness" similarly became a new experience during this time. New movements, many communal in character, sprang up among the lately radical youth and their nonpolitical successors in the college generation of the 1970s who flocked into scores of newly created programs of Jewish studies. Many young adults, brought up in the assimilationist environment or more mildly religious style of their parents, began looking for their own ways of being more "Jewish," whether in these new and experimental fellowships or in the older-established affiliations. Some moved all the way back toward the older-style Orthodoxy, which also experienced a new access of strength and authority at this time. "Our stock in trade is tradition," said the Hasidic rabbi who was directing his group's activities on eight campuses in California, "our concern is with young Jews who feel themselves rootless, left adrift in a political and computerized society."[17] Insofar as these young Jews were still interested in politics, it was Jewish-connected politics, having to do mainly with the plight of Jews in the Soviet Union or relations with Israel.

These tendencies, whatever their numerical or social weight or staying power might prove to be, were part of the larger flight from normlessness and formlessness, part of a search for the greater security of more structure, more certainty, more coherence, more order, more authority. Describing the Jesus Movement at Stanford University, a professor of religion there said: "I think it's an authority structure in a society that's at a loss for authority structures. There's a real authoritative simplicity about the evangelical Christian position that's very appealing." Commenting disapprovingly on the movement's flight from social activism, the Dean of Chapel at Stanford said: "The Jesus Movement is not going to lift a finger to change the status quo. They're waiting for the Second Coming and Christ is going to take care of all that."[18]

While they are waiting, however, they are presumably experiencing some greater peace, that being the whole point of the exercise. But it has to be noted that whatever relief the individual might get by making this kind of religious retreat, he plainly gets it not as an individual alone but as a member of a group. Even in the most contemplative or the more exotic sects and certainly in all revivalist and millennial sects, fellow contemplators and fellow believers are always necessary to the process. It is not just an inner peace that is being sought, but an outer bond of definition, the sense of belonging with others who are feeling the same way. These seekers for salvation are not withdrawing alone to lonely mountain or desert vigils with the infinite, but they are flocking together in churches, temples, communes, fellowships. "It's difficult to be Jewish alone," said a young woman member of a Jewish fellowship on an Ohio campus. "Watching each other pray, you pick up this incredible warmth."[19]

Any larger assessment of these fluid facts has to wait on events yet to unfold. Not only is their relative social significance still unclear—cults come and go and evangelical religion has always been with us—but the depth of the crisis to which they respond is not clear either. As the experience of Weimar Germany of the 1920s showed, a breakdown of this kind, if it breaks down far enough, finds its own "solution" not in the religious but in the political sphere. It was not at all certain in the American condition of the mid-1970s where any parallels could be accurately drawn. But by withdrawing from the actualities while waiting to see what they might bring, many Americans so disposed could ease their fears and hold off despair by reaching into the back rooms of their various Houses of Muumbi for the old warming comforters of their several old-time religions.

✦

In other places, finally, old-time religion has by contrast been made a means of challenging or at least passively resisting political systems. In parts of Latin America and in the Philippines, radical priests march with guerrillas; and in both the Philippines and Korea, the Catholic Church hierarchy itself has openly entered into opposition to ruling dictators. For an especially striking example of how religion appears in this role, however, one can turn to the Soviet Union and its satellites.

Religion in Russia was too deeply imbedded, even for the Bolsheviks, to be abolished at a stroke like other institutions of the old order. Instead, religion, left formally and legally "free," was made a major target of the regime from the beginning. Vigorous campaigns were waged against all religious beliefs. Crippling limitations were put on opportunities for worship and religious education. Church establishments and hierarchies generally became pliantly submissive tools of the regime. Still, the churches, mosques, and synagogues in Russia remained refuges for old believers and makers of new ones. As the source—or even just as the symbol —of an alternative set of beliefs and moral concepts, religion offered a choice to those who could not take what the regime had to offer. This is obviously a matter that no simple formula can define, but the conversion of Solzhenitsyn in a labor camp is one example that testifies to the strength that could be mobilized by such a choice. The daring use of the pulpit as a platform for criticism, even protest, by an occasional bold priest has also testified to the use of the church as a channel for resistance, or at least for expressing resistant feelings. In Lithuania, Latvia, and Estonia, demands for greater religious freedom—as guaranteed nominally by the constitution—have been explicitly used to spearhead pressure for greater national self-assertion in other spheres.

In Soviet Armenia, the Armenian Apostolic Church has enjoyed a notable resurgence in the post-Stalin era, even while docilely accommodating to the government in all political matters. In those Soviet republics where Islam was traditionally the prevailing religion, it still remains difficult, after more than half a century of authoritarian pressure and constraint, for the center to win the desired conformity to the Communist models it seeks to impose.[20]

Most visible in recent years, probably, has been the remarkable case of the Soviet Jews, more repressed as both a national and a religious group than most others, driven back into their Jewishness not only by a stubbornly surviving attachment to their origins but by the even more stubbornly surviving anti-Semitism in the regime and in the Russian society generally. Least able of all the many nationalities in the Soviet Union to implement the limited opportunities to preserve their "national culture," many Jews demonstratively flocked to the synagogues that did remain open for worship on Jewish holy days and in the face of costly personal risks came finally to demand and openly struggle for the right to emigrate to join their fellow Jews in Israel or elsewhere abroad. The issue of Jewish emigration became an element in American-Soviet relations between 1972 and 1974, and through the openings thus created, many thousands of Soviet Jews did leave the country. Soviet Jews arriving in Israel have included members of a distinctive traditionalist Jewish sect that kept itself intact over the years in Soviet Georgia, large numbers of assimilated Jews professing varied degrees of Jewish religiosity, and many like the much-publicized Soviet ballet dancer Valery Panov, who, when asked by a television interviewer after his arrival in Israel whether his non-Jewish wife would now convert to Judaism, with a surprised look replied: "No, my wife and I are atheists."[21]

As this response suggests, the case of religion and the group identity of the Jews may well be the most complicated and paradoxical of all. Since it is more inextricably tangled than most with what is called "peoplehood," we shall return to it in the discussion that follows of the element of group identity called "nationality."

IX

NATIONALITY

✦

Then all the elders said unto Samuel, Now make us a king.
And the Lord said unto Samuel, Hearken unto the voice of
the people, for they have not rejected thee, but they have rejected me, that I should not reign over them. And Samuel told
all the words of the Lord unto the people that asked of him a
king. This will be the manner of the king that shall reign over
you. He will take your sons to be his horsemen and some shall
run before his chariots. He will take your daughters, he will
take your fields and vineyards and he will take the tenth of
your seed. And ye shall cry out on that day because of your
king which ye shall have chosen you; and the Lord will not
hear you on that day. Nevertheless, the people refused to obey
the voice of Samuel and they said, Nay; but we will have a
king over us that we also may be like all the nations. And the
Lord said to Samuel, Hearken unto their voice, and make
them a king.
—ABRIDGED FROM SAMUEL I, 8:4–22

FROM RELIGION to the nation it is but a step, historically and psychologically. As we take that step now, we seem finally to come
face to face, indeed eyeball to eyeball, with that abominable snowman himself. For basic group identity comes into view most often
dressed in its national colors, marching under its national flag,
wearing its national tag. In its many definitions and usages, the
"nation" or "nationality" appears as the ultimate, the most inclusive, even the "terminal" form of the basic group identity itself.

The nation, writes Rupert Emerson, is "the largest community which, when the chips are down, effectively commands men's loyalty . . . it is for present purposes the effective end of the road for man as a social animal, the end point of working solidarity between men." Other groupings have played this role, the family, the tribe, religious communities, but "all of these, without vanishing from the scene, have bit by bit, often after harsh struggle, yielded pride of place to the nation in the sense that for constantly growing numbers of men the claims of the nation have come to be accepted as taking priority over claims coming from any other source," the nation having come to be seen as "the community which makes the nearest approach to embracing all aspects of their lives."[1]

In one form or another, the strong identification and feeling of loyalty attached to the idea of the "nation" has always been present in human affairs. "It has been a mark of nature, if not nurture," wrote Carlton Hayes, "for human beings since the dawn of history to possess some consciousness of nationality, some feeling that the linguistic, historical, and cultural peculiarities of a group make its members akin among themselves and alien from all other groups."[2] Attachment to one's own family and the locality where one is born has always been part of its beginning; hence *patria,* one's birthplace, and on from there to all that "fatherland" and "motherland" eventually came to mean. The very use of these terms carries the powerful primordial associations projected from one's own birth and one's own parents to all others born in the same place, the same country. The word "nation" itself is from the Latin *nasci,* "to be born." The emotions and attachments first focused on family, tribe, clan, or other kinship group extended gradually outward to larger bodies of belonging and connectedness, to local regions, towns, cities, city-states, religious bodies, the realms of lords and kings. These came to command, in the words of a fourteenth-century Arab philosopher, that "unique mutual affection and willingness to fight and die for each other."

In western Europe three to four centuries ago, these various claimants on group loyalty began to be absorbed into what became the modern "nation," a political entity whose demand for loyalty overrode all others. "Love of fatherland," said a bishop at the court of Louis XIV, is "all the things which unite citizens together: the altars, the sacrifices, glory, peace, and security, in a word the society of divine and human things." A century later the French Revolution made the transfer from the divine to the national quite literal and explicit: it built its altars only to the fatherland; *la Patrie* took over from God. From Napoleon's time until now, taking on its modern shapes in Europe in the nineteenth century and in Asia and Africa in the twentieth, the idea of the "nation" and the driving force of "nationalism" have dominated the making and the wielding of political, economic, and military power in every kind of society and under every kind of ideological banner. The presence of nationalism is everywhere, its prints on our history and our lives huge and deep.[3]

Yet for all this pervasiveness, all this dominance in all our affairs, an extraordinary fact: even at eyeball range, neither "nation" nor "nationality" come clearly into view. As in so much else, it depends on who is looking. One distinguished scholar after another has made the safari over time and come back to describe what he has seen; but each, like an artist, has painted his own vision of what he saw, and no two portraits have been quite alike. All writers of this century make the same acknowledgment to those of the last—almost always, for example, to John Stuart Mill, Lord Acton, Ernest Renan—who had preceded them on the same quest. Nearly fifty years ago, Carlton Hayes began his own classic study of the subject (published in 1926) with the observation that the word "nation" was "tantalizingly ambiguous," that "nationalism" appeared as "vague and intangible and mysterious," and that "there is no agreement as to precisely what it is."[4] Twenty years later, the British historian E. H. Carr, who headed up a special commission to examine the subject, concluded that "the nation is not a definable and clearly recognizable entity."[5] Others, estimable scholars all, have written landmark works on the matter —Alfred Cobban, Boyd Shafer, Hans Kohn, Louis Snyder, Rupert Emerson among them—without coming, even among themselves, to any commonly accepted view of what "nation" and "nationality" actually look like, full face on. We obviously do know a great deal about the subject, thanks in good part to their works, but what we do not know, as Rupert Emerson ruefully acknowledged in his own notable study (published in 1960), "adds up to an impressive body of ignorance and uncertainty.[6]

Everyone has his own list of the parts that go into the making of a nation. Give or take an item or two, they all include the elements of what I have called the basic group identity, usually mentioning shared culture, history, tradition, language, religion, some adding "race" as well as the elements of territory, politics, and economics that all go in their varying measures into the making of what is called a "nation." On closer examination, it seems, no single part could be shown to be unique or indispensable to nationhood, except perhaps for some version of the idea of a shared past and a shared common will noted earlier by Mill and Renan and included as standard elements in every definition offered since their time. His own search through these thickets of definition led Emerson to join most of his predecessors in concluding: "The simplest statement that can be made about a nation is that it is a body of people who feel that they are a nation; and it may be that when all the fine-spun analysis is concluded, this will be the ultimate statement as well." We cannot ever really be certain what it is that makes "the existence of a singularly important national 'we' which is distinguished from all others who make up an alien 'they.' "[7] As state of mind, shared consciousness, or other version of Renan's "soul" or "spiritual principle" or Otto Bauer's "community of fate," the "nation"—so formidably real in the real world of everyone's everyday existence—has eluded all efforts of scholars to agree on what precisely it is. The abominable snowman again.

Finding such imprecision more abhorrent than any vacuum ever was, latter-day social scientific political science has tried to reobjectify the "nation" and "nationalism." Karl Deutsch, notably, has tried to sort out the graspable, countable, measurable "building blocks" of technology and communications that go into the making of a "nation." To this beacon, many of the tired and weary of academia have flocked in these years, only belatedly to find nestling among Deutsch's tidy formulas, diagrams, and tables, the same old ambiguities, elusive, subjective, uncontrollable as ever. They pollute the scientifically antiseptic precincts from which some thought they had finally been banished, or where, at least, it was thought they could simply be ignored.[8] If there is some arrangement of the various indicated ingredients which somehow creates a "nation" as hydrogen and oxygen at two to one make water, no one has found the formula. "The combinations in which they appear," concluded the quietly despairing Emerson after long toil, "defy orderly analysis."[9]

This uncertainty about the meaning of "nation" and "nationality" has been reflected and compounded by a corresponding confusion in how these words are used, whether by official bodies, scholars, lexicon makers, or in the common parlance of various languages. As with the substance, so with the names: the same words arise in different meanings and versions out of different outlooks and experience. In all that there is to read about the politics, diplomacy, wars, and revolutions of the last several centuries, these terms contradict and trip over one another, adding their additional blur to the miasmalike quality of the history itself. In one text or context or another, the word "nation" has been used interchangeably with "tribe," "people," "ethnic group," "race," "religion," "nationality," "country," and "state," among others. Distinctions are variously made among and between these terms, having to do with ideas about size, territory, "stage of development" or measure of "backwardness," the level of "consciousness," or, in the end, just how the particular writer feels about it.

The facts, past and present, seem to suggest that the formula whereby a "tribe" or a "people" does or does not become or remain a "nation" depends mainly on the conditions of power or the lack of it, and the given political circumstances of the time. The World War I peace settlement promised "self-determination of nations," presumably to all. As the victors rearranged the map at the expense of the vanquished, new "nations" were carved accordingly out of the lands of the defeated central European empires, each new "nation," to be sure, made up of a mix of subnationalities, each of which in turn would have dearly wished to become a "nation" on its own. But the Versailles formula was not considered to apply at all to the multitude of "nations" locked into the colonial empires of the Western powers: when *they* tried in the next few years to exercise self-determination, they were put down by main force. One world war later, the United Nations went the League one better and proclaimed the universal right of "self-determination of peoples." But no formula about what constituted a "nation" or a "people" was applied to any specific outcome, only the concrete circumstances of the forces in play. Only these circumstances could explain why, after World War II, the ex-colonies in Asia and Africa were simply converted from quite arbitrary colonial administrative conveniences into "nations." No formula, only particular conditions and relations of power and interest, could explain why, in the decades following 1945, little Gambia and the tiny islands of Fiji, Nauru, and Grenada could become "nations," while big Biafra could not; why Pakistan, a patchwork of Punjabis, Sindis, Pathans, Baluchis, etc., could become a nation, while Nagaland, with *its* patchwork of separate tribes, could not; why the Pathans of Pakistan could not have their own Pushtunistan, at least not yet, while the Bengalis could, after a bloody amputation, finally create their own Bangladesh. Tiny Abu Dhabi could become a "nation," but the Kurds must still fight on to establish their own Kurdistan. The Filipinos, Indonesians, and Burmese all acquired sovereignties of their own, but not the Muslims of Mindanao and Jolo, the Achinese of Sumatra, or the Kachins, Shans, or other peoples living on lands they held long before there was a "Burma."

If by "nation" we mean a culturally homogeneous group, then what is being said here is that some "nations" become states and some do not. If, as is so much more commonly the case, we use "nation" to mean the same thing as "state," then by some unkind fate, all claimants to nationhood who are unsuccessful in winning sovereignty for themselves cannot be referred to as "nations" but have to remain as "tribes" or "minorities." This fate, it should be clear, has nothing to do with whether they are indeed "nations" by this or that definition. It has to do only with the fact that at the given time they lack the power or other fortuitous conditions in which, weak as they might be, they could set up "states" of their own. This terminological blur between "nation" and "state," often blurred further as "nation-state," is probably the most common and the most important of all these confusions. Thus the League of Nations.[10] Thus the United Nations. Thus all the official bodies, agencies, and organizations that use the word "international" in their names, when, as Walker Connor has pointed out, they have to do not with "nations" but with sovereign states most of which are made up of many "nations." These confusions of usage have been noted, not always without further compounding, by various writers,[11] and it is happily not needful for us to review them at any greater length here.

One principal clarifying distinction does emerge. It lies between defining "nation" or "nationality" as in essence *cultural* or *political*. These two views do not appear or develop separately, but they do wind in and out of the design, making different patterns as they go.

The cultural concept of nationality in its modern European context is usually traced back to the eighteenth-century German poet-philosopher Johann Gottfried Herder, to whom we have already referred, who conceived of a *Volk* formed around the core of a common language as the keeper and carrier of the common heritage. This idea played a guiding role in much of the further course of nineteenth-century European nationalism—Mazzini adopted it and gave it his own rhetorically universalistic setting—and it appears and reappears in the turbulent history of European politics. Herder, who was more concerned with culture than with politics, apparently believed that if each *Volk* could be a nation unto itself, all would live happily ever after among themselves and in amity with others. The mystique of the German *Volk* he so passionately espoused ultimately became, as he could not have dreamed in his own universe, the driving spirit of Hitler's Reich. Believers in the positive power of self-determined homogeneous peoplehood of this kind do have to ponder the fact that the two most conspicuously successful examples of this type of national development occurred in modern times in Germany and Japan, with a third possibly in the making now in Maoist China.

The political concept of the nation took shape not out of any cultural or group matrix but out of the ideas and events that created the new states of post-Reformation western Europe. It came out of the social transformations and political revolutions in England, America, and France. This was essentially the great shift of power from the kings to the newly rising bourgeois class. The guiding ideas were Social Contract and General Will and democracy, in the tradition usually ascribed in its beginning to Rousseau. The evolution of the "nation" that grew out of these ideas moved, not like Herder's from the cultural to the political, but from the political to the cultural.[12] The rise of the bourgeoisie, the development of modern capitalism, the industrial revolution, the establishment of new systems of government based on popular sovereignty, all created their own new cultures in the "nations" that came into being in this process. Where this happened, "nationality" came most generally to mean, especially in official usage, passport-holding citizenship in the state regardless of the individual's country of birth or origin. But it also became the symbol of a new cultural identity that in some degree displaced or at least shared place with any older ancestral cultural legacy an individual might also have. Such were the degrees of relative assimilation of different peoples that took place in Britain and France and other European countries, but most especially in America. The stamp of a uniquely new Americanness became visible on all immigrant groups, especially as they moved into their second and third generations, becoming much deeper and more strongly marked without ever quite effacing the older imprints of remoter cultural origins.

In eastern Europe and beyond, on the other hand, "nationality" remained the term applied to particular communal groups whose cultural features were their own but whose political status was fixed by the places they held in some larger imperial power system, as under the Hapsburgs, Romanovs, and the Ottoman rulers. These groups were defined by region, by language, and, in the Ottoman empire especially, by religion. No Jew in Poland was ever a "Pole" by nationality, no Ukrainian or Georgian or Tatar or German in Russia a "Russian," no Greek or Bulgarian or Syrian or Kurd in old Turkey a "Turk." In the Ottoman empire, separate groups enjoyed separate local rule under the "millet system"—millet coming from the Arabic *millah,* meaning "a religious community." Under this system each group had a large measure of jurisdiction over its own purely internal civil affairs, usually as defined by its religious code and administered by its religious leaders. Out of these separate enclaves eventually came the various nationalisms that split the crumbling old empire and formed the new states that were carved out of it.[13] The millet system that existed in old Palestine under Turkish rule was maintained through the decades of the British mandate and provided the framework in which the Zionists were able to organize and maintain themselves as the national force that finally established its own power in Israel. The millet structure was carried over essentially untouched into the new state, which is in all respects a modern democratic state except that all matters touching on the civil status of its citizens—birth, death, marriage, divorce, recognition as "Jews"—remain under the effective control of an archaic religious establishment much as they did in Ottoman times, only now subject to contention in the secular courts set up by the new state.

In older times in much of the world, nationality and religion were commonly fused in the society—in the single body of the divine or divinely ordained ruler or in some other form of entwined religious and temporal power. Such was the case too in Europe until the Reformation. The creation of the modern European "nation" as we know it now began with the noble princes of the land taking over from the holy princes of the church and proceeded with the bourgeois princes of wealth taking over from the noble princes of the land. The newly risen bourgeois class created governments based, in theory at least, on the sovereignty of the people. The power and the glory passed from God's Chosen Church to God's Chosen Kings to God's Chosen People.*

In his discussion of the transfer of the "religious sense" from religion to nation, Hayes noted that, like declining Rome, where "pagan skepticism" among the elite led to the popular deification of the emperors, eighteenth-century Europe, amid similar elite skepticism about all religion, witnessed the elevation of the "nation" as the "central object of worship." In revolutionary France this was most ardently and explicitly done. Altars to the fatherland were erected everywhere bearing the words "The citizen is born, lives, and dies for *La Patrie*." The new regime instituted civic excommunication, civic baptism, civic marriage. It dedicated hymns, prayers, feasts to the new national deity. In modified and adapted forms this became the style of all the new European nationalisms. The believers in the Age of Reason who founded the American Republic believed in the higher calling, ideals, and mission of their new nation: the new American "civic religion."[14]

This was one of the great shifts in human affairs, one of those great turnings from all that had gone before toward much that would try to become new under the sun. For all its shoddy or

---

* Shakespeare had personified and glorified the England ruled by the Tudor kings, but it was Milton who registered the transfer of heaven's mandate from the kings to the people. "God is decreeing some new and great period," he wrote. "What does he, then, but reveal himself to his servants and, as his manner is, first to Englishmen?" Cromwell believed that the people of England were "a People that are to God as the apple of his eye." Quoted by Carlton Hayes, *Nationalism: A Religion,* New York, 1961, p. 41.

Since choosing the ancient Hebrews and then Cromwell's Englishmen, God has clearly collected an orchardful. "It would appear," said Nnamdi Azikiwe, the East Nigerian nationalist leader in 1949, "that the God of Africa has especially created the Ibo nation to lead the children of Africa from the bondage of the ages." Quoted by Emerson, loc. cit., p. 356. "As black preachers we must tell our people that we are God's chosen people and that God is fighting with us as we fight. When we march, when we take it to the streets in open conflict, we must understand that in the stamping feet and the thunder of violence we hear the voice of God." Albert Cleage, *The Black Messiah,* New York, 1968, p. 6.

ironic features and all its great failures, it was still one of history's finer hours of aspiration, as the historian J. L. Talmon's statement of it should remind us:

> The recognition of the right of the individual to be his own lawgiver, the challenge directed to him to express his personality spontaneously instead of submitting to god-given or time-hallowed prescriptions for the expiation of his sins, to work for the triumph of progress on earth instead of waiting for divine judgment—all these were extended to the collective personality of the nation. Moreover man's own smallness and unworthiness could be sublimated into the greatness and power of the nation, as they were formerly into the glory of the Church.[15]

These rearrangements of religious and secular value systems and interests were all part of a revolution that was taking place. As Weber, Tawney, and of course much earlier in their sharper way, Marx and Engels, showed, it was not always possible to distinguish between the lofty and the low, the heavenly and the earthly orders of self-interest that operated in those turbulent times of change. It was a massive transfer of power between classes and it was quite possible, even reasonable, to interpret the whole process as one of identifying the interests of God with those of the creators of the new capitalist system and with the cause of each of the aggressively contending national powers they created to advance their own particular interests. To put it in its bluntest and nonloftiest form, it was a matter of refashioning the old-style religion to fit the new-style rapacity. "The upshot of the whole process," to quote Hayes once more, was "that a nationalist theology of the intellectuals" and, he might have added, of the new ruling classes became "a nationalist mythology for the masses." A new religious syncretism was achieved, the continued adherence to the various ancestral faiths adapting obediently to "the exigencies of nationalist worship and discipline." The cult of the nation, the worship and reverence of national symbols and heroes—the cult of Washington in early America came close to using the language of deification—became entwined and incorporated into the more traditional religious symbols and objects of worship, characteristic behavior that history had known long before and has known only too well since. Traditional religion was duly bent to all these purposes and the autonomy of religion progressively brought under the control of these new national forces. "The universal in religion," as Rupert Emerson put it, was made "to bow to the tribal gods of nations."[16]

Tribal gods were obviously much better suited to national purposes than any other kind, especially the kind that spoke for the brotherhood of man. Tribal gods, plainly earthier, more practical, and more "national" in every way, required brotherhood only among fellow members of the tribe, and that only when faced by their natural enemies, or all who belonged to other tribes. One of the great advantages of tribal-nationalist religion was its ability to blunt contradictions between universal moral professions and parochial self-serving practice. Believers in God usually require their God to be always right; in the cult of patriotism—the highest form of nationalist religion—believers were licensed, indeed required, to believe in their country, right or wrong. Before this time there had been tribal wars, dynastic wars, religious wars, but national wars have surely outdone them all, as David did Saul, in the business of mutual slaughter. In the celebrations of nationhood in song, story, and sacred ritual, indeed, no matter how far back one goes, these slaughters and their heroes and exploits are celebrated most of all, as a look at the words of almost any national anthem will attest.[17]

Some of the loftiest spirits and best minds of many generations have struggled to see how it might be otherwise, but the "nation" and the power of "nationality" have bested them all, whether as political fact, fiction, goal, idea, myth, or state of mind.

"Nationality," then, comes in different sizes, shapes, and colors, and, as always in such matters, styles have been subject to change. But "variable and malleable" as Alfred Cobban suggested it might be, it remains in all its varieties a primary shaping ingredient in the formula of every person's life.

As identification by birth with a "nation"—meaning a group

with certain shared holdings of history and culture—it fixes certain features of every person's existence no matter what other features he takes on. It establishes where one belongs or is seen by others to belong. It fixes the place that is "home," whether it be a country, a region, a neighborhood, or simply the bosom of the group. It is where one lives or is entitled to live, physically, emotionally, psychologically, and it underpins and in some way shapes us, no matter how we change or how far away we move. From this basic attachment, as so much art and literature attest, much nourishment has come. "Nationalities," wrote Aleksandr Solzhenitsyn in his undelivered Nobel Prize lecture in 1970, "are the wealth of humanity, they are its crystalized personalities; even the smallest among them has its own special colors, hides within itself a particular facet of God's design." From it too, and presumably also part of God's design, has come the hatred, violence, and bloodshed that resulted as these colors clashed, as these crystalized personalities confronted one another over their differences and over how to distribute humanity's wealth, whether spiritual or material.

As citizenship in a state, "nationality" has been hardly any less governing or influential, providing the individual with whatever security—both physical and emotional—it can create in a remarkably insecure and unsafe world. However oppressed, disaffected, or alienated the individual might be within his own "nation," the unhappy fact is that everywhere else in the world he is more alien still, unless, as so many immigrants to America in the century past were uniquely able to do, he could carry his "nation" with him and acquire a new "nationality" that served him better than his old one. To be deprived of nationality in the sense of having citizenship in a state is to be cast out into the desert of homelessness, out among the beasts of prey that roam the wild world outside. To suffer this fate, as millions have in this era of the Refugee, the Stateless, and the Displaced Person, is to learn, as Hannah Arendt has written, that "the abstract nakedness of being human" is not enough to entitle one even to the least of so-called "human rights," that in our age nationality has become "the only remaining and recognized tie with humanity."[18] To belong to a nationality that is defined by birth rather than by citizenship has meant for millions of people in our time to be doomed to banishment and death. In Hitler's Germany, German Jews who thought they were Germans turned out, for purposes of the slaughter, to be Jews. In Stalin's Russia, millions of Ukrainians, Germans, Tatars, and other peoples were transported to exile and death. Even in Franklin Roosevelt's America, Japanese-Americans who thought they were Americans were abruptly uprooted and moved to detention camps because they were seen as Japanese.

By its various definitions, in all its varied appearances, "nationality" is clearly, however, the most inclusive and the most explicitly political of all the elements that go into the making of every person's basic group identity. If "group belongingness is the haven of personality," as R. M. MacIver has written, "it is strongest and most enduring when it achieves the form of nationhood."[19] The "nation" is the most persistently surviving unit of political organization in human affairs, remaining so in a world that has outgrown its limitations and can no longer afford its drawbacks and dangers. Since it is politics—relative power or powerlessness—that decides the fate of any community of people, nationality is in the end the most critical of all the identifications an individual carries as part of his group identity.

The history of world politics during the last two centuries has consisted primarily of the increasingly more explosive appearance, disappearance, and reappearance of "nations" or states, wars and revolutions changing their placement and displacement in relation to one another and to the distribution of resources and power. In the tour of the world's political landscape with which we opened this work, we took a wide look at many of the current particulars and we do not need to redraw any of that large picture here. Every aspect of it—postcolonial, postimperial, postrevolutionary, and in the United States postillusionary—is dominated by the problems of nation, nationality, nationalism. These impinge on every person's existence. They press their reshaping forms on all our group identities as we come through the great political changes that are now the common experience of all.[20] For purposes of illustration here, I will deal briefly with two examples, the Japanese in Japan and the Jews in Israel, because each one in its quite unique way shows the element of nation or nationality in a peculiarly central role. The experience of Jewish Americans and black Americans, with which I conclude, illustrates other aspects and other measures of the role of nationality in group identity; their experience, along with that of other groups in the society, is giving new shape to the nationality we call "American," indeed is creating a new American group identity.

By almost all the definitions, Japan is probably the truest "nation" on earth and one of the few that can accurately be called a "nation-state." Its people are physically and culturally homogeneous to a unique degree, even taking into account all their urban-rural, modern-traditional, intra-insular particularities, and the odd survival of their untouchable minority. They have their own long-established and clearly defined island territory standing by itself out to sea. They have their own long-recorded history, rich tradition, mythology, folklore, their language and art, partly derived long ago from nearby China but long since made into something peculiarly their own. These underpinnings play an important part in the self-awareness and the self-esteem of the Japanese, giving them the relatively firm ground on which, more currently, they feel uncertain about themselves. It is Japan's more recent history as a modern nation, little more than a century long, that figures dynamically in the group identity problem that now presses so strongly on so many thoughtful Japanese. This was essentially the history of Japan's effort to imitate and overtake the national-power-wielding style of its modern national rivals in Europe and the United States; it was in the concept of the *nation* that everything in the Japanese culture-past and culture-present of the past hundred years has come into focus.

The Meiji transformation that began in 1868 created a nation that generated new kinds of power. It put ancient myths to work to serve new ends. It began deliberately and systematically to acquire the industrial and military technologies developed in the West and set out under the leadership of its newly armed forces to challenge Western mastery in Asia. The nation was pulled together in a system of authority rising through the hierarchies of the society to the Emperor at its apex, the great age of his dynasty and the divinity of his origin fully mobilized to lend force to the commanding mystiques of the regime. Japan was transformed in a few decades into a modern military power. The shrewd use of old beliefs and new drives built an economic and political system capable of totally mobilizing a notably energetic and mobilizable people.[21] Within barely fifty years, its leaders came remarkably close to achieving their daring military objectives. But they failed politically by failing to lead a real mobilization of Asian nationalism against the West. Their successes were made of ingenuity and energy, their failure was of the imagination. Japan's military power alone, based on very narrow resources, was not and never could have been a match for that of the United States, and Japan went down to defeat. As it was, Japan's conquests did trigger political revolutions overdue in most of Asia, but they did not come with Japan but against it and did not come to a head until Japan itself was crushed.

What was crushed by the defeat of 1945 was the nation created by the Meiji generation. Under American occupation, Japanese of all classes waited with a certain numbness to discover how they might be able to reassemble themselves as a group again. The prewar generation hoped to salvage the system they had known. The wartime generation was all but paralyzed by the loss of confidence and authority suffered in the betrayal and the fall of what they had so believingly accepted. The postwar youth generation vainly looked for larger new coherences to replace the nation as the object of their faith and allegiance. The process of change in Japan in the postwar decades centered on the concept of the nation, getting away from the one that was, getting back to it, changing it, re-creating it, somehow to fill with new substance or at least with something different the great empty space created at the center of Japanese life by the defeat.

Japan's postwar radical youth reached hard for something supranational to fill the void, international pacifism, international communism. But they found themselves grabbing at empty air. The emotions and symbols of international pacifism were cynically manipulated by international communism; but worse still, international communism during these years was breaking up everywhere into its separate national parts, forcing even Communist Japanese back to a new "Japanism," a new "national communism" of their own. This produced split perspectives among the radicals bearing on Russia or China, both of which filled most Japanese with fear or uncertainty or both. It drove tiny groups of ultraradicals to the politics of international terrorism where no one would follow them.

What did come to fill that great empty space—helped by American aid policies, the Korean war, and the cold-war strategic calculations of the 1950s and 1960s—was the extraordinary economic reconstruction of Japan and its spurt in less than two decades to the front ranks of world production and trade in a whole series of key sectors. This came on with a spectacular rush. Japanese industry set out to accomplish what Japanese militarism had failed to do, to win and to maintain a position as one of the world's premier powers. The remarkable success of this effort in the 1960s was accompanied by a quickening recovery and reshaping of Japanese national consciousness at many levels and in many forms, the gradual reappearance in the public vocabulary of the long-banned phrase "national interests"—words associated with Japan's militarist period—the restoration of flag and anthem as national symbols, the flocking of millions to Shinto shrines on traditional occasions, the beginning of revision of the history of the war, providing a more self-justifying view of Japan's wars of conquest in Asia and the Pacific during the first half of the century.[22] Even without subscribing to this rehabilitating view of the past, Japanese leaders were clearly being forced by their new role and by events to take a new view of Japan's place in the world, especially after the sudden reopening of American contact with China in 1971 shifted the terms of the world power struggle. It was clear that, ready, willing, or able or not, Japanese leaders were going to have to begin defining and looking after those same old "national interests" that had led Japan into the world power struggle in the first place.

Some old and painful disabilities, however, soon reappeared. Some of Japan's "economic animals" began repeating in Southeast Asia some of the history made there a generation before by some of Japan's military animals. The ghost of the wartime "East Asia Co-Prosperity Sphere" reappeared in the results of the damaging lack of sensitivity to the needs and feelings of the peoples whose countries the Japanese penetrated with thought only for their own short-term gain. The other new appearance of an old weakness was even more ominous. The world energy crisis brought on by the Arab oil-producing countries in 1973–74 reminded Japan sharply of the fact, unchanged by all that had happened in the intervening years, that Japan's own national resource base was painfully narrow, that its growth, strength, and survival still rested on access to resources of almost every kind that could only be found elsewhere in the world. But as Japanese, especially Japanese intellectuals, ruminated, worried, even agonized over the recurring questions of what the Japanese national identity really was, and Japanese economic and political leaders mulled worriedly over what path to take to serve their national interests in an unstable and dangerous world situation, it was clear that reconstitution of the nation was already well under way, that it was geared up to go, suffering only from not knowing what direction to take.

Despite these uncertainties of national definition and direction, however, the question "What is a Japanese?" is quite different from, say, the question "What is a Jew?" The difference, made of many things, is, I suspect, also a matter of how each group identity has fared in the matter of its nationality, its enclosure in a nation. The Japanese are characterized above all by their physical homogeneity, their territorial compactness, their shared existence in one island county over a long period of time: the stereotype of the neatly tied package fits the picture. All the elements of the Japanese group identity are tightly congruent and they are wrapped —colorfully and beautifully, of course—in the cultural *and* political wrappings of Japanese nationality. One might not always know what the contents are, but one can never mistake where it comes from. By contrast, the question "What is a Jew?" calls for trying to bring together a great untidy scatter of physical and cultural varieties and experiences shaped in many different places in different ways over a long period of time.[23] It makes by way of group identity a package not neatly tied together at all, some of whose contents you might sometimes be able to know, but which from the outside you could rarely identify at all.

✦

The mix of history, religion, and nationhood in the Jewish group identity is more difficult than most to reduce to any formula that might suggest how these separate parts produce their result. It is peculiarly difficult to begin with because there is no agreement on what the result is. Writing on the subject is without end, and its riddles remain unanswered. The question "What is a Jew?" remains at the center of Jewish existence in Israel, where Jewish nationality has regained its own political life under the name "Israeli," and elsewhere in the world where Jews remain Jews while being citizens of other states. There is no consensus or clarity as to whether a Jew is a Jew by virtue of being born to a Jewish mother, as Orthodox doctrine holds, or by his belief in a religious creed set forth in the Law, or by his undivestible holding of a share in the history of a "people" or "nation" built around this creed in which many Jews believe in different ways and many others do not believe at all. These questions appear and reappear in all the ongoing varieties of Jewish experience. It is not the purpose of these paragraphs to suggest answers but only to reflect briefly about the role of "nationality" in the makeup of the Jewish group identity.

In the sense of being anything other than "Jewish," the problem of "nationality" has been part of the riddle of Jewish identity for only about two hundred years and only in parts of western Europe and in America. For more than 1500 years before that, the Jews, having lost Israel, been dispersed, resisted absorption, survived extermination, failed to disappear, had remained "Jews," everywhere a people apart. They were kept apart by the unrelenting hostility of the Gentile world, especially the Christian world, and by their own unyielding maintenance of their own beliefs and their own separateness. These were preserved by the rabbinical tradition set forth in the Talmud and other works of refinement and interpretation of the Law, which Jews believed God had given them to serve as a model for the whole world. The world, however, developed its own versions of God's law and kept the Jews and their version outside its pales, locked up in its ghettos, occasionally tolerating their separateness, more commonly victimizing them for it.

Not until the emancipation from the ghetto that followed the French revolution did Jews began to acquire west European nationalities. They did so to some extent at the cost of their identity as Jews. The liberal Gentiles who pressed for Jewish emancipation saw it as a way for Jews to shed their Jewishness, i.e., to shed whatever it was that caused them to be rejected. They could thus become part of the modernizing world in the new era in which Reason, perhaps, but the Nation, surely, was going to replace Religion. For this, the "Jews as a nation"—common phrase of the time—had to give way. This was the meaning of the principle proclaimed in 1789 by the French champion of rights for the Jews, Clermont-Tonnerre: "To the Jews as individuals, everything; to the Jews as a nation, nothing." There were many Jews ready to accept this invitation to drop the burden of centuries at last, to break out of stifling isolation and parochial confinement, to join the rest of the enlightened human race on its march toward universal betterment. Many such Jews chose accordingly to disappear into the non-Jewish mass. But there were many others who were glad to become citizens of the world outside the ghetto by becoming citizens in the new "nations" coming into being, but at the same time had no wish to cease being Jews. What such Jews did was to adapt the old traditions to new modernizing needs, some to embrace the new Reform Judaism founded for this purpose, others choosing more casual ways to subordinate their Jewish to their new European identities. The Jews in western Europe who chose this path during the rest of the nineteenth century lived on in varying patterns of continuing apartness, rejection, exclusion, and victimization. The anomalies were many, illustrated by this description of Gustav Mahler: "As a Bohemian among Austrians, as an Austrian among Germans, as a Jew in the world, he was always on the outside." Or of Heine: "an apostate to the Jews, Jew to the Germans, German to the French . . . and all too often, a stranger to himself." The Enlightenment did not successfully humanize Europe but unfortunately became subject itself to the success of nationalism. Neither did the emancipation emancipate all who had to be emancipated. Anti-Semitism flourished just as virulently under the pure clear light of Science and Reason as it had in the shadow of Faith and Doctrine, or, as some had it, superstition and dogma. As someone of the time remarked, had the Enlightenment worked, there would have been no Zionism.[24]

Neither emancipation from the ghettos nor the subsequent ambiguities of life for Jews in western Europe ever did spread to eastern Europe, where the Middle Ages continued right on through the nineteenth century. By its closing decades, continued persecution had led to a mass exodus of Jews, most of them going to America. The precariousness of the Jews' position—dramatized by the pogroms in the unemancipated east and the Dreyfus affair in the emancipated west—brought the rise of political Zionism, the search for a national-territorial answer to the "Jewish Question," the problem of their persistent separateness among their fellow Europeans. It was in Germany finally, where assimilation had gone furthest and cosmopolitanism had borne some of its best fruits, that anti-Semitism reached the level of ultimate violence. The passports acquired by Jews with their European nationalities proved good in the end only for one journey, one way, to the gas ovens. Hitler's Europe became the graveyard for all but a handful of its

Jews. The rest of the world, including America, did not open its doors to many survivors. The re-creation of a Jewish nationality in Israel became the only way most of them could stay alive; and quite like a biblical miracle, it came to pass.

The new Jewish state came into being to house the old Jewish nation, a new Israeli "nationality"—in the sense of citizenship in a state—to protect the old Jewish "nationality"—in the sense of a culturally homogeneous people with common holdings. But the Jews who came to Israel were not homogeneous and held their common holdings quite differently. The existence of Israel may have "solved" what used to be called the "Jewish Question" in Europe, but it did not by any means solve the riddle of Jewishness. By coming together from seventy countries after two thousand years, the Jews in Israel found it not easier but more difficult than ever to define what a Jew is, what Jewishness is.

For most of these Jews, however, this difficulty of definition had little or nothing to do with "nationality." Those who came from Germany and western European countries had no reason left to trust in the security offered them by the "nationality" most of those countries offered them. But the larger number by far never did hold the nationalities of the countries from which they came, in Europe from Germany eastward, or in North Africa from Morocco to Egypt, or from Yemen, Iraq, or anywhere else in the Arab world. Whatever else it meant to these Jews, to gain haven and a new Israeli nationality meant to *survive,* to win whatever security the creation of a Jewish state could give them in an inhospitable and hostile world.

But the question of what *else* it meant remained. This was the problem of redefining their common identity as Jews, of defining what it was, exactly, that was surviving. This was, to be sure, an intensely personal matter for a great many people; but beyond them as individuals it had to do also with the meaning of Judaism as a religion, the relation between religion and the state in Israel, between Judaism as Israel's state religion and Judaism elsewhere in the world, between religious Judaism and secular Zionism, between orthodoxy, reform, or freethinking, between the universal values of the religion and the parochial values of nationhood and the pressing needs of the state. These issues were raised, moreover, in the very context of survival itself, for Jewish nationalism was not left to work out these problems by itself. It had to confront and combat Arab nationalism, not only of the Arab states that surrounded it but of the Palestinian Arabs whose counternationalism laid claim to the very land of Israel itself. Through four wars and constant strain, this had become for many Israelis not just a matter of facing enemies who wanted to destroy them but also of defining the meaning of their own survival. Creation of the state of Israel had come out of the most desperate need simply to stay alive. Now there was clearly a deep and somber growing need among many of Israel's Jews, especially among its thoughtful young, to understand what it was that made their Jewish nationhood different. Was their nationality unique in some commanding way meaningful to all human beings, or were they, like their ancestors of old who first pressed Samuel to give them a king, going through all this simply to be, after all, "like all the other nations"? This was the question not only for Jews in Israel but for Jews elsewhere in the world, especially in America, who also had to decide how they distinguished between their religion and their nationality, and to find out where, if anywhere, finally, they do belong.

In the matter of "nationality," the Jews who migrated from Europe to America had a different and, for Jews, a unique experience. They became part of a society and a national history that for all its legacies from Europe was moving along different paths toward different outcomes. The uniqueness of the American experience had to do with the uniqueness of the American credo: it was the only society in the world that had taken as its explicit goal the building of an open society, the making of one "nation" out of many. There was obviously a wide gap between rhetoric and reality, between profession and practice, between the tale and the truth. Immigrants who did not come from Protestant northern

Europe found few hearts of gold in their golden new land. They did find virulent bigotry of the anti-Catholic, anti-Semitic, anti-Negro, and all the anti-other varieties. Group behavior in America was like all group behavior where differences of race, religion, origin, and culture were involved. That is to say, it was full of hate, fear, contempt, and was organized in pecking orders of scales and levels of dominating and being dominated. Several generations of Jews in America, like other immigrant and minority groups, suffered much of the same apartness, rejection, and exclusion that was the common lot of Jews in Europe. The difference was that the dominant credo of the society was in constant contradiction with this behavior. It proclaimed secular equality; its dominant religion preached brotherhood. Weak as the spirit was compared to the flesh, it still made life different in America from life in Europe.

If this difference was not yet working for the blacks and other nonwhites who occupied the bottom rungs of the society, it did soon begin to make a significant difference for the European immigrants who poured into the country during the nineteenth century and up to about 1920. The Jews who came to America from eastern Europe found the barriers against them located much farther out than any that had hemmed them in before. By comparison with Czarist eastern Europe, the new land was for them an egalitarian haven free of the old fears and full of new opportunities and great mobility for all. The American direction, moreover, was different. The American evolution in succeeding generations was not the European evolution. While Jews in Europe were arriving at the gates of extermination camps, Jews in America were approaching the thresholds of successful integration in the American society, an integration that involved not their disappearance but their survival as Jews in whatever form they chose to give their American Jewishness.[25]

Like blacks and other distinctive minorities in the society, Jews in America are familiar with the experience of a blurred two-ness, of being both *Jewish* and *American,* the mix of the two and the lines between them never clear. For a long time the conventional way of defining—and often of dismissing—the distinction was for a Jew to see himself as Jewish by religion and American by "nationality," essentially meaning citizenship. But this oversimple formula never quite covered the matter. If being a Jew is a condition that cannot be exactly or precisely described to everyone's satisfaction or agreement, so is the condition of being American. Jewishness is seen as a "peoplehood" that takes in more than religion: nonreligious Jews are still Jews, their "cultural" nationality is still Jewish. In 1947, the Jews who created Israel created a new "political" nationality that also makes a claim on the loyalty of Jews wherever they might be: any Jew who migrates to Israel is entitled by Israeli law to opt for Israeli citizenship by simply declaring himself to that effect.

Being "American," on the other hand, means having a nationality that takes in a good deal more than just citizenship. The "political" character of American "nationality" has been acquiring a "cultural" character to go with it. With all its flaws and warts and deformities, an American "peoplehood" has been coming into being; and Jews, like members of other European immigrant groups, began increasingly to share the sense of *belonging* to it, especially during the two decades after World War II when the American society began to move so much more swiftly toward actually becoming more and more the open society it had always professed to be.

This sense of having American "nationality," in the meaning of peoplehood as well as citizenship, culturally as well as politically, grew steadily as one increasingly mobile generation of Jews followed another, becoming more and more "American" in the process. Still it remained ever fragile, tentative, always hedged by a certain awareness of persisting limits on how far and how fully they belonged in the American society and of how far the experience of Jews elsewhere in the world still governed their own. American Jews became a primary source of financial and political support for the Zionist movement in Europe and Palestine. The impact of the Nazi holocaust on American Jews included the complex experience of being survivors, safe and far away from the disaster that had befallen their kin. There was a deeply troubled and troubling ambivalence in the time when Roosevelt's America was opened to let in only a trickle of refugees from Hitler, a surge of passionate relief when President Truman gave his ultimately decisive support to the creation of Israel. American Jews related intensely to Israel, their support having much to do, indeed, with its survival. But for all the complexity and ambiguity of its emotional underpinnings, this intense relationship never included for the overwhelming bulk of America's Jews any impulse to heed the Zionist call to join in the Return, to migrate to Israel themselves, to give up their American nationality to become Israelis.

Only a tiny handful of American Jews, some twenty thousand, did migrate and remain in Israel as settlers during its first twenty-five years. I have reported elsewhere my own glimpse of the dilemma of identity into which most of these American migrants were plunged.[26] What needs to be said about it here is that much of it revolved quite explicitly until mid-1967 around the issues of their nationality, the literal and legal as well as emotional and moral problem of choosing to remain American citizens or becoming Israelis. Only a few hundred up to that time did choose Israeli nationality. The rest stayed on in Israel as noncitizen residents, agonizing in a limbo of their own on this side of an uncrossed desert. This particular aspect of their dilemma was greatly eased— at precisely the moment when the 1967 war had put it under enormously heightened strain—by a decision of the United States Supreme Court which voided laws penalizing American citizens with loss of citizenship if they served in foreign armies or voted in foreign elections. In effect this decision left Americans in Israel free to enjoy dual citizenship; in the political sense of "nationality" they could now enjoy being both "American" and "Israeli."

This left untouched many other still more deeply rooted difficulties in bridging their American and Jewish identities while in Israel. In whatever way their cultural nationality was Jewish, it had also become, in equally ineradicable ways, American. It was precisely the values and circumstances that had made it possible for American Jews to become Jewish Americans that made it difficult for so many of these American Jews to become Israelis. These touch on such deep and crucial matters as the nature of politics, the relation of church and state, and even more deeply, perhaps, their concepts of the nature and practice of Judaism as a religion and of the link between religion and nationhood. Whatever it was in their view of themselves as Jews that had led these individuals to leave America and go to Israel, there was no way that those who had been born and brought up as Americans could leave behind the outlooks they had acquired in the process; this was precisely the "cultural" identity as Americans they acquired along with their American nationality. From this came the built-in conceptions that made it extremely difficult for them to choose between what seemed to be a limited national-religious parochialism and what still promised to be an unlimitedly broad, diverse, and open pluralism.

In the great trials and crises that beset both the American and the Israeli societies in the 1960s and 1970s, these choices and these conceptions were all coming under test and question by Jews in both America and in Israel. In both countries, the nature and role of "nationality" in the group identities called "Jewish," "American," and "Israeli" were being shaped by great confused and confusing events whose outcomes could not be foreseen. Some were going to depend on the high politics of the world power struggle as it unfolded in the eastern Mediterranean, some on the further evolution of the American society and the further course of the nationalist confrontation between Israeli and Arab. Somewhere along there, amid those great further unfoldings, it might become clearer than it is now what it signifies to be a *Jew,* an *Israeli,* an *American.*

Even more than for Jews, the question of nationality for black Americans has long been obscured behind a heavy veil of alienation and exclusion, ambivalence and duality. Always present in the complex of Negro life in America from the beginning, the issue of nationality was stirred in new ways by the end of the colonial system in Africa and the appearance of newly independent African states. A noted scholar who made a journey to the then Gold Coast—it was in 1955 before it became Ghana—told me of a conversation he had there with an African:

> He asked me what *nation* I came from. I was confused by this until I realized that he meant what *tribe* I derived from, and I explained that no American Negro was in a position to identify his tribal origin, that *my* nation was America. He said: "You see, this is one of the errors in trying to equate Africans and American Negroes. Why *every* African knows *his* nation!" [27]

The irony in this exchange had more to it than mere semantic confusion. The African was just being caught up in events that required him to enlarge his idea of his "nation" from his tribe to the larger national idea of a Ghana, an enlargement that was plainly not going to be easy for him to make. On the other hand, the black visitor from America could reply that he was "American," that he knew *his* nation well enough, the only question being whether his nation knew *him*.

Of this condition, W. E. B. Du Bois had long ago written these vivid oft-quoted words:

> The Negro is a sort of seventh son, born with a veil, and gifted with second sight in this American world—a world which yields him no true self-consciousness, but only lets him see himself through the revelation of the other world. It is a peculiar sensation, this double-consciousness, this sense of always looking at one's self through the eyes of others, of measuring oneself by the tape of a world that looks on in amused contempt and pity. One ever feels his two-ness—an American, a Negro; two souls, two thoughts, two unreconciled strivings; two warring ideals in one dark body whose dogged strength alone keeps it from being torn asunder.[28]

No small part of the black man's long struggle for identity in America has been to resolve this two-ness, to shake the blur into some single or coherent image he could have of himself as a person who is black and as an American. He has been in America much longer than most of those around him now who are so unquestioningly "American." He was cut off more completely from his roots than any others who came here after him. He shaped his culture and personality out of the materials of his life in America. That life was dominated by his subjection, by his exclusion from the surrounding society, the denial of his manhood, even his humanhood, and even that most elementary of birthrights that went so automatically to everyone else, his nationality. A war was fought over his status and one result was that his rights as an American citizen were at last formally and constitutionally guaranteed to him. But even after this, for another hundred years, he continued to stand outside the pale while wave after wave of latercomers rolled past him and over him and within a generation or two, even though they also experienced exclusion and discrimination, took on their new identities as Americans, made their way upward through the society, and began in varying measures to belong to it. Black Americans, however, continued not to belong. They remained firmly placed but always displaced, rooted yet held rootless, included yet relentlessly excluded: their *two-ness, American* and *Negro,* made them national and alien at the same time.

The struggle of blacks in America was to win the same legal, political, social, and human rights enjoyed by other Americans but denied to them. Defeated again and again during the long history of that struggle, in almost every generation some despairing black men concluded that if they were denied their nationality as Americans their only option was to leave America, to go to some other land, to found a nation and acquire a nationality of their own. During more than two hundred years there were recurring attempts, always small and obscure, to organize migration to this end, from Paul Cuffee's first voyage to Sierra Leone in 1815 and Martin Delany's exploratory voyages to the Niger in the 1850s, to Marcus Garvey's "Back to Africa" movement in the 1920s. With the exception of the movement that resulted in the founding of Liberia in 1820, which took place under rather different auspices, none of these efforts ever led to any significant migration from America. Some tiny black nationalist and migrationist groups continued to exist through the years, but they have continued to be ignored by the great mass of American blacks. In their numbers, blacks in this country remained where they were planted in American life, holding fast to the fact, which Du Bois did not until the end of his long life tire of stressing, that "there is nothing so indigenous, so completely 'made in America,' as black Americans are."[29]

It took generations of struggle, and two world wars had to happen, before the civil rights revolution of the 1950s and 1960s seemed to begin at last to vindicate this conviction. That first great wave of change brought down the legally established system of white supremacy in the United States. But after washing over most of the old system that stood in the South, it broke against the stronger walls of the northern urban ghettos and all the thickly encrusted economic, social, and psychological legacies of the long past. In the disenchantment with the promise of integration and the great turmoil of frustrated expectations and released feelings among blacks that filled the years 1965 to 1970, new forms of black nationalism appeared. They appeared in small ultrarevolutionary groups that summoned the black masses not to migrate but to join the "Third World" in armed struggle for "national liberation" on the Algerian, Cuban, Chinese, and Vietnamese models. Products of the same kind of despair as had come in generations past, these movements came to nothing, just as earlier ones had. The mass of black Americans remained stubbornly rooted, despite everything, in their American identity. They were not going to be severed from it, either by leaving the country or by following desperate young men down nihilist paths. Migrationists continued to be heard at the margins of the new black radicalism. Surviving followers of Marcus Garvey still called on blacks to return en masse to Africa. But independent Africa apparently offered no greater attractions for black Americans as migrants than colonial Africa had in Garvey's time. More generally the separationists among black radicals in America in the 1960s and 1970s proposed to do their separating on American soil, some groups adopting for this purpose some version of the formula espoused by the Black Muslims for the creation of "a separate, free, independent nation for black people" somewhere on American territory.

One form this took was the attempt to create self-contained black communities that would control their own affairs. Several small groups, like the black nationalist "New Africa" or the more conservative ex-CORE leader Floyd McKissick's band of community builders in North Carolina, purchased tracts of land in hopes of becoming self-sufficient by themselves. McKissick would give a national cast to his program for a "parallel society" by half-jestingly invoking the example of Indonesia, a land of many islands scattered over a vast area of sea. The black nation of America, he liked to say to bemused black audiences, would consist of black islands called Harlem, Newark, Hough, South Side, Watts, etc., dotting the vast white sea of America.

The reality in this whimsical image was the fact of great concentration of urban black populations in decaying central cities. If it had any black nationalist content in it at all, it evoked the grim prospect of a set of peculiarly American Bantustans, urban black reservations South African style, self-governing communities surviving in the rot amid a general social and political deterioration that would have to include political repression on a large scale. On the other hand, assuming not a deterioration but a recovery and renovation of the American society, this same concentration carried with it, and, indeed, already heralded, the possibility of quite another prospect. Along with increased voter registration and participation in all parts of the country, it was leading not toward separation and isolation but toward greater participation by blacks in the American political system. By 1974, there were some three thousand elected black officials in the country, a threefold increase in three years. There were 108 mayors of cities, including such far from all-black cities as Los Angeles, Detroit, Atlanta, Cincinnati, and Gary.[30] This appeared to suggest that the great mass of black Americans was moving not toward separation and isolation but toward greater participation in the American political system. They were showing the same patterns of ethnic voting solidarity that had accompanied the upward political mobility of other population groups like the Irish, Italians, Poles, and Jews as they moved toward some fuller integration in the society as a whole.

No one could yet be sure of the direction and the quality and the pace of change for black Americans. The social and economic struggle upward out of poverty had a long way to go. The problem of becoming more integrated—of belonging to the society as least as others did—continued to present deep and gnawing difficulties of many kinds. These included the somber question of whether the newly opening society was in fact going to open far enough to admit its black population at least on the same basis that it was finally admitting other hitherto excluded groups. The ambiguities and uncertainties of the new situation were made all the more insupportable by the quickened pace of change and heightened expectations unfulfilled. The consequent feelings of impatience, anger, and despair might be expressed by a radical few in unrealistic and unrealizable programs for political and geographic separation. But for most, especially for intellectuals and members of the rising middle class standing at the edge of change, it could and did in this time take the form of many other kinds of psychological, emotional, and social withdrawal. One result in the 1960s and 1970s was the spectacle of some blacks trying to rebuild the walls which other blacks before them had spent their lives fighting to pull down.

This was in some cases a complicated first effect of change itself, as among the young black men and women who poured in their new thousands into the mainstream colleges and universities of the country. A first impulse was to retreat into their own study programs, their own cafeteria corners, their own all-black dormitories, as though the fight against segregation in these places had never been fought, never been won. The only seeming difference, besides the greatly increased numbers, was between the old segregation imposed by bigoted whites and the new self-segregation self-imposed by those who expressed an aggressive counterbigotry to shield their fear and uncertainty in this new world without the old racial street signs and markers. The same behavior appeared as part of the power-seeking tactic of the "black caucus" that aimed to separate and mobilize blacks as a distinct interest group in all kinds of organizations and institutions in the society. This was seen by some as a hardheaded tactic, a pulling-in so that they could later step out and move forward, a retreat—a strategic withdrawal, if you will—into a safe haven, a place where they could cluster with their own, deal collectively with the white foe outside, and, as far as they could, avoid the friction, the hurt, and the heavily pressing demands of the free-for-all world outside. It was a way of carrying the ghetto with them as they left it for a world that still largely wanted to keep them ghettoized.

Still, the irreversible had happened. The political and legal breakthroughs had taken place and there could be no going back. Short of the replacement of the present political system by some other, there could never be a return to anything resembling the disenfranchisement and legal segregation of the past. To this rock-bottom extent, as a matter of nationality and law, black Americans had finally been recognized as *Americans* with rights equal to those of all other citizens of the country.

This did not mean that Du Bois's double image had been shaken by this great turbulence into any greater singular clarity. Black Americans, by no means sure as yet what it meant to be American, had only begun to examine in new ways the old question of what it meant to be *black*. This was taking place in the new "black" consciousness of the time, beginning with the rehabilitation of the very word itself. It was implicit and explicit in the veritable explosion of self-assertion and self-expression by blacks in all the arts, the reach to redefine blackness, to re-examine the relation of black Americans to their African origins, to modern Africa and Africans, to all other cultures, to discover what their unique place was in the American culture itself. If there could really be no question that their "nationality" was American, in what way, if any, were they also a "nation" as blacks? The answer had to do with much more than the winning of civil and political rights. It had to do with emerging from generations of being alienated and suppressed. It was not going to come soon or easily or without pain. Only one thing was sure: as this generation of black Americans gets on with the business of trying to determine what it is to be black, it will also be determining, along with many other Americans similarly engaged, what it means in terms of both political and cultural nationality to be American.

X

WHAT NEW PLURALISMS?

✦

During a lull in the 1974 hostilities on Cyprus, units of young Greek Cypriot and Turkish Cypriot soldiers faced each other across a narrow stream at the edge of Nicosia and began to exchange talk and visits. As a correspondent talked with an officer on the Greek side, "a sudden cry, like Tarzan's jungle cry, came from the Turkish side. A Greek soldier returned it. 'It has no meaning,' the Greek officer explained. 'It cannot be translated. We made it up. It means we have nothing to do and there is nothing sane to say.' "
                    —*The New York Times*, September 6, 1974

HERE TO STAY, then, are the idols of our tribes, full of their enchanting beauties and crushing brutalities, granitelike in their power to survive, mobile and vital in their power to reproduce themselves, to be reborn, to evolve. They preside over all our altars. They give us what they give us to meet our needs, and we give them all the human sacrifices on which they feed. Despite occasional impulses and even efforts in a number of cultures to see if it could be otherwise, this remains the essential order of human existence. The more things change, the more this remains the same.

The same, but not static. Basic group identity is not as fixed and crusted as it can come to seem when one discusses it in shorthand ways. On the contrary, it is remarkably dynamic, in an almost constant state of becoming. To define and describe it, I have had to try to take basic group identity apart, to examine each of its main elements to see where the strength and persistence come from and how each works in the cluster of the whole, especially under the impact of ongoing political and social change. In so doing, I have shown that these elements are inseparable and inextricably mixed into the whole, that you cannot in the end get at the essence of basic group identity simply by disassembling it and laying it out on the workbench like the pieces of a machine. The separate parts of group identity come melded to each other in highly varied and often quite distinctive or eccentric ways. They are not machine-pressed products but works of art. Despite great and universal resemblances among them, no two are alike or necessarily follow any common rule of growth or survival. Each has to be seen not only for what it was and what it came out of but for what it has become, for what it is, in this place, at this time, among these people, in these circumstances. Basic group identity is not like a dead rock lying unchanged since it was formed by some movement of matter in eons past. It is a living thing that grows, changes, and thrives or withers according to the rise or decline of its own vitality and the conditions in which it exists. It dies too, or is fossilized. It disappears into some other evolving group organism, or it reappears in some new union of old elements that come together in some new way. When we look at this phenomenon, it is not like looking at the still surface of a stone but at the surface of a moving stream. Moreover, the prisms through which we look are differently placed for every observer and are never still, are always in motion.

The dynamism of basic group identity is a function of the mix of what people have inherited and what they have acquired, the mix of culture past and culture present. In every case, including even those that look most fossilized, each is made up of some version or variety of the primordial holdings acquired by every person from the past and in one way or another modified or even transformed by the circumstances of the present. All aspects of each group's interaction with others come to bear on the outcome: each one's share of economic well-being or deprivation, of relative power or powerlessness. There have been periods of time in various cultures that we think of as having been static, the terms of life in whole societies unchanging generation after generation. To the extent that this did occur in times past—and I suspect that more often than not this is a view more in the eye of the distant beholder than in the fact itself—it can hardly recur anywhere now. Given the rate and spread of social, economic, and political change in the modern era, it seems safe to say that whatever was fixed almost anywhere in this respect has by now become fluid, all flowing, as Heraclitus said of everything so long ago, into all.

Like everything, of course, this too is a matter of degree, and the degrees arrange themselves in a spectrum of quantities and qualities measurable, if not by numbers, then at least by words like "little," "some," "much." Thus at one end there are still even now groups of people for whom by chance or by choice things have largely stood still, preserved over time as they were, or at least as people believed they always were. But in such cases, the past has been kept alive only under sentence deferred. The modern world with its great power to undo all kinds of stable life reaches into the high hidden valleys of the Himalayas and the Andes and into the farms of the Amish in Pennsylvania. Even the Stone Age Tasadays, so long "lost" in the Cotabato forest in the Philippines, are finally, to their great misfortune, "found."

Across the middle and farther ends of this spectrum are people in identifiable groups who could perhaps be sorted out in a sequence by some measure of their relative rootedness or rootlessness. Here are all the many different groups we have glimpsed in these pages, the ground they stand on all but disappearing in the quakelike onset of the forces of political change. Here are all those thrown by these upheavals from their safe places, stumbling for refuge into their Houses of Muumbi as into storm cellars, or carrying their ancestral tablets with them as they flee from the wildness looking for any place where, with these tablets, they can feel at home again.

Then we come upon the more rootless still, the great numbers of different kinds of people in the world who are themselves already the changeling products of the modern era. They are the products of social and economic and technological change, of migrations, of cross-cultural mingling, of beliefs, visions, quests for something beyond parochial ties that would link them in some way more broadly to others. In all their varieties, these are people who by chance, choice, or need have become something quite different from what their forebears ever were. Few still carry any remnant of their ancestral tablets with them, although many may still carry on them the marks of their origins. Most have no Houses of Muumbi to which they can return. At the same time, their need to belong and to feel secure is no less great than those who do. So they are forced to try to satisfy those old needs in some new way. If they cannot rediscover some old Muumbi-like refuge, then they have to improvise or create a new one. They will be found now piecing together new group identities out of what they have acquired, giving new shapes to whatever is left of the old forms they inherited from their pasts. Nowhere is this highly non-static form of the current group identity experience more dramatically on display now than in the American society.

"Americans" are a great array of diverse peoples of many kinds and origins. More than most, the American group identity has always been and still is coming into being. New people, new forces, new circumstances have worked constantly to shape it, sometimes—although not always—trying to make it begin to fit more of the vision with which it was originally created. This was eighteenth-century Enlightenment vision at its loftiest: popular sovereignty, inalienable rights guaranteed to all individual citizens in their pursuit of life, liberty, and happiness in whatever form they might find it. The actuality was more than flawed; it carried within it from the beginning the cancer of slavery. It is far from certain, after all the crises and remissions and recurrences of all the years, that the body politic is not still mortally sick with it, failures as an open society overtaking successes and finally striking it in some vital part.

In their great variety of kinds, Americans live in a society whose ethos has long nominally been to make "one" out of these "many."

Its practice until quite recently was to make "one" only out of some (essentially white Americans of northern European Protestant origin) while partly excluding others (mainly whites of other origins) and more or less totally excluding others (its nonwhites: the blacks, browns, reds, yellows). This was still for all practical purposes the structure of American society as recently as 1945. In the decades since then, as we all know, great changes have taken place. The system of white supremacy was brought down in uneven ways and with uneven results. But this happened as part of the beginning of the revision of all mutual relations among all groups in the society, a great shaking-up of its long-established pecking order. These events raised anew the possibility that the "many" might finally become "one" or at least more "one" than it had been until now. During a tumultuous quarter century, we have touched highs and lows of expectations and outcomes in this ongoing process. In the civil rights revolution that at long last finally brought down legal racial segregation, it was possible to see the beginning of the closing of the gap between what the society had claimed to be and what it actually was. In the America of the burning ghettos, Vietnam, and Watergate, what had begun to put itself together after 1945 seemed to be falling apart. New illusions about the coming of racial justice and old ones about the nature of the society, its political system, its role in the world, lay punctured on all sides. Even the success of school desegregation in the South, the breakthrough that had opened these decades of change, was obscured as we measured how far we had come, even in this one matter, from the battle of Little Rock in 1957 to the battle of Boston in 1974. In the ongoing process of the making of the American group identity, the question remained: What was the "one" we were trying to create? And what, in making this "one," became of the "many"?

One feature of this turmoil, largely triggered by the black reassertion of the 1950s and 1960s, was an "ethnic revival," a reawakening of ethnic group consciousness among members of various other groups in the American population. This has been a complicated happening that remains a poorly reported part of the much-reported American scene. No one has yet distinguished its sounds—which are loud, especially on television—from its substance, which must be considerable. The message that comes via these amplified channels is that if it is beautiful to be black, Chicano, Puerto Rican, or Indian, then it has to be more beautiful still to be Irish, Italian, Jewish, Polish, Ukrainian, Slovak, Greek, Armenian, or whatever your origins indicate that you can now be proud to know that you are. We need to know what is "old" and what is "new" in this rise of ethnic consciousness, what is sound and what is substance, especially among that large population of second- and third-generation immigrant "stock," mainly Catholic and of central and southern European origin, that became the core of the working population of the industrial Northeast. This great slice of "middle" America has in these years suffered massive discontent and disaffection and economic hardship aggravated by racial tensions, struggles over neighborhoods, schools, jobs. These immigrant populations characteristically became more "American" even than the older Americans among whom they came, even while retaining their old-country languages and styles of life. In the classic American experience, their children drifted from the old ways, and their children's children began to rediscover them. The old shapes of this experience in America are the subject of a vast literature. Its new shapes have barely begun to be examined.[1] The question, in our present context, is how salient any new ethnic group consciousness has become among these Americans confronting the new circumstances of these years.

Among newly converted ethnic revivalists, it has become fashionable to say that ethnic differences among Americans did not melt at all in that melting pot. Indeed, as some of them now seem to see it,[2] the pot itself was used by the wicked Wasps of the Old Northeast to boil away all the rich pure stuff of non-Waspness and cook up a great thin mess of pasty second-class Waspness, which then became the essence of the common American culture. It all took place in the American dream/nightmare from which some of these rediscoverers of ethnicity see themselves as happily waking at last, looking with newly rubbed and cleared eyes on their own non-Wasp heritage.[3] There is surely in all this a measure of healthy recovery from self-deprecation and denial because of undervalued origins. But some "ethnic romantics" of the current passage make it hard to resist paraphrasing Harry Truman's famous aphorism about politics and suggesting that it has to be those who could not stand the heat of the melting pot who have come out so half-cooked. For the reality of the matter seems to be that all group identities, all ethnicity, especially all the American varieties, are made in melting pots and always have been. What is being produced in the American society by this process is not a second-class Wasp but what is becoming, for better or worse, a one-class American who is often also something else at the same time.

Just how these elements are melding still remains to be seen. One can catch dramatic glimpses of the process-in-being in the experience of Americans who go, out of some feeling of lostness, in search of their remoter roots—the many black Americans who have made pilgrimages to Africa in recent years, American Jews who have gone to Israel to try to become Israelis, Japanese-Americans who have gone to Japan, Italian-Americans who have gone to Italy. Whatever new view they acquire of their ancestral cultures, and whatever the feeling of need and alienation that drives them to seek it, there is a remarkably uniform experience that turns up during these quests. The seekers find out that they are not African, not Japanese, not Italian, or whatever, but something quite else, something quite distinctive: they are Afro-American, Japanese-American, Italian-American. A striking vignette of such a moment of discovery appears in a mostly lighthearted account of a journey back to Italy by a New York reporter who described his feelings as he stood at last before the house in the Abruzzo where his father was born:

I didn't cry. My heart didn't beat faster. But I was very glad I came. For the house, like the town and even Italy in general, confirmed my suspicions. I wasn't underneath *really* Italian. Neither was I just another good old red-blooded American. I was an Italian American—a unique breed, an identity in itself.[4]

New sets of values, outlooks, and styles of behavior turned up in these individuals, marking off their resemblances to one another and their differences from their non-American kin. These features of being "American" had worked their way into their own cultural bloodstreams more deeply than these seekers after ancestral roots had imagined; discovering it was often a disconcerting or rueful experience. The attempt to define just what these features are already fills many books and will fill many more to come: it is work in progress. What these individuals shared, in all their separate and distinctive ways, I do venture to say here, was a part of the core of the American group identity they were all engaged in creating.

The making of this new American group identity is a matter of old theory and new facts. In old theory, the American system is color blind, its rights guaranteed to all regardless of race, creed, or national origin, open to the pursuit of any uniqueness that any citizens might seek, so long as the pursuit of it does not impinge on the common rights of others. Obviously, the system has not worked this way. There was slavery. There have been crippling and deforming exclusions at all public levels, and prejudice and bigotry in the everyday life of the society. The exclusions were finally barred by law only in the last twenty years. The prejudice and bigotry still rampantly exist. The question is still how much old theory has been becoming new fact in these years. The new facts are unfolding all around us, and there is argument over how to read them. Under the many new pressures and counterpressures, the system is being molded into new shapes to accommodate the new needs. These new facts are creating new thresholds, new situations, new conflicts, new dilemmas. Whether and how they are carrying us into the making of a new American pluralism only time, our present time, will tell.

The pressure to revise relations between groups, for example, has led to pressure to revise the relative positions in the society of the group and the individual. This touches the bedrock of the whole American system, which is based on rights that belong to individuals, not to groups. This comes as part of the effort to correct former inequities and to enforce new laws requiring equality of status for all citizens. The struggle against discrimination produced laws barring exclusions based on race, religion, sex, or national origin. Out went the discriminating lines in job applications, out went the telltale photos that used to have to accompany such applications. But in the process of enforcing the new laws, all the old practices were revived, and what had been declared illegal for purposes of discriminating against various groups now became if not legal, then common practice for the opposite purpose of discriminating in their favor. The setting of quotas for hiring, for selection, for admission to various institutions in both the public and private domains became an issue, full of complexity and mixed motives, on its way through the courts. Their decisions will ultimately decide this critical aspect of the new pluralist system now being shaped.

Such new facts crowd the worlds of politics, of education, of business, of government. New attitudes appear. New conflicts arise. The problem is the striking of new balances between the "one" and the "many," between the individual as a single American citizen enjoying the same basic rights as every other American citizen, and the individual as a member of some group, an identity he shares only with the other members of that group, whether it be defined by racial, religious, or national origin. It remains the essence of the American theory and largely, indeed, of the American fact that one is "American" only as an individual. The American individual is free to associate with any kind of group to which he feels he belongs, and each such group is free to exist, to function, to live and grow according to its own genius and its own vitality. It does so on its own, however, in the great private domain where every person retains his own individual freedom of choice.

In our present time of passage, individuals are coming to new perceptions of themselves and of their groups. For what is still a great majority of the American population, there is no question at all of the relative places of these identifications. But for some members of some groups, the issue takes the form not of their individual rights as individuals but of their groups' rights *as groups*. Not going as far as the separatists who seek to establish nations of their own on their own lands, some of these group enthusiasts see their interests best served by the development within the American society of something resembling the Ottoman millet system, whereby designated groups have a corporate and legally recognized existence of their own and a measure of self-governance, or at least something resembling the old Czarist system, the communal electoral system in British India, or even in part the new Soviet system, in which "nationalities" enjoy a certain limited separate existence and serve to group individuals for various public purposes. These notions, expressed or implied by some self-styled "new pluralists,"[5] are not likely to make much headway in the American political and cultural environment. They do raise questions about the relative weights that these newly asserted group identifications may acquire in the future—at law, politically, culturally, in the educational system, in establishing bilingualism, or, in some areas, multilingualism, in economic life, in all the other institutions of the society. This is the kind of question the makers of a new American pluralism are going to have to answer as we move on through the process of deciding just what kind of a society we want the American society to be.

In theory, the American system was uniquely designed to provide a social and political framework in which differences of race and culture could be maintained and enhanced according to their own genius and vitality at the same time that all individual members of the society are fused into a political and social system that assures equality of status and a decent measure of common belongingness and self-esteem to all. This always has been and is more than ever a tall, tall order. Events of the last twenty-five years have both quickened and dampened the belief that such a thing could come to pass, and that the American group identity could be based on belonging to a society put together this way. Each one of us sees the picture from where we are in it. This allows, in our present pass, a wide range between relative optimism and bleak pessimism. At the very least, one needs stamina and needs to believe that the world *is* new, if only one's nerves are strong enough. It becomes a matter of believing that enough will change, even if so much remains the same.

✦

Things, of course, continue to change quite drastically. We come back to the paradox with which we opened this examination of our condition. We are fragmenting and globalizing at the same time. We spin out as from a centrifuge, flying apart socially and politically, at the same time that enormous centripetal forces press us all into more and more of a single mass every year. World power is more concentrated and more diffused than ever before. We reach the limits of the earth's resources while increasing every year the numbers of people who have to share in them. We have entered the postindustrial age before two thirds of the world has barely begun to emerge from the preindustrial era and before most of the world's people could glean any advantages at all from industrialization and modernization. The fundamental and decisive conflicts grow ever sharper over the hard stuff of wealth, access to sources of energy and other raw materials, over production, food, trade, and military power. These are the conflicts that will decide the fate of the world and its peoples. But these conflicts continue to be ribbed and shaped and fleshed by the soft stuff of group identities, by the ways people see themselves and are seen, how they feel about themselves and about others, and how these feelings cause them to behave.

We have now looked at length at that soft stuff of which group identities are made: the varieties of skin color and other physical characteristics, names and language, history and origins, religion, nationality. We looked at it afresh as though it had never been looked at before, because generations of students of society, unlike its artists and poets and ordinary people, had indeed stopped looking at it except in its national forms and as an incidental feature of evolving human affairs. Some of them did so because they simply took for granted the governing conceptions of their own times and their own national cultures about human differences, about progress and backwardness, superiority and inferiority, power and powerlessness. At another level, some believed that insofar as these differences were unfortunate or undesirable, they would be flattened out under the pressures of modernization or kept under control by the benign power of superior peoples carrying out their divinely ordained civilizing missions.

At best, possibly, they believed that conflict over differences of this kind rose out of ignorance and superstition and would be erased by advancing knowledge and enlightenment and improved well-being; or else that they rose out of class and economic exploitation, in which event they would be done away with—"nations" and all—by revolutions that would create a seamless and classless world socialist order. For socialists, more than for any other aspiring improvers of the human lot, the element of "class" dominated both description and prescription. All traditional systems were hopelessly reactionary—"feudal"—and all national governments in bourgeois states were simply executive committees of capitalist ruling classes. The tribal gods must have had a good laugh in their caves as they watched the socialist hope for a better future based on international working-class solidarity founder precisely on the rocks of "national" and "ethnic" differences.

With all appropriate humility, then, one has to state as a conclusion what has been well known to great masses of people for a long time but not to generations of elite humanistic scholars and strivers for human perfectibility: namely, that our tribal separatenesses are here to stay. Barring total extermination, they cannot be indefinitely contained. They are not about to dissolve into any new, larger human order. And a good thing too, some argue, since, as Solzhenitsyn said, these diversities are the wealth of humanity, inheritances from the past that are the main sources of the enhancement of life, of art and beauty and elevation of the human spirit. They stand as a present bar to the aridity and homogenized cultures created by modern industrial societies. This is strongly argued and there is certainly more in human experience to support it than any contrary notion that we might still be able to create some better kind of existence than we now have by detribalizing ourselves and ordering our lives by some set of more universal human and humane values.

On the other hand, with all the beauty goes all the blood. If tribal separateness and its life-giving qualities are here to stay, so are intertribal hostility and the death-dealing consequences. The coin of this realm, like all others, has two sides. Along with all it has contributed to the enhancement of the human spirit, tribal distinctiveness has contributed more than any other single cause to the brutalization of human existence. If anything emerges plainly from our long look at the nature and functioning of basic group identity, it is the fact that the we-they syndrome is built in. It does not merely distinguish, it divides. It provides the substance of an active value-laden, emotionally supported separation of one's own kind from all others. It develops in virulence and violence in direct ratio to the extent of contact with others. The relative license or relative constraint with which this hostility is expressed depends on the prevailing system of power, that is, who is ruling whom, and how. Where there is contact or propinquity between sufficiently different groups, the normal responses run from avoidance to suspicion, to fear, to hostility, to violence. Such violence occurs along a scale, depending on the power relations between them and the interplay of other interests, from indifference to deprecation, to contempt, to victimization, and, not at all seldom, to slaughter. There is nothing in our present condition to suggest that any significant numbers of people are any more prepared now than they ever were to act any differently in these matters, even—and perhaps especially—when they have just emerged from being victims and acquire the power to become victimizers in their turn. The only "new" question has to do with what kind of power systems, what kind of politics, might cope with this condition in its present form in any "new" way. The problem as always, if we wish to preserve and enjoy the enhancing pluses of our tribal uniquenesses, is what to do with their destructive minuses.

The underlying issue is still: can human existence be made more humane, and if so, how? For a long time answers to this question bore on varieties of the belief that the tribes of men would eventually, through Reason or Faith, come around to discover their One Humanity and would thereupon organize themselves to live more happily thereafter with one another. This belief survives only with the greatest difficulty in some of its religious versions. In its secular/

political forms, whether in the humanistic tradition created by the Enlightenment or the materialistic tradition of socialism, it barely survives at all. But the question remains and one must still doggedly ask it: How can we live with our differences without, as always heretofore, being driven by them to tear each other limb from limb? This is at bottom a question of power, of the relative power or powerlessness of groups in relation to one another. If there is any substance to the now-universal demand of all groups for some more decent equality of status in all societies, how might this demand be met? What new politics might meet these needs, what new institutions? What new pluralisms?

This is a "new" question, of course, only in a relative sense. Up until now, it was generally "solved" by the creation and main-tenance of power systems based on pecking orders, rulers and ruled, masters and subjects, empires and colonies, etc. These systems were usually created by the sword and usually came to an end the same way, falling apart or being cut to pieces, whereupon the old pieces would be rearranged by another ruling group in some new design. The repetition of this process and the reproduction of some such system remains the most possible, even the most probable, outcome of the present centrifugal whirl. Examples are common enough in the so-called socialist world and among recent ex-colonies. New models more in tune with modern capabilities suggest themselves in the control system created by positive reinforcement and the meeting of primary physical needs of masses of people, as in Maoist China, where results—no one yet knows how effective or how fragile—are achieved through a combination of physical force and high suggestibility. Much surer methods are being developed in laboratories at the frontiers of biology and biochemistry, where it begins to appear that the stuff of group identities and behavior in the future may be put together not in the messy confusion of human existence but in tidy test tubes. Black boxes already in the hands of some power holders can destroy part or, it is said, all of the human race. Further scientific "progress," it now appears, may before too long give the button pushers the means to homogenize it instead. This would certainly "solve" a great many of the problems created by human diversity. Nuclear war would of course "solve" all our problems even more radically. Doomsday speculation of this kind may be profitless, fruitless, or at least premature. But the least that has to be said, it seems to me, is that we are creating systems for total control or total destruction far more rapidly than we are creating any new political systems that promise more tolerable outcomes.

Still the options continue open. This is still a time of confused and chaotic passage. All the old pecking orders have been pulled down or at least been pulled apart for some rearrangement. In all kinds of clusterings, people hitherto deprived are reaching for some better distribution of the rights and privileges of belongingness and the satisfactions of self-esteem. There are still choices, still directions open, still new outcomes to seek. It is still possible to imagine systems of power, new pluralisms, in which human beings may be able to live with one another in some more satisfying and mutually satisfactory way. Those who still believe in the face of all the irreducible and stubborn facts to the contrary that some more humane arrangement of human affairs is possible must still gamble on some right things happening even if—as is most likely—they happen for some wrong reasons.

NOTES

II. THE SNOWMAN

1. A recent study of this matter begins: "Very few researchers of ethnic relations ever define the meaning of ethnicity. To find out how often social scientists use explicit definitions of ethnicity in their empirical research, 65 sociological and anthropological studies dealing with one or another aspect of ethnicity were examined. Only 13 of these included some definition of ethnicity; 52 had no explicit definition at all." In addition, "27 definitions of ethnicity, taken from more theoretically oriented works, were examined," but the most commonly mentioned attributes of ethnicity—common origin, culture, religion, race, language—were mentioned in many fewer than half of them. Wsevolod W. Isijiw, "Definitions of Ethnicity," *Ethnicity,* 1, 111–124 (1974).

2. William L. Eilers, "The Uses of Identity," unpublished ms. thesis, M.I.T., 1966; "Primary Groups," in Broom and Selznick, *Sociology,* text with readings, New York, 1963, pp. 135–175; Parsons and Shils, eds., *Toward a General Theory of Action,* Cambridge, 1951, pp. 192–195; Ward Goodenough, *Cooperation in Change,* New York, 1963, chaps. 8, 9; Ali A. Mazrui, "Pluralism and National Integration," in Kuper and Smith, eds., *Pluralism in Africa,* Berkeley, 1969; Gordon Allport, "The Historical Background of Modern Social Psychology," in Lindzey, ed., *Handbook of Social Psychology,* Cambridge, 1954, vol. 1, pp. 31–40.

3. Bruce Mazlish, "Group Psychology and the Problems of Contemporary History," *Journal of Contemporary History,* 3:2, 1968, p. 163.

4. Sigmund Freud, *Group Psychology and the Analysis of the Ego,* Anchor edition, pp. 169–70.

5. Ibid., p. 194.

6. Ibid., p. 196.

7. Included in Erik Erikson, "Identity and the Life Cycle: Selected Papers," *Psychological Issues,* 1:1, 1959, pp. 18–49; also in same selection, "The Problem of Ego Identity," pp. 101–164. Other sources by Erikson used here include *Childhood and Society,* New York, 1950, and *Identity, Youth and Crisis,* New York, 1968.

8. Erikson, *Identity, Youth and Crisis,* p. 22.

9. See Erikson's chapter on "Reflections on the American Identity" in the 1963 edition of his *Childhood and Society,* and a late work, *Dimensions of a New Identity,* New York, 1974.

10. An example of Erikson's visionary-hortatory style: "As in the near future peoples of different tribal and national pasts join what must eventually become the identity of one mankind, they can find an initial common language only in the workings of science and technology. This in turn may well help them to make transparent the superstitions of their traditional moralities and may even permit them to advance rapidly through a historical period during which they must put a vain superidentity of neonationalism in the place of their much-exploited historical identity weakness. But they must also look beyond the major ideologies of the new 'established' world, offered them as ceremonial masks to frighten and attract them. The overriding issue is the creation not of a new ideology but of a universal ethics growing out of a universal technological civilization [whose test is] . . . the care it inspires." *Identity, Youth and Crisis,* p. 260.

11. All quotations here are from Erich Fromm, *Escape from Freedom,* New York, 1941.

12. Edward Shils, "Primordial, Personal, Sacred and Civil Ties," *British Journal of Sociology,* 8, 1957, p. 139.

13. Clifford Geertz, "The Integrative Revolution, Primordial Sentiments and Civil Politics in the New States," in Geertz, ed., *Old Societies and New States,* New York, 1963.

14. "Group Identity and Political Change," adapted from a lecture at the International House, Tokyo, December 6, 1963, *Bulletin of the International House,* April 1964.

15. For details of these studies and related treatments, cf. *Scratches On Our Minds: American Images of China and India,* New York, 1958 (paperback as *Images of Asia,* New York, 1972); *Emergent Americans,* New York, 1961; *The New World of Negro Americans,* New York, 1963; *India's Ex-Untouchables,* New York, 1965 (paperback edition, 1974); *American Jews in Israel,* New York, 1967; "Group Identity and Political Change: The Role of Color and Physical Characteristics," *Daedalus,* Spring 1967; "Group Identity and Political Change: Nationalism Revisited," *Survey,* October 1968; "Color in World Affairs," *Foreign Affairs,* January 1969.

III. IDOLS OF THE TRIBE

1. A. H. Maslow lists "belongingness" and "esteem" second and third in his list of five basic needs—the first two are physiological needs and safety and security needs, the fifth is self-actualization. Cf. *Motivation and Personality,* New York, 1954. See also Frank Goble, *The Third Force: The Psychology of Abraham Maslow,* New York, 1970, chap. 4; for studies that try to relate Maslow's narrowly based treatment of these needs to broader cultural and political settings, see especially Jeanne Knutson, *The Human Basis of the Polity,* New York, 1972, and Joel Aronoff, *Psychological Needs and Cultural Systems,* New York, 1967, especially pp. 51–80. On "belongingness," see also Leonard Doob, *Social Psychology: An Analysis of Human Behavior* (1952), Westport, Conn., 1971, pp. 230–236. Some political con-

sequences of feelings of "homelessness" are discussed by R. E. Lane, *Political Ideology,* New York, 1962, pp. 179–181. On "anomie" as a state of normlessness in society, see Knutson, op. cit., pp. 145 et seq.

2. For an essay on some current aspects of the need of people to have, hold, or regain their *homes,* see Ferdinand Mount, "The Sense of Dispossession," *Encounter,* December 1972, pp. 9–16.

3. Cf. "Group Identity and Political Change," loc. cit., pp. 24–25.

IV. BODY

1. Hajime Nakamura, *Ways of Thinking of Eastern Peoples: India-China-Tibet-Japan,* Honolulu, 1964, pp. 162–63, 180.

2. Quoted by Samuel J. Todes, "The Human Body as the Material Subject of the World," PhD thesis, Dept. of Philosophy, Harvard University, 1963, p. iv.

3. Ibid., p. 7.

4. Helen Lynd, *On Shame and the Search for Identity,* New York, 1958, p. 137. Cf. Paul Schilder, *Image and Appearance of the Human Body* (1935), New York, 1950, pp. 212, 240–241.

5. See Mary Douglas, *Purity and Danger, An Analysis of Concepts of Pollution and Taboo,* London 1966. Cf. Hiroshi Wagatsuma, "The Social Perception of Skin Color in Japan, *Daedalus,* Spring 1967; also his "Mixed Blood Children in Japan, An Exploratory Study," ms., October 1972; Frederic Wakeman Jr., *Strangers at the Gate,* Berkeley (1966), 1974, pp. 55–57.

6. A lively look at what has been done to the body and its coverings in various cultures can be had in Bernard Rudofsky, *The Unfashionable Body,* New York, 1971.

7. Mircea Eliade, *The Myth of the Eternal Return, or, Cosmos and History,* Princeton (1954), 1971, chap. 1; Octavio Paz, *The Labyrinth of Solitude,* pp. 205–206, 208.

8. "The party chief of the Central Asian highland republic of Kirghizia charged in a major ideological speech recently that local poets sought to glorify their mountains as a force 'supposedly capable of benefiting the life of the Kirghiz people. The writers seem to forget that it is the Communist Party and the Soviet people who produce cultural and economic gains for the Kirghiz. . . . There is, of course, nothing wrong with a writer's lovingly depicting mountains which have always served as a symbol for poetic national feelings. But . . . for many of our poets, the mountains have become a fetish, a subject to be revered as a deity.' " *The New York Times,* July 15, 1973.

9. Colin Turnbull, *The Mountain People,* New York, 1972, pp. 157, 161–162.

10. For a fuller treatment than I am going to be able to give here of the place of "race" in current world affairs see my "Color in World Affairs," *Foreign Affairs,* January 1969, pp. 235–250, and other studies included

along with it in George W. Shepherd, Jr., *Racial Influences on American Foreign Policy,* New York, 1970.

11. See my *Scratches On Our Minds: American Images of China and India,* New York, 1958 (paperback edition title *Images of Asia,* New York, 1972), pp. 280–290.

12. See my *India's Ex-Untouchables,* New York (1965), 1974; Pulin Garg, "Some Notes on Importance of Skin Color in India," unpublished memorandum, 1965.

13. An anthropologist has reported some Yunnan villagers' idea of female beauty: "The lighter her skin and the rosier and smaller the mouth, the better. A high-bridged, narrow, pointed nose was preferred." The skin of the ideal man, he added, "was expected to be darker." In the village, he reported, "complexions varied somewhat and a lighter color was considered preferable to a dark. The noses of boys and girls were pinched to make the bridges higher, a form which was considered particularly attractive." Cornelius Osgood, *Village Life in Old China: A Community Study of Kao Yao, Yunnan,* New York, 1963, pp. 253–54, 273–74. Other citations from the Chinese used here come for the most part from a research memorandum prepared for me at M.I.T. in 1965 by Alan P. L. Liu.

14. Emmanuel John Hevi, *An African Student in Red China,* New York, 1963.

15. Cf. Bruce D. Larkin, *China and Africa 1949–1970,* Berkeley, 1971, chap. 6; David Albright, "The Soviet Union, Communist China, and Ghana, 1955–1966," PhD thesis, Dept. of Political Science, Columbia University, 1970, pp 327, 329. See also Robin A. Remington, *Revolutionary Role of the Afro-American: An Analysis of Sino-Soviet Polemics on the Historical Importance of the American Negro,* Center for International Studies, M.I.T., Cambridge, Mass., October 1968.

16. Alan Liu quotes from an account published by an overseas Chinese traveler in Communist China: "In every nursery school or kindergarten, the following questions-and-answers were often heard:

" 'Who are the villains?'

" 'The American wolves!'

" 'Why have the Americans turned into wolves?'

" 'Because the Americans have the wolf's heart and dog's lung.' "

Classrooms were described as being decorated with pictures showing American soldiers killing, cooking, and eating children. The soldiers were usually depicted with "their skin full of black hair . . . face painted light blue, long teeth protruding from their mouths." From Lin Tae, *Ta-lu Chien-wen* (What I Saw on the Mainland), Hong Kong, 1954.

17. Some of the scattered and inadequate information we have about some groups of this kind will be found in Noel P. Gist and Anthony Gary Dworkin, eds., *The Blending of Races: Marginality and Identity in World Perspective,* New York, 1972.

18. For an examination of the details of what I learned myself about this matter from a study of the literature but mainly from a long series of in-

tensive interviews with individuals going through this experience—including Du Bois, Randolph, Frazier, Hughes, and many others—I have to refer the reader to my *New World of Negro Americans,* especially "Black Stand Back," pp. 72–101, and "The Heart of the Matter," pp. 155–172.

19. Cf. John M. Goering, "Changing Perceptions and Evaluations of Physical Characteristics among Blacks, 1950–1970," *Phylon,* 33:3, Fall 1972, 231–241.

V. NAME

1. John Dewey and Arthur F. Bentley, *Knowing and the Known* (1949), Boston, 1960, p. 147; cf. Anselm Strauss, *Mirrors and Masks,* Glencoe, Ill., 1959, chap. 1.

2. Dewey, ibid., xii, 156 ff.

3. William James, *Pragmatism: A New Way for Some Old Ways of Thinking* (1907), New York, 1948, pp. 64–65.

4. Alfred Cobban, *The Nation State and National Self-Determination,* New York, 1969, p. 22.

5. Fung Yu-lan, *Short History of Chinese Philosophy,* New York, 1948, pp. 83, 92, 153; James, op. cit., p. 52.

6. For numerous examples, see J. G. Frazer, *The Golden Bough: A Study in Magic and Religion* (1890), Toronto, 1969, chap. 22, "Tabooed Words."

7. James, op. cit., p. 53.

8. Quoted by Hiroshi Wagatsuma, "Problems of East and West in Japanese Culture," ms., December 1972.

9. *The New York Times,* March 8, 1973.

10. Nakamura, op. cit., p. 121.

11. Lynd, op. cit., p. 65.

12. Final Report, Meeting of Experts on Educational Methods Designed to Combat Racial Prejudice, Unesco House, Paris, June 24–28, 1968, issued at Paris, October 24, 1968.

13. See "Name to Go By: The 'Anglo-Saxons,' " chap. 3 in my *American Jews in Israel,* New York, 1967, pp. 54–69.

14. *The New York Times,* February 16, 1970; July 30, 1972.

15. Hazel W. Hertzberg, *The Search for An American Indian Identity: Modern Pan-Indian Movements,* Syracuse, 1971.

16. For references to sources and for a fuller account based on extensive interview material, see my *India's Ex-Untouchables,* especially chap. 2, "The Name to Go By."

17. Cited by E. Franklin Frazier, *The Negro in the United States,* New York, 1949, p. 358. For references to sources and a fuller account based on extensive interview material, see my *New World of Negro Americans,* especially "A Name to Go By," pp. 62–71.

18. See Gunnar Myrdal et al., *American Dilemma,* New York, 1944, p. 133 and notes thereto.

VI. LANGUAGE

1. Lynd, op. cit., p. 242; Erikson, "The Problem of Ego Identity," loc. cit., p. 115.

2. Herbert C. Kelman, "Language as Aid and Barrier to Involvement in the National System," Conference on Language Planning, East-West Center, Honolulu, April 7–10, 1969.

3. Dell Hymes, "Linguistic Aspect of Comparative Political Research," in R. T. Holt and J. E. Turner, *The Methodology of Comparative Research,* New York, 1970, pp. 297–98, 315.

4. Cited in *International Encyclopedia of Social Science,* 9:22, from Sapir's *Selected Writings in Language, Culture and Personality,* David Mandelbaum, ed., Berkeley, Cal., 1949.

5. "Science and Linguistics," in Maccoby, Newcomb, and Hartley, *Readings in Social Psychology,* New York, 3rd ed., 1958.

6. Lynd, op. cit., p. 175.

7. Hymes, loc. cit., p. 311–12; Karl Deutsch, *Nationalism and Social Communication,* Cambridge, Mass., 1953, 2nd ed., 1966, p. 66.

8. See especially remarks by Kenneth Fearing, Joseph Greenberg, and Charles Hockett in Harry Hoijer, ed., *Language in Culture,* Proceedings of a Conference on the Interrelations of Language and other Aspects of Culture, *The American Anthropologist,* 56:2, Memoir #79, December 1954.

9. Ibid., p. 122–23.

10. Lynd, op. cit., pp. 177, 246–247.

11. Kenneth Fearing in *Language in Culture,* p. 55.

12. Hymes, loc. cit., p. 315.

13. Quoted by Fearing, loc. cit., pp. 50–52.

14. Joshua Fishman, ed., *Sociology of Language,* The Hague, 1971, p. 313.

15. In Joshua Fishman, Charles Ferguson, Jyo Tindra Das Gupta, eds., *Language Problems of Developing Nations,* New York, 1968, p. 216.

16. Deutsch, op. cit., p. 97.

17. William Peterson, "Ethnic Structure in Western Europe," ms., October, 1972.

18. E.g., see Heinz Kloss, "Notes Concerning a Language-Nation Typology," in *Language Problems of Developing Nations,* pp. 69–85.

19. Dankwart Rustow, "Language, Modernization, and Nationhood," *Language Problems of Developing Nations,* pp. 87–105.

20. For an unusually sensitive treatment of the bilingual, biculturated North African Arab French-speakers, see Charles Gallagher, "North African Problems and Prospects: Language and Identity," in *Language Problems of Developing Nations,* pp. 129–151; cf. also Herbert Passin, "Writer and Journalist in the Transitional Society," in *Communication and Development,* Lucian Pye, ed., Princeton, 1963, pp. 82–97.

21. Ali Mazrui, "Some Sociopolitical Functions of English Literature in Africa," in *Language Problems of Developing Nations,* p. 184.

22. Ali Mazrui, *The Trial of Christopher Okigbo,* New York, 1972, p. 102.

23. Lyndon Harries, "Swahili in Modern East Africa," in *Language Problems of Developing Nations,* pp. 415–429.

24. Cited by Robert Armstrong, "Language Policies and Language Practices in West Africa," ibid., pp. 228–230.

25. *American Jews in Israel,* p. 225.

VII. HISTORY AND ORIGINS

1. Mircea Eliade, *Myth and Reality,* New York, 1968, p. 33.

2. Ibid., p. 21.

3. "Those sociologists and anthropologists who are interested in personal identity tend to treat historical matters more as stage settings, or backdrops, than as crucial to the study of persons . . . A man must be viewed as embedded in a temporal matrix not simply of his own making, but which is peculiarly and subtly related to something of his own making—his conception of the past as it impinges on himself . . . Personal identity is meshed with group identity, which itself rests upon an historical past." Anselm Strauss, *Mirrors and Masks: The Search for Identity,* Glencoe, Ill., 1959, pp. 164, 173.

4. J. H. Plumb, *The Death of the Past* (1969), New York, 1971, pp. 31, 33.

5. A Boston ancestry tracer reported in the year following the naming of Humberto Medeiros as cardinal that an "unusually large number of Portuguese" had been seeking her services. *Boston Globe,* May 10, 1973.

6. E.g., William Maxwell, *Ancestors,* New York, 1971.

7. Cf. Alex Haley, "My Furthest-Back Person—'The African,' " *The New York Times Magazine,* July 16, 1972. The *Boston Globe,* coincidentally of the same date, carried an account of some current efforts by persons adopted in infancy to seek out their natural parents, a complicatedly painful variation on the same theme.

8. Fritz Stern, ed., *The Varieties of History from Voltaire to the Present,* New York, 1956, p. 19.

9. Plumb, op. cit., p. 60.

10. In defense of violent passages about Jews in textbooks used in Palestinian refugee camps, a Syrian minister of education said: "The hatred we instill in our children from birth is a sacred emotion." Quoted by David Gordon, *Self-determination and History in the Third World,* Princeton, 1971, p. 115.

11. Octavio Paz, *Labyrinth of Solitude,* New York, 1961, p. 11. E.g., in Ulster, a 1690 battle between Catholics and Protestants is symbolically relived in each year's Orange Day Parade, and periodically re-enacted by new mutual killing—more than 1000 dead in the most recent of the renewals up to mid-1974. A thirteen-year-old Protestant boy explained to an inquiring reporter: "They hate us because of what King Billy done. You see, King Billy was a Protestant and his army beat the Catholics and they can't forget.

It's history. I learned it in school." Nursery rhymes taught to Protestant children drop time and tense altogether from their sense of this event: "If I had a penny/Do you know what I would do/I would buy a rope/and Hang the Pope/And let King Billy through." A "rope skipping song . . . still shrilled by Catholic girls" goes: "St. Patrick's Day will be jolly and gay/And we'll kick the Protestants out of the way/And if that won't do, we'll cut them in two/And send them to hell with their red white and blue." "Ulster: Children of Violence," *Newsweek,* April 19, 1971.

To trace the shape of some of these matters in other ancient and irrepressible conflicts, see, e.g., concerning the Croat-Serb experience, Rebecca West, *Black Lamb and Grey Falcon,* New York, 1940. For an examination of how Greek Cypriot and Turkish Cypriot children learn about their respective histories in their respective schools, see Barbara Hodge and G. L. Lewis, *Cyprus School History Textbooks: A Study in Education for International Misunderstanding,* Education Advisory Committee of the Parliamentary Group for World Government, London (1966). On the Flemish-Walloon conflict in Belgium—the "Germano-Latin scar that cuts across Europe" that has been there since the fourth and fifth centuries, when the Franks invaded what is now Belgium—see "Notes of MIT-Harvard Joint Faculty Seminar," December 3, 1969; Aristide Zolberg, "Crises of Political Development in Belgium," ms., 1972, and his "The Making of Flemings and Walloons, Belgium 1830–1914," *Journal of Interdisciplinary History,* Fall 1974.

12. Cf. David Lowenthal, "Past Time, Present Place: Landscape and Memory, the Age of Nostalgia," ms., University College, London, 1974.

13. J. Nehru, *Discovery of India,* New York, 1946, p. 434.

14. *The New York Times,* October 16, 1966. In the Soviet Union itself, the struggle between the wielders of Russian central power and provincial glorifiers of non-Russian local history goes on, less bloody now than it was in Stalin's day, but with no end in sight. A recurring sample: "An unorthodox historical study, glorifying the independent and anti-Bolshevik state of Georgia before it was absorbed into the Soviet Union, has stirred a political scandal in Georgia by its bold challenge to the Kremlin's policy on national minorities. The Communist Party . . . has issued a decree condemning the author of the work, the publishing house editor who let it pass, and several academic and party officials who had endorsed the controversial book." *The New York Times,* May 14, 1972.

15. Gordon, op. cit., pp. 70, 76, 89–95.

16. *India's Ex-Untouchables;* for material on the *burakumin,* see George DeVos and Hiroshi Wagatsuma, *Japan's Invisible Race: Caste in Culture and Personality,* Berkeley, Cal., 1966.

17. See John Hope Franklin, *From Slavery to Freedom,* New York, 1947; also his "Rediscovering Black America: A Historical Roundup," *The New York Times Magazine,* September 8, 1968.

18. See Franklin's comments in bibliographic notes of the fourth edition of his *From Slavery to Freedom* (1947), 1974.

19. In *The New World of Negro Americans*, especially Part III, "Negroes and Africa," pp. 105–322.

20. James Baldwin, *Notes of a Native Son*, New York, 1955, pp. 6, 7, 163, 165.

21. Cited by Rupert Emerson, *Empire to Nation*, Boston, 1960, p. 154; cf. Gordon, op. cit., p. 34n.

22. Soedjatmoko et al., eds., *An Introduction to Indonesian Historiography*, Ithaca, New York, 1965, p. xiv.

23. For a study of some of the available models, in this case the writing of French history, see Carlton J. Hayes, *France, a Nation of Patriots*, New York, 1930. For a discussion of how "history itself becomes a weapon in the conquest of national identity," see Arthur Schlesinger, Jr., "Nationalism and History," *Journal of Negro History*, LIV:1, 1969, 19–31; also David M. Potter, "The Historian's Use of Nationalism and Vice Versa," in *History and American Society*, New York, 1973. For a sensitive examination of the problems of the new nationalist historian who also wants to respect the demands of scholarship, see Soedjatmoko, "The Indonesian Historian and His Time," in *An Introduction to Indonesian Historiography*. For a famous example of a reconstruction and rediscovery of history by a nationalist leader, see the already cited J. Nehru, *The Discovery of India*. For a more current treatment of the use and abuse of history and historians in the decolonization process, in this case drawing mainly on contemporary Arab experience, see David Gordon, *Self-determination and History in the Third World*, Princeton, 1971. Concerning Africa, see J. F. A. Ajayi and E. J. Alagoa, "Black Africa: The Historian's Perspective," *Daedalus*, Spring 1974, pp. 125–134; K. O. Dike and J. F. A. Ajayi, "African Historiography," *International Encyclopedia of the Social Sciences*, 6:394–399; Philip D. Curtin, *Precolonial African History*, American Historical Association pamphlets, Washington, D.C., 1974. For the role of history in another setting, see Ann L. Craig, "History and Origins: An Element in Mexico's Group Identity," *Revista Interamericana Review*, III:4, Winter 1974.

24. *Boston Globe*, April 14, 1974.

25. For an illuminating review of a century of Japanese concern with cultural identity, see Hiroshi Wagatsuma, "Problems of Cultural Identity in Modern Japan," in Theodore Schwartz and George DeVos, eds., *Ethnic Identity, Cultural Continuity and Change*, forthcoming.

26. Conversation with the author, Tokyo, January 1973. Dr. Doi is the author of *The Anatomy of Dependence*, New York, 1973.

27. Professor Tsurumi is the author of *Social Change and the Individual: Japan Before and After Defeat in World War II*, Princeton, 1970.

28. The history of the Jews is the subject of a vast and highly varied literature. For an introduction to the subject in a single volume see Abram Sachar, *History of the Jews* (1953), New York, 1971. For an essay that attempts to put Jewish history in its larger Western or world context, see J. L. Talmon, "Suggestions for Isolating the Jewish Component in World

History," *Midstream,* March 1972. For an introduction to the history of the religion, see Jacob Neusner, *Way of Torah: An Introduction to Judaism,* Belmont, Cal., 1974.

29. Cf. Robert Alter, "The Masada Complex," *Commentary,* July 1973.

30. During a lecture in Boston in February 1974. Jacob Neusner strikes a similar note under the title "Now We're All Jews—Again," in *Response: A Contemporary Jewish Review,* Winter 1973–4, p. 151. Amos Elon writes of the generational experience in Israel in *The Israelis: Founders and Sons,* New York, 1971.

31. Cf. Jonathan Mirsky, "Writing Textbook History: Two Current Examples," *Journal of Asian Studies,* 33:1, November 1973, p. 91; C. P. Fitzgerald, "The Chinese View of Their Place in the World," *Chatham House Essays,* London, 1964, pp. 5–6.

32. *Scratches On Our Minds: American Images of China and India* (*Images of Asia*).

33. Cf. Albert Feuerwerker, ed., *History in Communist China,* Cambridge, 1968, especially "China's History in Marxian Dress," pp. 39 ff; Joseph Levenson, "The Place of Confucius in Communist China," pp. 56–73; David Farquhar, "Chinese Assessments of a Foreign Conquest Dynasty," pp. 175–188.

34. Cited by Stuart Schram, *The Political Thought of Mao Tse-tung,* New York, 1963, pp. 105–107, 109–110.

VIII. RELIGION

1. The word origins and usages cited come from a variety of dictionaries and encyclopedias; from Wilfred Cantwell Smith, *The Meaning and End of Religion,* New York, 1963, chaps. 3 and 4, especially the notes thereto; and from Yu Zunvair, former reference librarian, Harvard-Yenching Library, and Dr. Ai-li Chin.

2. Cf. Guenter Lewy, *Religion and Revolution,* New York, 1974.

3. For studies of the political role of religion and the process of secularization in a number of Muslim, Buddhist, Hindu, and Catholic Latin American countries, see Donald E. Smith, ed., *Religion and Political Modernization,* New Haven, 1974.

4. R. H. Tawney, *Religion and the Rise of Capitalism,* New York, 1926, pp. 6–7.

5. In a summary of the state of our knowledge about the psychology of religion, we learn that there is "a single frequently replicated empirical finding in social psychology: the positive correlation between indices of religion ["especially as measured by institutional loyalty and conservative doctrines"] and of prejudice, authoritarianism, and other conservative attitudes," suggesting that a common condition of personal inadequacy finds relief in the "strict categorizing and self-enhancement provided by ethnocentric doctrines." *International Encyclopedia of the Social Sciences,* 13:415, 420.

6. E.g., Asoka Mehta and Achyut Patwardham, *The Communal Triangle in India*, Allahabad, 1942; Richard Rose, *Governing Without Consensus: An Irish Perspective*, Boston, 1972, especially chap 8, "Two Bodies in Christ."

7. "It is going to be difficult to speak of *the* Roman Catholic position on any issue from now on. In effect, there is no specifically Catholic ethic anymore. We used to have a very poor understanding of sin . . . But having jettisoned this impoverished sense of sin, we still have failed to replace it with anything else." Father Charles Curran, professor of moral theology, Catholic University of America, *Newsweek,* October 4, 1971. For a sample of the ferment churned up by these changes, see Garry Wills, *Bare Ruined Choirs: Doubt, Prophecy, and Radical Religion,* New York, 1972.

8. William Petersen, "Report on Ethnic Minorities in Switzerland, Belgium, and the Netherlands," ms., October 1972.

9. Cf. "The National Pact in Lebanon," in Donald E. Smith, ed., *Religion, Politics and Social Change in the Third World,* New York, 1971, pp. 190–193; Gordon, op. cit., pp. 99–104; Leonard Binder, ed., *Politics in Lebanon,* New York, 1966; Lliya F. Harik, "The Ethnic Revolution and Political Integration in the Middle East," *International Journal of Middle Eastern Studies,* III:3, 1972, pp. 303–323.

10. *India's Ex-Untouchables.*

11. Nearly 100 persons were killed in Pakistan in May-June 1974 in a renewal of rioting between Muslims and a dissident Muslim sect known as the Ahmadis or Qadianis. Some 2,000 were killed in similar riots in 1953. *The New York Times,* July 4, 1974.

12. Cf. Thomas Hodgkin, *Nationalism in Colonial Africa,* London, 1956, pp. 93–114.

13. *The New York Times,* March 8, 1972, June 30, 1972, March 25, 1973, June 20, 1974; Marcia Wright, "African History in the 1960s: Religion," and John Ralph Wills, "The Historiography of Islam in Africa: The Last Decade (1960–1970)" in *African Studies Review,* XIV:3, December 1971.

14. See C. Eric Lincoln, ed., *The Black Experience in Religion, A Book of Readings,* New York, 1974; also his *The Black Church Since Frazier,* published in the same paperback volume with E. Franklin Frazier, *The Negro Church in America,* New York, 1974. For bibliography on Christianity, religion, and the black experience, see Elizabeth W. Miller, *The Negro in America, A Bibliography,* Cambridge, Mass., pp. 18–20; for a study of black cults, see especially Arthur Fauset, *Black Gods of the Metropolis,* Philadelphia, 1944, and C. Eric Lincoln, *The Black Muslims in America* (1961), Boston, 1973. For a brief but pungent statement of the subject, see E. Franklin Frazier, *The Negro in the United States,* New York, 1949, Chap. XIV; also my *New World of Negro Americans,* especially pp. 122–128, 332–336, and passim.

15. By mid-1974 there were said to be 5,000 religious cults registered in the U.S. as non-profit organizations claiming a membership of more than two million. *The New York Times,* Sept. 2, 1974.

16. Dean M. Kelley, *Why Conservative Churches Are Growing*, New York, 1972; Edward B. Fiske, "The Strong Current of Spiritual Revival," *New York Times*, Mar. 5, 1972; "The New Counter-Reformation," *Time*, July 8, 1974. Cf. Will Herberg, *Protestant-Catholic-Jew, an Essay in American Religious Sociology*, New York (1955), revised edition 1960.

17. *The New York Times*, Aug. 2, 1974; see also David Singer, "Voices of Orthodoxy," *Commentary*, July 1974.

18. *The New York Times*, Dec. 26, 1971.

19. *The New York Times*, April 3, 1973.

20. "Islam is more aggressive and reactionary than other religions," a local Communist editor in Baku complained to a visiting correspondent. "This religion teaches people to think about themselves and their families." *The New York Times*, Dec. 13, 1971.

21. NBC, June 23, 1974.

IX. NATIONALITY

1. Rupert Emerson, *From Empire to Nation*, pp. 96–97.

2. Carlton Hayes, *Essays on Nationalism*, New York, 1926, p. 26.

3. Ibid., pp. 26–29; Boyd C. Shafer, *Faces of Nationalism*, New York, 1972, pp. 8–10; Emerson, op. cit., chap 5.

4. Hayes, op. cit., p. 89.

5. E. H. Carr, *Nationalism and After*, New York, 1945, p. 40.

6. Emerson, op. cit., p. 89.

7. Ibid., p. 102. See also Karl Deutsch, op. cit., chap 1; Leonard Doob, *Patriotism and Nationalism*, New Haven, 1964, pp. 4–9; Louis L. Snyder, *The Meaning of Nationalism*, New Brunswick. N.J., pp. 72–73.

8. In an examination of Deutsch's theories about nationalism, Walker Connor lists ten major works of the 1960s by important American political scientists concerned with theories of "nation-building" and "integration." Not one, he found, "dedicates a section, chapter, or major subheading to the matter of ethnic diversity," and in six the indexes show "not a single reference to ethnic groups, ethnicity, or minorities." "Nation-Building or Nation-Destroying?" *World Politics*, April 24, 1972.

9. Emerson, op. cit., p. 102.

10. At Versailles in 1919, when the delegate of Portugal "suggested that the new organization would more correctly be called a League of States, Lord Robert Cecil replied that he thought the difference between the word 'nation' and 'state' was a very small one." Cobban, op. cit., p. 123.

11. Hayes, op. cit., pp. 4–6; Shafer, op. cit., pp. 7–18, 13–16, and especially notes thereto; Emerson, op. cit., pp. 96, 114 ff., 298 ff., Connor, loc. cit., pp. 332–336; Cobban, op. cit., chaps. 2 and 7.

12. For useful treatments of this development see Cobban, op. cit., chap 7; J. L. Talmon, *The Unique and the Universal*, New York, 1966, chap. 1.

13. Cf. Kemal Karpat, "An Inquiry into the Social Foundations of Nationalism in the Ottoman State: From Social Estates to Classes, From Mil-

lets to Nations," Center of International Studies, Woodrow Wilson School of Public and International Affairs, Princeton, July 1973, mimeo.

14. For a lively treatment of this history see Hayes, *Nationalism: A Religion,* New York, 1960, also his *Essays on Nationalism,* chap. 7.

15. Talmon, op. cit., p. 19.

16. Hayes, *Essays on Nationalism,* p. 110; S. M. Lipset, *First New Nation,* New York,, 1963, pp. 18–19; Emerson, op. cit., p. 169.

17. See Martin Shaw and Henry Coleman, eds., *National Anthems of the World,* London, 1963; cf. Oliver Jensen, "Letter from the Editor," *American Heritage,* August 1974, p. 2.

18. Hannah Arendt, *The Origins of Totalitarianism,* New York, 1958, p. 300.

19. R. M. MacIver, *The Challenge of the Passing Years: My Encounter with Time,* New York, 1962, pp. 77, 79.

20. For a sharply perceptive treatment of many of the matters dealt with in this same context, see Walker Connor, "The Politics of Ethnonationalism," in *Journal of International Affairs,* 27:1, New York, 1973. This issue of the journal contains useful articles on nationality and nation-building problems in the Soviet Union, India, Canada, Czechoslovakia, Malaysia, Israel, and Uganda and Tanzania.

21. Cf. Kimitada Miwa, *Crossroads of Patriotism in Imperial Japan,* ms., 1971.

22. Takeo Uchida, "A Study of Concepts of the Nation in Postwar Japan," PhD thesis, Fletcher School of Law and Diplomacy, 1969.

23. One of the more unexpected features of the Japanese quest for clearer self-definition in the last few years was the immense popularity of a book called *The Japanese and the Jews,* written pseudonymously by one "Isaiah Ben Dasan," which tried to compare and contrast Japanese and Jewish history and cultural styles. The work was much more penetrating about the Japanese than it was about the Jews, whom it treated primarily in their biblical period and aspect, and touched only scantily on the aspects of group identity dealt with here. Published in Japanese in 1970, the book sold over two million copies. An English translation was issued by Weatherhill, Tokyo and New York, in 1972. A comment of my own on the book appeared in *The Japan Times,* Tokyo, March 7, 1973.

24. This is history placed by many writers in many settings. The interested reader new to it can find starting points in Ben Halpern, *The Idea of the Jewish State,* Cambridge, Mass., 1961; Talmon's *The Unique and the Universal,* chap. 1, and his *Israel Among the Nations,* New York, 1970; N.D. Segre, *Israel: A Society in Transition,* New York, 1971, chap. 2.

25. Cf. Jacob Neusner, *American Judaism: Adventure in Modernity,* Englewood Cliffs, N.J., 1972.

26. *American Jews in Israel.*

27. *New World of Negro Americans,* especially "Souls So Dead," pp. 97–101; also my "Nationalism Revisited: Group Identity and Political Change," *Survey,* 69, October 1968.

28. W. E. B. Du Bois, *Souls of Black Folk* (1903), New York, 1953, p. 3.

29. For a fuller review of this history, with references, see *New World of Negro Americans,* "Back to Africa," pp. 114–154.

30. *National Roster of Black Elected Officials,* Joint Center for Political Studies, Washington, D.C., vol. 4, April 1974.

X. WHAT NEW PLURALISMS?

1. Classic works in the field are led by those of Marcus Hansen and Oscar Handlin. For fresh starting points, see Milton M. Gordon, *Assimilation in American Life,* New York, 1964; Nathan Glazer and Daniel Patrick Moynihan, *Beyond the Melting Pot,* Cambridge, Mass., 1963.

2. E.g., Michael Novak, *The Rise of the Unmeltable Ethnics,* New York, 1972.

3. Andrew M. Greeley, "The Ethnic Revival," Center for the Study of American Pluralism, University of Chicago, September 1974.

4. Anthony Mancini, "Ethnic Travel: When You Find Your Roots You Eat Them," *The New York Times,* August 1, 1971. For my own glimpses of the Afro-American experience in Africa—a highly controverted subject— see my report of interviews with black Americans in West Africa in 1963, in *New World of Negro Americans,* pp. 294–322. Cf. also my *American Jews in Israel.* For Japanese-American experiences, see a novel, Dan Okimoto, *American in Disguise,* New York, 1971; also Don Nakanishi, "The Visual Panacea: Japanese Americans in the City of Smog," in Akira Iriye, ed., *Mutual Images: Essays in Japanese-American Relations,* Cambridge Mass., forthcoming in 1975.

5. See, for example, Murray Friedman, ed., *Overcoming Middle Class Rage,* Philadelphia, 1971, and my comments on it, "The New Pluralists," *Commentary,* March 1972.

INDEX